John Cassian and the Creation of
Monastic Subjectivity

Studies in Ancient Religion and Culture

Series Editors:

Philip L. Tite, University of Virginia

Michael Ng, Seattle University

Studies in Ancient Religion and Culture (SARC) is concerned with religious and cultural aspects of the ancient world, with a special emphasis on studies that utilize social scientific methods of analysis. By "ancient world," the series is not limited to Greco-Roman and ancient Near Eastern cultures, though that is the primary regional focus. The underlying presupposition is that the study of religion in antiquity needs to be located within cultural and social analysis, situating religious traditions within the broader cultural and geopolitical dynamics within which those traditions are located.

This series also encourages cross-disciplinary research in the study of the ancient world. Due to the historical development of various academic disciplines, there has arisen a set of largely isolated and competing fields of study of the ancient world. Often this fragmentation in academia results in outdated or caricatured scholarly products when one discipline does use research from another discipline. A key goal of this series is to help facilitate greater cross- and inter-disciplinary work, bringing together those who study ancient history (especially social history), archaeology (of various methods and geographic focuses, as well as theorists in archaeology), ancient philosophy, biblical studies, early patristics/church history, Second Temple and formative Judaism, and Greek and Roman classics, as well as philologists.

Given the focus on the social and cultural context within which religion functions, the series also publishes studies which explore the various social locations in which real people in antiquity practiced or interacted with their religious traditions. Examples include the domestic cult, food production and consumption, temple worship, funerary practices/monuments, development of social networks, military cult, and ancient medicine.

Finally, the series encourages a broader application of theoretical and methodological tools to the study of the ancient world. While the main perspective is social-scientific (understood broadly), specific analyses from the reservoir of critical theory, narrative theories, economic theory, bio-archaeology, gender analysis, anthropology of religion, and cognitive theory are welcome.

John Cassian and the Creation of Monastic Subjectivity

Joshua Schachterle

SHEFFIELD UK   BRISTOL CT

Published by Equinox Publishing Ltd.

UK: Office 415, The Workstation, 15 Paternoster Row, Sheffield, South Yorkshire S1 2BX

USA: ISD, 70 Enterprise Drive, Bristol, CT 06010

www.equinoxpub.com

First published 2023

© Joshua Schachterle 2023

All rights reserved. No part of this publication may be reproduced or transmitted in any form or by any means, electronic or mechanical, including photocopying, recording or any information storage or retrieval system, without prior permission in writing from the publishers.

British Library Cataloguing-in-Publication Data

A catalogue record for this book is available from the British Library.

ISBN-13   978 1 80050 148 5 (hardback)
          978 1 80050 149 2 (paperback)
          978 1 80050 150 8 (ePDF)
          978 1 80050 250 5 (ePub)

Library of Congress Cataloging-in-Publication Data

Names: Schachterle, Joshua, author.
Title: John Cassian and the creation of monastic subjectivity / by Joshua Schachterle.
Description: Sheffield, South Yorkshire ; Bristol, CT : Equinox Publishing Ltd, 2023. | Series: Studies in ancient religion and culture | Includes bibliographical references and index. | Summary: "This study of Cassian's writings is supplemented with Michel Foucault's analysis of the creation of subjects in order to examine Cassian's formation of a specifically Egyptian form of monastic subjectivity for his audience, the monks of Gaul. Foucault's concepts of disciplinary power and pastoral power are also employed to demonstrate the effect Cassian's rhetoric would have upon his direct audience, as well as many other monks throughout history"-- Provided by publisher.
Identifiers: LCCN 2022010844 (print) | LCCN 2022010845 (ebook) | ISBN 9781800501485 (hardback) | ISBN 9781800501492 (paperback) | ISBN 9781800501508 (pdf) | ISBN 9781800502505 (epub)
Subjects: LCSH: Cassian, John, approximately 360-approximately 435. | Foucault, Michel, 1926-1984. | Monastic and religious life--History--Early church, ca. 30-600. | Asceticism--History--Early church, ca. 30-600. | Subjectivity--Religious aspects--Christianity. | Church--Authority. | Church history--Primitive and early church, ca. 30-600.
Classification: LCC BR1720.C3 S23 2022 (print) | LCC BR1720.C3 (ebook) | DDC 271--dc23/eng/20220725
LC record available at https://lccn.loc.gov/2022010844
LC ebook record available at https://lccn.loc.gov/2022010845

Typeset by ISB Typesetting, Sheffield, UK

Contents

	Acknowledgements	vii
	Preface	ix
1.	Introduction: John Cassian's Journey	1
2.	Cassian's Context and Asceticism as Basis for Valid Authority	13
3.	Foucault, Cassian, and the Creation of Subjects	69
4.	Conflicts Between Monasticism and the Church	90
5.	Cassian's Rhetorical Attempts to Separate Monasticism from the Church	123
6.	Conclusion	155
	Bibliography	171
	Index of Ancient Sources	180
	Index of Subjects	186
	Index of Modern Authors	191

Acknowledgments

I am indebted to many people, without whom I could not have completed this book. I would first like to thank Thomas Nail, Pamela Eisenbaum, and Gregory Robbins. Their advice was indispensable. Next, I would like to thank Rob Heaton. Without his invaluable help this book would have remained unfinished and half as good.

Finally, I reserve my greatest thanks for my family. My wife Lisa encouraged me to start my doctoral program and then to transform my doctoral dissertation into this book. Throughout, she has kept me afloat more times than I can count with her love and support. This is her book as well as mine. In addition, my sons, Ben and Aidan, have been endlessly patient as I spent long hours away from them in libraries and my office. You both have my heartfelt gratitude.

Preface

John Cassian (360–435 CE) started his monastic career in Bethlehem. He later traveled to the Egyptian desert, living there as a monk, meeting the venerated Desert Fathers, and learning from them for some 15 years. Much later, he would travel to the region of Gaul to help establish a monastery there by writing monastic manuals, the *Institutes* and the *Conferences*. These seminal writings represent the first known attempt to bring the idealized monastic traditions from Egypt, long understood to be the cradle of monasticism, to the West.

In his *Institutes*, Cassian comments that "a monk ought by all means to flee from women and bishops" (*Inst.* 11.18). This is indeed an odd comment from a monk, apparently casting bishops as adversaries rather than models for the Christian life. In this book, therefore, I argue that Cassian, in both the *Institutes* and the *Conferences*, is advocating for a distinct separation between monastics and the institutional Church.

In Cassian's writings and the larger corpus of monastic writings from his era, monks never referred to early Church fathers such as Irenaeus or Tertullian as authorities; instead, they cited quotes and stories exclusively from earlier, venerated monks. In that sense, monastic discourse such as Cassian's formed a closed discursive system, consciously excluding the hierarchical institutional Church. Furthermore, Cassian argues for a separate monastic authority based not on apostolic succession but rather on what I term apostolic praxis, the notion that monastic practices such as prayer and asceticism can be traced back to the primitive church.

I supplement my study of Cassian's writings with Michel Foucault's analysis of the creation of subjects in order to examine what I believe to be Cassian's formation of a specifically Egyptian form of monastic subjectivity for his audience, the monks of Gaul. In addition, I employ Foucault's concepts of disciplinary power and pastoral power to demonstrate the effect Cassian's rhetoric would have on his direct audience, as well as many other monks throughout history.

Chapter One

Introduction: John Cassian's Journey

At the end of the fourth century CE, a war had started between two factions of Egyptian monks. The alleged subject of the dispute was the corporeality (or incorporeality) of God. According to the fifth century Church History written by Socrates Scholasticus, the less educated monks all posited that God had a body, that in fact this body was the divine image in which humans were created (Gen. 1.26). Socrates also notes that the more educated monks believed the opposite: God, as an unlimited being, could not be circumscribed by a body or be subject to the passions associated with bodies.[1] In fact, the controversy had been stirred up not by the monks themselves but by Theophilus, bishop of Alexandria.

Socrates notes that Theophilus had originally been "expressly teaching that the Divine Being is wholly incorporeal."[2] This apparently enraged a sizable group of uneducated monks who then essentially rioted outside Theophilus's home, even threatening to put him to death.[3] Theophilus, fearing for his life, approached the monks and contritely offered to change his mind on the matter. The monks then demanded that Theophilus explicitly condemn not only his previous position, but also the works of Origen, the third-century scholar and theologian these monks viewed as the pernicious source of the notion of a disembodied divinity. Indeed, Socrates quotes Theophilus as telling these monks: "'I will readily do what you require: and be not angry with me, for I myself also disapprove of Origen's works, and consider those who countenance them deserving of censure.'"[4] Theophilus's life was saved, and the monks were appeased. However, this was not the end of the controversy.

---

1. Socrates Scholasticus. *Historia Ecclesisastica.* In *Patrologia Graeca.* Edited by J.-P. Migne, vol. 3. Paris: 1864. Translated by A.C. Zenos. From *Nicene and Post-Nicene Fathers, Second Series*, Vol. 2. Edited by Philip Schaff and Henry Wace (Buffalo, NY: Christian Literature Publishing Co, 1890), 6.7.
2. Socrates, *Historia Ecclesisastica, 6.7.* ἀσώματον δὲ αὐτὸν δογματίσαι τὸν θεόν.
3. Socrates, *EH*, 6.7.
4. Socrates, *EH*, 6.7. Ἀλλ᾽ ἐγὼ ἔφη Θεόφιλος, ποιήσω τὰ δεδομένα ὑμῖν, καὶ μὴ χαλεπαίνετε πρὸς μέ. Καί γὰρ ἐγὼ ἀπεχθῶς ἔχω πρὸς τὰ Ὀριγένους βιβλία, καί μέμφομαι τοὺς δεχομένους αὐτά.

There were, during Theophilus's time as bishop, four monks, known collectively as the Tall Brothers (οἱ Μακροὶ), who were well-respected in and around Alexandria. Theophilus himself admired them, both for their holiness and their learning. This resulted in his forcibly ordaining one of them, Dioscorus, as bishop of Hermopolis against his will (as I will discuss later, this was a common practice among Egyptian bishops in late antiquity).[5] Theophilus also asked two of the other Tall Brothers to work in the church with Dioscorus, which the brothers reluctantly agreed to do. However, Socrates writes that the monks "were dissatisfied because they were unable to follow philosophical pursuits and ascetic exercises" and that in addition, "they thought they were being spiritually injured, observing [Theophilus] to be devoted to gain, and greedily intent on the acquisition of wealth."[6] Eventually, the monks were sufficiently frustrated with this behavior and returned to their cells in the desert. In retaliation for their abandonment of him, Theophilus sent out a letter to the surrounding monasteries, telling them that the Tall Brothers, in direct conflict with his official decree, believed God to be incorporeal and that therefore no monk should listen to or credit any doctrines they espoused.[7] The result, according to Socrates, was that "the more ignorant [of the monks] who greatly exceeded the others in number, inflamed by an ardent zeal and without knowledge, immediately raised an outcry against their brethren."[8]

The end of this conflict came when Theophilus, having armed the uneducated monks for use as his henchmen, marched with them to Nitria, the monastic settlement of the Tall Brothers and their faction in the Egyptian desert, and forcibly evicted them from the area.

> A division being thus made, both parties branded each other as impious; and some listening to Theophilus called their brethren 'Origenists,' and 'impious' and the others termed those who were convinced by Theophilus 'Anthropomorphitæ.' On this account a violent altercation arose, and an inextinguishable war between the monks. Theophilus on receiving intimation of the success of his device, went to Nitria where the monasteries are, accompanied by a multitude of persons, and armed the monks against Dioscorus and his brethren; who being in danger of losing their lives, made their escape with great difficulty.[9]

---

5. Socrates, *EH*, 6.7.
6. Socrates, *EH*, 6.7. ἠνιῶντο δὲ ὅμως, ὅτι μὴ ἐφιλοσόφουν ὡς ἤθελον, τῇ ἀσκήσει προσκείμενοι. Ἐπεὶ δὲ προϊόντος τοῦ χρόνου, καὶ προσβλάπτεσθαι τὴν ψυχὴν ἐνόμιζον, ὁρῶντες τὸν ἐπίσκοπον χρηματιστίκον τε μετερκόμενον βίον, καὶ πολλὴν σπουδὴν περὶ χρεμάτων κτῆσιν τιθέμενον.
7. Socrates, *EH*, 6.7
8. Socrates, *EH*, 6.7. Οἱ δὲ ἁπλούστεροι, πλείους τε ὄντες καὶ ζῆλον ἔχοντες θερμὸν, κατὰ τῶν ἀδελφῶν εὐθέως ἐχώρουν.
9. Socrates, *EH*, 6.7. Ἦν οὖν διαίρεσις ἐν αὐτοῖς, καὶ ἀλλήλους ὡς ἀσεβοῦντας

The Tall Brothers escaped and fled to Jerusalem with approximately 80 other monks. To this day, the Eastern Orthodox Church mourns this occasion on July 10.[10] It is likely that among those fleeing was a monk named John Cassian.[11]

Cassian was born around 360 CE, probably in the region of Scythia Minor (now Romania and Bulgaria) and well-educated in Latin and Greek. He started his monastic career at a monastery in Bethlehem where he spent three years as a novice.[12] He later traveled with a friend and fellow monk, Germanus, to the Egyptian desert, visiting well-known monasteries, living there as a monk, meeting some of the most eminent senior monks, and learning from them for about 15 years.[13] Much later, he secured his place in the history of monasticism when he went to Gaul to help establish two monasteries there by writing monastic manuals, the *Institutes* and the *Conferences*. These seminal writings represent the first known attempt to bring the idealized monastic traditions from Egypt, long understood by Cassian's time to be the cradle of Christian monasticism, to the West. Eventually, these writings became one of the bases of the *Rule of St. Benedict* and subsequent Western monastic rules. Cassian is venerated as a saint by both the Roman Catholic and the Eastern Orthodox Churches. His monastic writings

---

διέσυρον΄ καὶ οἱ μὲν Θεοφίλῳ προσέχοντες ʽ Ὠριγενιαστὰς καὶ ἀσεβεῖς ʽ ἐκάλουν τοὺς ἀδελφούς. Οἱ δὲ ἕτεροι ʽ Ἀνθρωπομορφιανοὺς ʽ τοὺς ὑπὸ Θεοφίλου ἀναπεισθέντας ὠνόμαζον. Ἐκ τούτου παρατιβὴ γίνεται οὐ μικρὰ, καὶ ἦν μεταξὺ τῶν μοναχῶν πόλεμος ἄσπονδος. Θεόφιλος δὲ ὡς ἔγνω προβάντα τὸν σκοπὸν, ἅμα πλήσει καταλαβὼν τὴν Νιτρὶαν, ἔνθα εἰσί τὰ ἀσκετήρια, ἐξοπλίζει τοὺς μοναχοὺς κατά τε Διοσκόρου καὶ τῶν αὐτοῦ ἀδελφῶν. Οἱ δὲ κινδυνεύσαντες ἀπολέσθαι μόλις διέφυγον.

10. The Eastern Orthodox Church commemorates this occasion as the "Myriad (10,000) Venerable Fathers of the desert and caves of Nitria, martyred by the impious Patriarch Theophilus of Alexandria." Socrates, however, says nothing of any monks being killed in this altercation. Moreover, even if some were martyred, the number 10,000 is almost certainly hyperbolic.

11. Although we know that Cassian lived and practiced in Scetis at the time of the Tall Brothers' expulsion, he does not write of his exit from Egypt explicitly. However, the next time he is referred to in ancient writings he is with the Tall Brothers in Constantinople under the protection of John Chrysostom. He then goes to Rome to advocate for Chrysostom in Sozomen, Eccl. Hist., 7.26.

12. John Cassian. *Conferences*, edited and translated by E. Picherry. Conférences. 3 vols. *Sources Chrétiennes*, 42, 54, 64 (Paris: *Éditions du Cerf*, 1955–59). Translated by Boniface Ramsey. *John Cassian: The Institutes*. Ancient Christian Writers, 57 (New York, NY: Paulist Press, 1997), I.1. All English quotations from *The Conferences* will be from this translation unless otherwise noted.

13. John Cassian, *The Institutes*, translated by Colm Luibheid, *Conferences* (New York: NY: Paulist Press, 1985). See Introduction to this translation of *Conferences*, written by Owen Chadwick.

continued to have an immense influence on other Christian writers well into the Middle Ages.[14]

One of the first things a reader notices in Cassian's writings is his insistence on the practice of solitude, increasing gradually and systematically throughout a monk's life, as necessary for the achievement of spiritual and moral perfection. He writes, for example, that solitude allows the monk "to have a mind bare of all earthly things and, as much as human frailty permits, to unite it thus with Christ."[15] Such prescriptive solitude shapes the subjectivity of individual monks by purging all external human influence from monastic selves, and then reconstituting them with only the divine as a formative source. However, Cassian's recommendation for individual perfection, which he had no doubt learned from his Egyptian elders, had a far more ambitious aim.

By the beginning of the fifth century when Cassian was writing, monks in Egypt and Palestine could refer to a veritable litany of their own monastic traditions, both oral and written, which appear to have all but ignored much of earlier Christian theological tradition. In Cassian's writings, as well as the larger corpus of monastic writings from his era, monks never referred to early Church fathers such as Irenaeus or Tertullian as authorities; instead, they cited either scripture—almost always in allegorical interpretations—or quotes and stories exclusively from earlier, venerated monks.[16] In that sense,

---

14. "Already in the fifth century two abridgments of *The Institutes* were made in Gaul and Africa, the former of which, by Eucherius of Lyons and entitled Epitomes operum Cassiani, has survived and appears in PL 50.867–94. In the sixth century Benedict prescribed the reading of *The Conferences* (in Reg. 42.3) and of both *The Institutes* and *The Conferences* (in Reg. 73.5), while Cassiodorus recommended *The Institutes* to his monks at Vivarium in his work *De inst div. litt.* 29 (PL 70.1144). Cassian inspired, sometimes without even being mentioned by name, such major Western thinkers as Gregory the Great (d. 604), Alcuin (d. 804), Rhabanus Maurus (d. 856), Rupert of Deutz (d. 1129), and Thomas Aquinas (d. 1274), who cites him more than a dozen times in the section on moral theology of his *Summa Theologiae*." Cassian, John and Boniface Ramsey, translator, *The Conferences* (New York, NY: Newman, 1997), preface, 7.

15. Cassian, *Conferences*, XIX.8.4. Heremitae uero perfectio est exutam mentem a cunctis habere terrenis eamque, quantum humana inbecillitas ualet, sic unire cum Christo.

16. "This emphasis on principles, on techniques that had little reference to the personalities involved, shows how the discipline of the spiritual life had come to depend less on the insight and authority of holy men, and more on a sense of corporate tradition, custom, and experience." Philip Rousseau, *Ascetics, Authority, and the Church in the Age of Jerome and Cassian* (Notre Dame, IN: University of Notre Dame Press, 2010), 198. In an apothegm, one monk tells a novice : "If you can't be silent, you had better talk about the sayings of the [monastic] Fathers than about the Scriptures; it is not so dangerous." *Apophthegmata Patrum* (Greek Alphabetic). Edited by Jean-Baptiste Cotelier

monastic discourse such as Cassian's formed a closed system, consciously excluding the hierarchical institutional Church. Thus, the thesis of this book is that Cassian insisted on the maintenance of monasticism as a closed discursive system so that it could achieve autonomy, becoming separate from, rather than subject to, the institutional church. That is, all monastic discourse would ultimately refer only to itself, even if this meant stretching the definition of "monastic" to include prophets from the Hebrew Bible and the apostles. In this sense, I believe that the solitary monk may have been, for Cassian, a kind of synecdoche for a larger, ideal monastic system.

I would add that I am not arguing that Cassian was a revolutionary. I find no evidence that he was looking to destroy the institutional church. Rather, I believe he wanted to establish monasticism and the institutional church as parallel tracks, both fully functioning toward the *telos* of salvation, but not overlapping in terms of authority. In fact, I will argue that Cassian establishes the basis for monasticism's authority in a manner paralleling that of the church's authority. In contradistinction to apostolic succession, the dominant mode of authority in the church, I have chosen to call this second basis *apostolic praxis*.[17] In short, Cassian will place far greater emphasis on practice than belief, surely a dangerous undertaking in post-Nicene Egypt where heresiology was reaching its peak. In addition, just as the institutional church traces its authority back through each successive bishop to the apostles, Cassian will trace the practices he defines as proper monastic living back to the apostles and the primitive church. Ideally, this would grant monks an autonomy that, as is clear from the conflict above, was not bestowed on them and, despite Cassian's efforts, never would be.

It is beyond the scope of this book to make an argument about the entire institution of early Christian monasticism. In fact, because there is such a large corpus of writings both by and about early monastics, I will limit myself to Cassian's writings –principally the *Conferences* and the *Institutes*—with additional contributions from the *Apophthegmata Patrum* (*AP*), and other monastic documents from roughly the same era (late fourth and early fifth centuries CE). My intent is not to argue that all late antique

---

in *Ecclisiae Graecae Monumenta*. Paris: 1677. 1.338–712. Reprinted by Jacques-Paul Migne. In *Patrologia Graeca* 65:71–440. Paris: J-P Migne, 1864. Edited by Jean-Claude Guy. *Recherches sur la tradition grecque des Apophthegmata Patrum*, 13–58. *Subsidia Hagiographica*, 36. Brussels: Société des Bollandiste, 1962. Translated by Benedicta Ward, *The Sayings of the Desert Fathers: the Alphabetical Collection*. Kalamazoo, MI: Cistercian, 2004. Amoun of Nitria, 2. Εἰ οὐ δύνασαι σιωπᾶν, καλόν ἐστι μᾶλλον ἐν τοῖς λό γοις τῶν γερόντων, καὶ μὴ ἐν τῇ Γραφῇ. Κίνδυνος γάρ ἐστι οὐ μικρός.

17. I would like to thank my colleague, Dr. Robert Heaton, for the neologism, suggested to me while he was reviewing a draft of this book.

monastics saw themselves as ideally separate from the Church. Rather, I plan to show that Cassian and the group of educated monks he associated with saw such a separation as an ideal form of Christianity. The violent conflict between the bishop of Alexandria and Cassian's monastic community, based as it was on the bishop's apparently self-serving political machinations, could only have confirmed Cassian's desire to separate monks from an often-errant Church hierarchy. Perhaps this explains his assertion that "a monk ought by all means to flee from women and bishops."[18]

A Brief Summary of Cassian Studies

To justify the scope of this book, the following is a brief survey of significant studies on John Cassian. The standard for Cassian studies was set in 1998 by Columba Stewart's *Cassian the Monk*. This monograph begins with a solid biographical sketch of Cassian, based though it is on the scanty source material available, followed by an analysis of his theology. This analysis includes confronting the accusations of Semi-pelagianism rendered against him by Augustine's follower Prosper of Aquitaine, a charge Stewart competently argues is nonsense. Instead, Stewart establishes clearly that while Cassian's ascetical theology required that monks put forth effort toward perfecting themselves, such effort would never be sufficient for salvation without that divine grace over which no person has control.[19] While Stewart does an admirable job connecting Cassian's life and theology, he does not address what I see as the political implications of Cassian's theology viz a viz the power dynamics inherent in the type of monastic system advocated for in both Cassian's *Institutes* and *Conferences*.

Another well-researched work addressing Cassian's theology is Robert Rea's dissertation *Grace and Free Will in John Cassian*. Like Stewart, Rea confronts the erroneous notion that Cassian rejected the necessity of divine grace in order to protect his robust conception of free will. Rea goes on to explicate Cassian's writings, finding that for Cassian, grace and free will are both necessary and coexistent. In fact, Rea concludes that Cassian finds grace and free will interacting in two distinct but compatible ways.

---

18. John Cassian, *Institutes*, edited and translated by Jean-Claude Guy. *Institutions cénobitiques. Sources Chrétiennes*, 109 (Paris: Éditions du Cerf, 1965). Translated by Boniface Ramsey, *John Cassian: The Institutes*. Ancient Christian Writers, 58. (New York, NY: The Newman Press, 2000), XI.18. All quotations from *The Institutes* will be from this translation unless otherwise noted. [O]mnimodis monachum fugere debere mulieres et episcopos.

19. Columba Andrew Stewart, *Cassian the Monk* (New York, NY: Oxford University Press, 1998), 78.

Sometimes grace acts directly on the heart, with the human will responding in kind. Other times, grace acts by waiting for human effort and then assisting it to come to fruition. Rea asserts that in both cases, however, Cassian sees the entire process overseen by God in the best interests of each human being.[20] As with Stewart's work, though, Rea's writing does not address or even acknowledge issues of power and subjectivity I find inherent and crucial in Cassian's writings.

One book that does address these dynamics, albeit in a different way from my own research, is *Tradition and Theology in St. John Cassian* written by Augustine Casiday. In particular, Casiday begins his book by acknowledging that while many monastic writers in Cassian's time wrote extensive histories of the monks of Egypt, Cassian's purpose was completely different. Cassian instead was attempting "to influence the history of the monks of Gaul" and indeed "acknowledged that in his writings he aimed to propagate a certain tradition."[21] In other words, the tradition of the book's title was the monastic way of life Cassian had learned in Egypt and was attempting to establish among existing monasteries in Gaul. This approach toward Cassian's goal in his writings aligns with my own in that it recognizes that Cassian was in a position of rhetorical power, having lived with and learned from the widely respected monks of Egypt. However, while Casiday looks carefully at Cassian's attempt to shape the subjectivity of Gallican monks he ignores what I find to be at least as important: how Cassian's attempt to shape monastic subjectivity influences power relations between monasticism and the institutional church.

Another work I found both revealing and highly useful to my own work, Richard Goodrich's *Contextualizing Cassian: Aristocrats, Asceticism, and Reformation in Fifth- century Gaul*, elucidates the Gallican sociopolitical context into which Cassian brought his Egyptian monastic teachings. While most books on Cassian deal primarily with his background as a monk in Egypt, Goodrich notes that attempting to reform already- established monasteries in Gaul was akin to stepping into a minefield. Monks and clerics in Gaul were generally drawn from the upper classes, and the whole notion of asceticism and renunciation which was *de rigueur* in Egypt was anathema to a culture in which the wealth and status into which one had been born continued to carry weight even in the monastery.[22] Goodrich's research

---

20. Robert F. Rea, "Grace and Free Will in John Cassian," (PhD dissertation, St. Louis University, Missouri, USA, 1990), 152–205.
21. Augustine Casiday, *Tradition and Theology in St John Cassian* (Oxford: Oxford University Press, 2010), 4.
22. Richard J. Goodrich, *Contextualizing Cassian: Aristocrats, Asceticism, and Reformation in Fifth-century Gaul* (New York, NY: Oxford University Press, 2007), 5.

exposes the conflicted world into which Cassian was attempting to bring reforms from an alien culture and theology. In other words, Cassian was not merely struggling to correct monks' behavior like a strict teacher entering an unruly classroom; rather, he was confronting an entire power dynamic in which his ideas of renunciation and asceticism as the *sine qua non* of monastic life would have seemed ridiculous if not heretical. To achieve his goal, Cassian used rhetoric which situated him as the latest in a long line of venerable ascetics, beginning with the apostolic age and continuing through Anthony and the later generation of monks in Egypt with whom he had lived and studied.[23] While Goodrich's book addressed these power dynamics and the role they played in Cassian's attempted reformation in Gaul, he kept his study strictly delimited within monastic circles, all but ignoring power relations between monks and clergy/bishops.

Finally, I would be remiss if I did not address and acknowledge what is at the time of writing this book the latest contribution to Cassian studies, *Sites of the Ascetic Self: John Cassian and Christian Ethical Formation*, by Niki Kasumi Clements. Clements's book examines the ascetic practices outlined by Cassian from the perspective of an ethical subjectivity. In this context, she notes that asceticism, like ethical formation of all kinds, is formed initially by a kind of imitative behavior in which the subject forms themself according to their teacher, primarily through imitation of the teacher's "behavior, attitude and orientation.[24] According to this view, Cassian's purpose in writing the *Institutes* and the *Conferences* was to offer literary forms of the ethical monastic exemplars with whom he was privileged to interact in Egypt to the monks of Gaul, who were separated from such venerable personages both in place and time.

In addition, Clements considered "Cassian's construction of asceticism through attention to cultivation and an ethics of daily practice," an orientation she calls "*ethical agency*, where Cassian roots ascetic formation in the practical, daily cultivation of desired dispositions and the human effort required to commit to such practices despite their many challenges."[25] Clements, uses the writings of Michel Foucault to argue that "constructions of power" in ascetic practice "need to be met with a corollary stress on constructions of ethics in asceticism."[26] Thus, she argues that Cassian is not merely prescribing an abject, docile obedience to superior monks, but rather the cultivation of one's own embodied, ethical self. While I find Clements's

---

23. Goodrich, Contextualizing Cassian, 6.
24. Niki Kasumi Clements, *Sites of the Ascetic Self: John Cassian and Christian Ethical Formation* (Notre Dame, IN: University of Notre Dame Press, 2020), 3.
25. Clements, *Sites of the Ascetic Self*, 4.
26. Clements, *Sites of the Ascetic Self*, 6.

premises both interesting and useful in the realm of ethics, I do not find the power dynamics between institutional church and monastic formation addressed in this book.

While this is hardly an exhaustive list, I believe my research, as presented in this book, fills a gap in Cassian studies, one that addresses power dynamics in Cassian's writings while also confronting Cassian's history and his antipathy toward the place of bishops and clergy in authority over monastics.

Cassian was a man haunted by a ghost. Since the Alexandrian bishop Theophilus had expelled the more meditative sect of monks like Cassian from the Egyptian desert, he would likely have viewed that form of contemplative, ascetic monasticism—the correct type of monastic practice, in his opinion—as dead, a murdered corpse to which he could not help but cling mournfully. After Cassian's sojourn in Constantinople with John Chrysostom and subsequent travels to Rome and elsewhere, his journey ended in Gaul, a place where according to him, monasticism and its accompanying asceticism were being practiced atrociously.[27] It is at this point, when Bishop Castor asked Cassian to write practice manuals for the region's monks, that Cassian saw the opportunity to resurrect, to reincarnate his beloved Egyptian monasticism.[28] He would start by embodying this form himself as an example to Gallican monks, showing them correct practice as fulfilled in his own aging, ascetic body. From there, with Cassian's knowledgeable instruction in writing, this embodiment could only spread through the bodies of other monks. Through this training, a stronghold of what Cassian clearly believed to be the proper form of monastic life could proliferate, apart from any meddlesome and destructive influence by priests and bishops who had never been monks or ascetics. Many of these hierarchs did not understand the ins and outs of reforming one's self, of breaking the old self down until nothing remained and then recreating that self according to divine sources only. This book is the story of Cassian's attempt, through his writings, to recreate the heaven on earth he believed he had experienced in the Egyptian desert with his monastic mentors, to reinvigorate the way of

---

27. In the preface to his *Institutes*, Cassian writes that his patron's "wish is to establish in [his] own province, which lacks such things, the institutes of the Eastern and especially of the Egyptian cenobia." Cassian, *Institutes*, preface, 3. In prouincia siquidem coenobiorum experti Orientalium maximeque Aegyptiorum uolens instituta fundari.

28. There is no extant evidence for why Cassian traveled to Gaul. He may have been summoned there from Rome by bishop Castor or sent there by the bishop of Rome at the time. Either way, the evidence stops at Cassian's journey to Rome and only picks up again with the writings he accomplished in Masillia (modern-day Marseilles).

life that would truly lead monks to salvation. To make my case, this book will proceed in the following order.

Outline of Chapters

Chapter two establishes the context in which Cassian is writing. I begin with his Egyptian context, the place and time in which he learned how to be a monk from the men he considered masters of the monastic vocation. This includes the backgrounds for Cassian's seminal monastic writings and their sources.

I then skip ahead to the context in which Cassian wrote both the *Institutes* and the *Conferences*. This is relevant because while I argue that Cassian is trying to separate the institution of monasticism from that of the church, it is necessary to formulate a picture of what the institutional church of Gaul was in the early fifth century. This picture includes the turbulent politics of the time in which Rome had lost the province to Germanic invaders and had only reconquered the region a few years before Cassian's arrival. This instability in turn had thrown the elite of Gaul into confusion, making it difficult to know whether it was most beneficial for them to support the various usurpers to the throne or to continue to advocate for Roman control in the region. Such turmoil among the wealthy had, strangely, convinced many wealthy men of Gaul to become monks, believing that if they "stored up treasure in heaven," then heaven would preserve their social rank in the world to come. Finally, we must look at the ways in which Gallican monasticism (and asceticism) differed greatly from that of Egypt, causing Cassian to accuse the Gallican monks of grave errors in their practice and eliciting suggestions, not to say commands, from him in order to right the listing ship of their monastic practice.

Chapter three aims to establish how Cassian's creation of monastic subjectivity creates monks for whom monastic identity is necessarily separate from other parts/roles within the institutional Church. Thus in chapter three, I use Michel Foucault's notion of the creation of subjects to analyze Cassian's formation of a specifically Egyptian form of monastic subjectivity for the Gallican monks. In discussing Foucault, I detail his three modes of subjectification: First, modes of investigation create subjects as objects of knowledge; second, practices and procedures divide subjects both from within, and from other subjects according to standards of norm and deviance; and third, practices and procedures of self-management encourage subjects to transform themselves as subjects in order to meet an ideal. After establishing examples of these three modes from Cassian's own writings, I discuss how Cassian's use of subjectification is geared toward the creation

1   *Introduction*   11

of self-governing monks who, even in total solitude, police themselves. In addition, I argue that Cassian's rhetorical shaping of monastic subjectivity uses three of Foucault's principal modalities of power: disciplinary power, achieved through surveillance and the creation of particular forms of knowledge around monastic and ascetic practice; pastoral power, in which Cassian himself plays the role of shepherd to the monasteries' flock; and biopower, in which power is exercised through the gathering of data about a population. The interplay and overlap of these three forms of power will then inform my analysis of Cassian's rhetorical aims and methods.

In chapter four I establish that conflicts between the Church and monasteries or individual monks were not simply figments of Cassian's (or my) imagination but rather matters of historical, or at least rhetorical, record which I argue could have easily induced a type of monastic separatism in Cassian's writings. These conflicts include the Origenist Controversy, one manifestation of which resulted in Cassian and his faction being ousted from the monastic community of Scetis in Egypt, frequent attempts by the Church to ordain monks forcefully, due to the monks' overwhelming popularity and authority among laypeople, the extraordinary lengths to which some monks would go to avoid ordination (running away, self-mutilation, purposely ruining their own reputations, etc.), and the *Life of Antony*, written by a prominent and outspoken bishop, which portrayed Antony as a heresy fighter on the side of bishops versus Antony's own letters which show him to be a contemplative focused on right practice over against right belief. This last analysis will establish that many bishops, aware of the popularity as well as the reputation for holiness and wisdom the monks had among laypeople, attempted in myriad ways to co-opt the lives of these monks, including forcing them to become part of the institutional church and rewriting their histories with a bias toward church hierarchies.

Chapter five will verify that Cassian is advocating for a clear separation between monasticism and the Church. In this chapter, I appeal to evidence from Cassian's writings where he envisions an increasing distance between the spheres of monasticism and the Church. Cassian writes, for example, that monks should "flee from women and bishops;"[29] both are a temptation and distraction to the ascetic monk. Lest one think that Cassian has invented this phrase himself and is thus something of a rogue in the monastic world, he prefaces the phrase by noting that it is "an old maxim of the Fathers that is

---

29. Cassian, *Institutes*, 11.18. Omnimodis monachum fugere debere mulieres et episcopos.

still current."[30] In other words, such sentiments acknowledging the dangers of both women and bishops for monks are both deeply rooted in monastic tradition and contemporary with Cassian's fifth-century context. Theophilus, bishop of the church of Alexandria, expelled Cassian and his fellow monks from their monastic paradise ostensibly because of particular theological differences, specifically those around the bishop's official decree that God was embodied. However, this also highlighted the comparison between bases of authority, with monastic authority based largely on proper ascetic practice and ecclesial authority based on title and claims of apostolic succession. Cassian also encourages total dependence on the traditions and practices of his monastic predecessors, implicitly excluding other Church fathers and theologians. In addition, he writes that monks should treat their ascetic way of life as the Christian norm—only ascetics are truly living the ideal Christian life. Finally, Cassian and other monastic writings quote only two authoritative sources: Scripture and the sayings/stories of other monks.

To conclude, chapter six will sum up the case I have made, arguing that indeed Cassian's intention was not simply to correct a well-intentioned but ill-informed Gallican monastic practice, but rather to gather the monks of Gaul together to create a correct and separate institution, uncorrupted by the church's whims, both political and theological. I then discuss the implications of such a conclusion (the "so what," if you will). First, had this been executed as Cassian may have intended, it very well may have created a very early "reformation," in which the church would have been split between monastics and clergy. In this scenario, the popularity of monks among lay people might easily have caused the decline of clergy-centered Christianity, causing a complete turnabout in church orthodoxy. Had this occurred, with monasticism's emphasis on ascetic practice, it is safe to say that the wealth of the church might never have accrued in the way it did, quite possibly lessening church political power and influence.

---

30. Cassian, *Institutes*, 11.18. Quapropter haec est antiquitus patrum permanens nunc usque sententia.

Chapter Two
Cassian's Context and Asceticism as Basis for Valid Authority

In the *Institutes*, Cassian begins his discussion of the vice of gluttony (*gastrimargium*) by reestablishing the basis of his authority for writing on best practices for combating the vices: "[W]e have recourse once more to the traditions and laws of the Egyptians. Everyone knows that they contain a loftier discipline with respect to abstinence and a perfect degree of discretion."[1] Having confirmed once again that his basis for authority is not his own ideas but rather those of the venerated monks of Egypt, Cassian here also conveys what remains the basis of authority for those famous monks: asceticism. Not only are the monks of Egypt known for their basic piety, but that piety itself is founded on correct ascetic practices. The fact that Cassian views true authority as centered on asceticism forms the basis of his entire monastic system. Like the compiler of the *AP*, Cassian does not reject, for example, all bishops out of hand. Rather, he sees anyone who practices asceticism sincerely and moderately as worthy of respect and authority. Note, for example, his devotion to and advocacy for John Chrysostom, bishop of Constantinople and noted ascetic. It was certainly not Chrysostom's ecclesiastical position that made him a figure of respect for Cassian but his commitment to ascetic practice.

I begin this chapter with an analysis of Cassian's former context in Egypt's monastic culture. It was this culture that shaped his views and convinced him of the correct way to live the monastic life which he would attempt to pass on to the monks of Marseilles. I then move on to the formative theological and ascetic sources of Cassian's thought and writing, namely Origen of Alexandria and Evagrius Ponticus. Next, I move on to the church of fifth-century Gaul, whence Cassian writes both his *Institutes* and *Conferences*. Since my ultimate argument is that Cassian wanted a monasticism separate from the institutional Church, as I stated in the introduction, we must determine what the "institutional church" was in the sociopolitical context in which Cassian was writing. Thereafter, I discuss Cassian's conception of asceticism as the mark of true authority. This section

---

1. Cassian, *Institutes*, V.3. Et in primis de ieiuniorum modo et escarum qualitate dicturi rursus ad traditiones ac statuta recurrimus Aegyptiorum, quibus sublimiorem discretionis continentiae disciplinam et perfectam rationem inesse nullus ignorat.

demonstrates that Cassian's definition of asceticism differed markedly from that of the Gallican monks to whom he was writing.

Gallican monks seemed to share the Church's notion of asceticism as occasional—perhaps even optional—but certainly secondary to participation in the sacraments. Cassian, again playing the role of expert on Egyptian monasticism, outlined the true practice of asceticism which would indeed confer authority on monks who practiced correctly. These practices included a moderate rule of fasting and prayer—though strictly adhered to—by which monks could mark themselves and their bodies as worthy of authority. Ascetics transformed themselves internally and gave visible evidence (through emaciated bodies, lack of sleep and few or no possessions) that they were perfected. Since the Church did not value or enforce asceticism as strictly as Egyptian monks, Cassian would have viewed its institutional aspects, including hierarchs—at least those hierarchs who did not practice asceticism—as therefore less authoritative than the traditions and practices of Egyptian monasticism.

Cassian in Egypt and the Origins of Monasticism

Alexandria was an abnormal city in the Roman Egypt of the third-century. For one thing, it was a Greek-speaking city surrounded by a sea of Coptic-speaking Egyptians.[2] More significantly for my purposes, its citizens considered themselves set apart from the rest of Egypt by virtue of their cosmopolitan lifestyle. Ancient documents refer to Alexandria as though it were next to Egypt, rather than part of it (*Alexandria ad Aegyptum*).[3] Throughout the centuries, it could boast of a sophisticated and varied intellectual environment, including the Great Library which was destroyed during the civil war there (48–47 BCE), as well as renowned intellectuals and philosophers such as Euclid, Ptolemy, Philo, and Plotinus. It is thus no surprise that most of the monastic literature, connected as it was to the city of Alexandria, was first written in Greek.[4] As Christianity began to spread into the majority of the Roman Empire, monastics would become its new philosophers.

Three distinct types of monasticism formed in Egypt: eremitic, or the solitary life; cenobitic, or large communities living in monasteries; and small groups of monks called 'lavras' or 'sketes,' usually formed around a senior monk or teacher. While there is no unambiguous historical record of who

---

2. William Harmless, *Desert Christians: An Introduction to the Literature of Early Monasticism* (Oxford: Oxford University Press, 2004), 6.
3. Harmless, *Desert Christians*, 6.
4. Harmless, *Desert Christians*, 11.

2. Cassian's Context and Asceticism as Basis for Valid Authority 15

the first Christian monk was, Antony (c. 251–356 CE) has traditionally been named father of Christian monasticism, and specifically, eremitic monasticism, at least since Athanasius, the bishop of Alexandria, wrote his hagiography in the fourth century. I will discuss Antony and his significance for Egyptian monasticism in a later chapter. For now, suffice it to say that Antony was a hermit, believed to have lived entirely alone in the Egyptian desert for at least the first 20 years of his monastic career. As a celebrated monk, Antony, as portrayed in Athanasius' hagiography, thus became the first model for monks, many of whom followed his example by moving to the desert and inhabiting caves, abandoned pagan temples or mausoleums, or simple cells made from mud bricks.[5] Later, a former Roman soldier named Pachomius formed the first cenobitic monastery (ca. 318–23) at Tabennisi in the Thebaid, going on to form several more thereafter.[6] Finally, though there is no such origin story about lavras, there are ample examples of stories and sayings coming out of such small communities in the monastic literature of the time.[7]

As noted before, Cassian began his monastic career in Palestine, living in a monastery in Bethlehem.[8] After living there for several years, he departed in the mid-380s CE, with another monk named Germanus. They headed for the Egyptian desert, first the Nile Delta and then subsequently to Kellia and Scetis, to meet some of the monastic heroes Cassian had heard about from a traveling Egyptian monk who had visited Cassian's Bethlehem monastery.[9] In addition to leaving Bethlehem in order to meet the Egyptian monks, Cassian writes also that his cenobitic community in Bethlehem was deficient in its discipline, a foreshadowing of the polemic tone he would later take with the Gallican monks.[10] Specifically, Cassian writes that the Bethlehem monks liked to go to sleep after the night office and at the same time, were inflexible in their rule of fasting, refusing to meet the far more important

---

5. Harmless, *Desert Christians*, 18.
6. Harmless, *Desert Christians*, 18.
7. Harmless, *Desert Christians*, 18.
8. Columba Stewart, *Cassian the Monk* (New York, NY: Oxford University Press, 1998), 6. Cassian specifically writes of "our own monastery, where our Lord Jesus Christ was born of a virgin and deigned to go through the states of his human infancy" (*Inst.*, 3.4.1) Nostroque monasterio primitus institutam, ubi dominus noster Iesus Christus natus ex uirgine humanae infantiae.
9. Cassian, *Conferences*, 20.1. See also Stewart, *Cassian the Monk*, 7. Cassian's lack of detail about his own past, while perhaps an admirable sign of humility in the ethos of monks in Egypt, is often frustrating for Cassian scholars.
10. Cassian, *Institutes*, 5.24. See also Stewart, *Cassian the Monk*, 7. Cassian also writes that the monks in Bethlehem would go back to sleep after morning prayers rather than doing some kind of manual labor as they should. Cassian, *Institutes*, 3.4.2.

requirements of hospitality for travelers on fast days.[11] That is, they were too lenient on some aspects of practice and too strict on others, a clear problem of incorrect priorities. The point, in Cassian's instructions to the monks of Gaul, was always to find the right balance of rigor and mercy.

Arriving in Egypt, Cassian and Germanus visited some of the most prominent monks, and eventually put down roots in the monastic settlement of Scetis, staying for about 15 years. Columba Stewart writes that Cassian left Bethlehem for Egypt some time in the 380's CE and, because Cassian mentions the festal letter of Theophilus which started the Origenist Controversy and ended with Cassian's exile, we can reliably date the controversy to approximately 399–400 CE.[12] Choosing neither the eremitic nor the cenobitic way of life, Cassian apparently lived in a small community which included the Tall Brothers and, more significantly, Evagrius Ponticus. Evagrius had abandoned a promising ecclesiastical career for the rigors of desert asceticism. His ideas, though Cassian never mentions him by name, would have a profound effect on Cassian's own notions of what correct monastic practice should be.[13] It is notable, given the purpose of this book, that in the biographical material on Evagrius, he is said to have started out as an ordained deacon and to have behaved unbecomingly while ordained. Thereafter, he became an ascetic monk and was hailed by numerous authors as a model monk and theologian.[14]

The most important mandate of Egyptian monasticism was renunciation. This was the key concept intended to completely remake the individual and thus included several levels. First, the monk was to renounce all social ties, including family, friends, and village, town, or city. The *AP* contains several stories in which a monk's distraught family members venture out into the merciless Egyptian desert in an attempt to reclaim the monk, only to find that not only do they no longer recognize him but also that the monk is unwilling to return, indicating that the transformation beyond his original social identity was already complete.[15] The fact that even a monk's mother no longer recognizes him uses the monk's appearance as a synecdoche for this profound inner change. In short, to renounce social ties in the late antique world was to undergo a kind of living death, or as Peter Brown puts

---

11. Cassian, *Institutes*, 5.24.
12. Stewart, *Cassian the Monk*, 8. See also Elizabeth A. Clark, *Origenist Controversy: The Cultural Construction of an Early Christian Debate* (Princeton, NJ: Princeton University Press, 2014), 44–46.
13. For biographical material on Evagrius see Palladius, *Lausiac History*, chapter 38.
14. Palladius, *Lausiac History*, 12–13.
15. See for example, *AP*, Poemen, 76 and Mark, Disciple of Abba Silvanus, 3.

it, "the self-imposed annihilation of [one's] social status."[16] One's entire identity was tied up with the community and family among whom one had been born and raised, which may be why exile was one of the severest punishments levied upon transgressors in the ancient world.

Next, monks were expected to renounce all personal possessions, including the security of wealth and any other physical objects to which they might be attached. Again, the point of such renunciation was untying the thread that bound the monk to a worldly identity. In one apothegm, for example, a monk named Gelasius, who is said to have lived a very austere, solitary existence, is given many material things, including beasts of burden and cattle, in order to establish a monastery. Another monk asks Gelasius if he is worried that he will become enslaved by all these possessions. Gelasius replies: "Your spirit is more enslaved by the needle with which you work than the spirit of Gelasius by these goods."[17] Apparently Gelasius, through years of profound austerity, had learned to detach entirely from any sentimental connection to material objects, even when they were at his disposal. Monks were to depend on God alone for their needs. An apothegm about Abba Bessarion makes this point clearly:

> Abba Doulas, the disciple of Abba Bessarion said, 'One day when we were walking beside the sea I was thirsty and I said to Abba Bessarion, "Father, I am very thirsty." He said a prayer and said to me, "Drink some of the sea water." The water proved sweet when I drank some. I even poured some into a leather bottle for fear of being thirsty later on. Seeing this, the old man asked me why I was taking some. I said to him, "Forgive me, it is for fear of being thirsty later on." Then the old man said, "God is here, God is everywhere."[18]

---

16. Brown, *Body and Society*, 214.

17. *Apophthegmata Patrum* (Greek Alphabetic) (AP), edited by Jean-Baptiste Cotelier, in *Ecclisiae Graecae Monumenta*. Paris: 1677, 1.338–712, Reprinted by Jacques-Paul Migne, in *Patrologia Graeca* 65: 71–440. Paris: J.-P. Migne, 1864, Edited by Jean-Claude Guy, *Recerches sur la tradition grecque des* Apophthegmata Patrum, 13–58. Subsidia Hagiographica, 36. Brussels: Société des Bollandiste, 1962, Translated by Benedicta Ward, *The Sayings of the Desert Fathers: the Alphabetical Collection*, Kalamazoo, MI: Cistercian, 2004. Gelasius, 5. Δέδεται μᾶλλον ὁ λογισμός σου εἰς τὸ κεντητῆριν ἐν ᾧ ἐργάζῃ, ἢ ὁ λογισμὸς Γελασίου εἰς τὰ κτήματα.

18. *AP*, Bessarion, 1. Ἔλεγεν ὁ ἀββᾶς Δουλᾶς ὁ μαθητὴς τοῦ ἀββᾶ Βισαρίωνος, ὅτι Ὁδευόντων ἡμῶν ποτε εἰς ὄχθαν τῆς θαλάσσης, ἐδίψησα, καὶ εἶπον τῷ ἀββᾷ Βισαρίωνι· Ἀββᾶ, διψῶ πάνυ. Καὶ ποιήσας εὐχὴν ὁ γέρων, λέ γει μοι· Πίε ἐκ τῆς θαλάσσης. Καὶ ἐγλυκάνθη τὸ ὕδωρ, καὶ ἔπιον. Ἐγὼ δὲ ἤντλησα εἰς τὸ ἀγγεῖον, μήποτε παρ᾽ ἐκεῖ διψήσω. Καὶ ἰδὼν ὁ γέρων,[140] λέγει μοι· Διατί ἤντλησας; Λέγω αὐτῷ· Συγχώρησόν μοι, μή ποτε παρ᾽ ἐκεῖ διψήσω. Καὶ εἶπεν ὁ γέρων· Ὁ Θεὸς ὧδε, καὶ πάντη Θεός.

Finally, monks were to renounce their very lives, no longer valuing their survival above all, but rather acting as if they were the least deserving of all creatures. In monastic parlance, this extreme renunciation of self was called humility (Greek: ταπεινότητα; Latin: *humilitas*): "Abba Anthony said, 'I saw the snares that the enemy spreads out over the world and I said groaning, "What can get through from such snares?" Then I heard a voice saying to me, "Humility."[19] This was the final renunciation and was considered by many to be the *sine qua non* of true monastic life. Abba John the Short is quoted as saying "Humility and the fear of God are above all virtues."[20] In another apothegm referring to the same Abba John, a monk asks: "Who is this John, who by his humility has all Scetis hanging from his little finger?"[21] This particular apothegm is notable in that it implies a sort of power, or at the very least esteem, gained by the practice of humility, perhaps best exemplified in the Gospel adage: "He who humbles himself will be exalted (Lk. 14.11)." Cassian has much to say about the absolute necessity for monks to be humble. In the *Conferences*, he writes of Abba Paphnutius that "by the practice of humility and obedience he mortified all his desires, and by this stamped out all his faults and acquired every virtue which the monastic system and the teaching of the ancient fathers produces."[22] Notice here that while Paphnutius surely practiced many forms of asceticism in his many years as a monk, including avoiding sleep, fasting, and long hours of prayer, it is humility and obedience, attitudes of mind in which one's own will is surrendered, which seem to have made the difference in transforming his character. Cassian here demonstrates through his rhetorical mouthpiece that relinquishing the personal will is the foundation of all other renunciations.

It was this theme of total renunciation that undergirded everything Cassian would attempt to teach Gallican monks in both the *Institutes* and the *Conferences*. As we shall see below, Gallican monks had not been required to renounce much of anything and must therefore have seemed all but heretical to Cassian for even calling themselves monks. Having shown the

---

19. *AP*, Antony, 7. Εἶπεν ὁ ἀββᾶς Ἀντώνιος· Εἶδον πάσας τὰς παγίδας τοῦ ἐχθροῦ ἡπλωμένας ἐπὶ τῆς γῆς· καὶ στενάξας εἶπον· Τίς ἄρα παρέρχεται ταύτας; Καὶ ἤκουσα φωνῆς λεγούσης μοι· Ἡ ταπεινοφροσύνη. See also Arsenius, 36; Euprepius, 5.

20. *AP*, John the Short, 22. Ἡ ταπεινοφροσύνη καὶ ὁ φόβος τοῦ Θεοῦ, ὑπεράνω εἰσὶ πασῶν τῶν ἀρετῶν.

21. *AP*, John the Short, 36. ὅτι Τίς ἐστιν ὁ Ἰωάννης, ὅτι διὰ τῆς ταπεινώσεως αὐτοῦ, ἐκρέμασεν ὅλην τὴν Σκῆτιν ἐν τῷ μικρῷ αὐτοῦ δακτύλῳ.

22. Cassian, *Conferences*, III.1. Humilitatis namque et oboedientiae disciplina omnes suas mortificans uoluntates et per hanc extinctis uniuersis uitiis cunctisque uirtutibus consummates.

2. Cassian's Context and Asceticism as Basis for Valid Authority 19

Egyptian monastic culture and values from which Cassian drew his ideas, we now turn to the context in which he was writing and the monks for whom he wrote.

Here, a bit of background information about the *Institutes* and the *Conferences*, Cassian's two principal writings, is appropriate.[23] The full Latin title of the *Institutes* was *De Institutis Coenobiorum et de Octo Principalium Uitiorum Remediis Libri XII*. The Latin word *instituta*, plural *institutum*, is derived from the verb *instituere*, best translated as "to establish" or "to lay down." This is entirely apt because the intention of the *Institutes* is to establish the correct form of monastic life in Gaul by laying down the specific rules and procedures for such an establishment. The word "institutes" also carries pedagogical weight, in that Cassian is not simply laying down rules and regulations but also teaching and passing down what he was taught by the monks of Egypt. He writes, for example,

> I shall faithfully attempt to explain, as well as I can with the Lord's help, just the institutes (*instituta*) of these men and the rules of their monasteries and, in particular, the origins and causes and remedies of the principal vices, which they number as eight, according to their traditions.[24]

Here, Cassian demonstrates the multivalent use of the word "institute": it is a teaching, meant to lay down the proper rules for the establishment of a proper monastery.

As for the *Conferences*, the original Latin title was *Conlationes XXIV*. The Latin word *conlatio* means "to bring or gather together," whether people or objects. In Cassian's parlance, the word means a gathering together of monks, usually to listen to the wisdom of an elder monk.[25] This indeed defines the entire genre of the *Conferences*. Each conference starts with young Cassian himself (as both narrator and infrequent interlocutor) and his friend Germanus as principal interlocutor and seeker of wisdom, asking questions of a more experienced and better-known elder monk, including some monks, such as Abba Moses, who were extremely famous in Cassian's time and appear in many late antique monastic sources. The bulk of each conference is given to the answers of these elder monks. The form is

---

23. Cassian also wrote *De Incarnatione Domini Contra Nestorium* (translated into English as *On the Incarnation*) as a defense against accusations that he was a Semipelagian. These accusations were made by a follower of Augustine's, Prosper of Aquitaine.

24. Cassian, *Institutes*, preface, 7. Instituta eorum tantummodo ac monasteriorum regulas maximeque principalium vitiorum, quae octo ab eis designantur, esider et causas curationesque secundum esideria eorum quantum domino adiuuante potuero, fideliter explicare contendam.

25. For Cassian's use of the term "conlatio" in this sense, see *Inst.* 5.29, 5.31, 12.27.2-4; *Conf.* 2.5.2, 2.15.3, 16.12.

somewhat Platonic as well in that each conference is in the form of a dialogue, as opposed to the unilateral direction of the teachings in the *Institutes*.

Finally, I have classified both the *Institutes* and the *Conferences* as works of rhetoric, and as such I will frequently refer throughout this book to Cassian's rhetoric. By rhetoric, I mean first that the works are meant to persuade their audience. Specifically, I rely on Aristotle's definition of rhetoric as the ability to perceive and implement what will be most persuasive to a given audience in every single situation.[26] In this case, while Cassian's patron, Bishop Castor of Apta Julia, will certainly read the final results, Cassian's intended audience is the monks of Gaul themselves. He is not only laying down rules, but also attempting to persuade them that following such rules will make them as holy and eventually perfect as their counterparts in Egypt. As we shall see in another section, Cassian uses established rhetorical methods from his own classical education in order to appeal to and persuade the educated monks of Gaul. I therefore use the term rhetoric to emphasize that, although Cassian seems to have a disdain for the classical learning of his time, he is clearly well-educated himself, an education which, in the fourth century when Cassian grew up, consisted in large part of training in rhetoric.[27] Thus, while Cassian is establishing the proper life of the monastery, he, like the similarly educated Augustine of Hippo, is also using his classical training to persuade his audience that what he says is true. His principal rhetorical tool, as I discuss below, is the use of the venerated Desert Fathers with their impeccable ethos as his mouthpieces in the *Conferences*, thus lending his discourse a force of holiness and authority that his own name might not have inspired. While the *Institutes* are clearly written from his own perspective, he refers constantly to the fact that he learned these rules and traditions from the eminent monks of Egypt. In other words, he does not speak on his own behalf but rather passes down what he learned from the holy men with whom he lived and practiced.

Cassian's Sources: Origen of Alexandria and Evagrius Ponticus

To elucidate further the conflict known to scholars as the Origenist Controversy, and Cassian's place within it, I turn here to the two most influential of Cassian's sources: Origen of Alexandria (184–253 CE) and Cassian's monastic contemporary and teacher, Evagrius Ponticus (345–99 CE). It is far

---

26. Aristotle, *Problems, Volume II: Books 20–38. Rhetoric to Alexander,* Edited and translated by Robert Mayhew, David C. Mirhady. Loeb Classical Library 317 (Cambridge, MA: Harvard University Press, 2011), I.2, 1355b26f.

27. George A. Kennedy, *Classical Rhetoric & Its Christian and Secular Tradition* (Chapel Hill, NC: The University of North Carolina Press, 1999), 167.

2. Cassian's Context and Asceticism as Basis for Valid Authority   21

beyond the scope of this book to make a full study of these two instrumental Christian thinkers.[28] However, their influence on Cassian's thought and writings was profound, and an overview of the two is thus essential to understanding Cassian's unique perspective on both theology and ascetic monasticism. While it is true that Cassian never mentions either Origen or Evagrius by name, this is likely for political reasons (which I will explain later).

Concerning the so-called Origenist Controversy, the most significant and controversial of Origen's opinions in late antique Egypt would prove to be on the nature of divinity. He begins *On First Principles* (Greek—Περι αρχων, Latin—*De principiis*), his *opus magnus*, with a discussion of the immateriality of God in reference to scriptural references. He notes first that some of his contemporaries argue that, following certain biblical passages such as "For the LORD your God is a consuming fire (Deut 4.24)," God is embodied. Origen views this and other bodily descriptions of God in scripture as metaphors, employed to explain divinity to less sophisticated readers. He argues therefore that "although many saints partake of the Holy Spirit, he is not on that account to be regarded as a kind of body, which is divided into material parts and distributed to each of the saints, but rather as a sanctifying power."[29]

After addressing God at the beginning of the world in the first chapter, in chapter six of *On First Principles*, Origen writes about "the end and consummation of all things."[30] He writes "the highest good, towards which all rational nature is progressing, and which is also called the end of all things… is to become as far as possible like God."[31] However, this is far

---

28. In addition to reading the voluminous works of Origen—especially *On First Principles*, I would recommend that anyone interested in an overview of Origen's life and thought read *Origen* by Joseph Trigg (London: Taylor and Francis, 2012). For a similar overview of Evagrius' life and thought, I recommend *Reconstructing the Theology of Evagrius Ponticus: Beyond Heresy*, by Augustine Casiday (Cambridge: Cambridge University Press, 2013).

29. Origen, G.W. Butterworth, and Henri De Lubac, translators, *On First Principles* (New York, NY: Harper & Row, 1966). I.1.3. Sed et cum de Spiritu sancto multi sancti participant, non utique corpus aliquod inteligi potest Spiritus sanctus quod divisum in partes esideria percipiat unusquisque sanctorum: sed virtus profecto sanctificans est." There is no complete extant copy of *On First Principles* in the original Greek. There are, however, Greek fragments preserved in an anthology of Origen's writings, the *Philokalia*, compiled by Basil the Great and Gregory Nazianzen. Most English translations are made from a Latin translation made by Rufinus of Aquileia in 397. For this reason, and for consistency, I will take all my translations here from Rufinus' Latin. For more on this manuscript history see John Anthony McGuckin, *The Westminster Handbook to Origen* (Louisville, KY: Westminster John Knox Press, 2004).

30. Origen, *On First Principles.*, 3.6.1. De fine vero mundi et desideria omnium.

31. Origen, *On First Principles*, 3.6.1. Igitur summum bonum ad quod natura

from a mere *Imitatio Christi* preached in later eras. In fact, Origen quite clearly believes that in the end, humans will attain union with God. He infers this from Genesis 1.26 in which God is said to have made man in his own image, concluding that while this indwelling image grants humans the possibility of achieving the perfection of God, "he should in the end… obtain for himself the perfect 'likeness.'"[32] Intimately entwined with this idea, however, is the question of what this conception of perfection will look like. Will human beings become perfect physical specimens in imitation of an embodied God, or will that perfection be uninhibited by physical limitations? Origen's opinion, citing John 17.21, is clear: "We are also led to believe that the end of all things will be incorporeal by the statement of our Savior, in which he says 'That as I and thou are one, so they also may be one in us.'"[33] Furthermore, he goes on to write that this putative union with the divine must signify God's lack of corporeality, not only at the end of days, but eternally. He writes, therefore, that this quotation on union with God from John 17.21 leaves us

> compelled to accept one of two alternatives and either despair of ever attaining the likeness of God if we are destined always to have bodies, or else, if there is promised to us a blessedness of the same life that God has, then we must live in the same condition in which God lives.[34]

Origen clearly believed that God was incorporeal, and that incorporeality was a higher state of being, fit only for God and those with whom God deigned to unite. This notion, among many others, would go on to heavily influence the monk who was likely John Cassian's primary monastic teacher, Evagrius Ponticus.[35] Equally significant for Cassian's thought was Origen's conception of the various levels of reading and interpreting

---

rationabilis universa festinate, quod etiam finis omnium dicitur… quia summum bonum sit, prout desideri est, similem fieri Deo.

32. Origen, *On First Principles*, 3.6.1. De fine vero mundi et desideria omnium.

33. Origen, *On First Principles*, 3.6.1. Nos quoque ducitur ad finem omnia credere quae a te dicitur Salvatoris passus esse dicatur, in qua dicit, 'quod sicut ego et tu unum sumus, ita et ipsi in nobis unum.'

34. Origen, *On First Principles*, III.6.1. Cogimur accipiunt duorum vel impetrandi similitudinem Dei sumus semper corpora uel si promissum est nobis illa uita Deum possumus, uiuunt in tali statu in quo Deus habitat.

35. While Evagrius' influence on Cassian is undeniable in both style and content, for reasons I will discuss shortly, Origen's influence is less obvious in both style and content. For this reason, I am unsure whether Cassian had actually read the works of Origen or if Origen's pervasive influence on certain types of monasticism were already so powerful by the fifth century that they merely formed the *habitus* in which Cassian lived, moved, and had his monastic being.

scripture. For Origen, there are three ways of interpreting scripture, each appropriate to the level of spiritual attainment of individual readers.

> Each one must therefore portray the meaning of the divine writings in a threefold way upon his own soul; that is, so that the simple may be edified by what we may call the body of the scriptures...while those who have begun to make a little progress and are able to perceive something more than that may be edified by the soul of scripture; and those who are perfect... may be edified by that spiritual law which has 'a shadow of the good things to come', as if by the Spirit. Just as a man, therefore, is said to consist of body, soul and spirit, so also does the holy scripture, which has been bestowed by the divine bounty for man's salvation. [36]

Note here that Origen ties the lower level of scriptural understanding, the literal, to the body, again affirming his schema of the disembodied as higher in state than the embodied. Cassian would employ a similar scheme of scriptural interpretation, designating the first and lowest level as tropology (*tropologia*) which was useful for moral and ascetic instruction, the second as allegory (*allegoria*), related to revelations from scripture conferred upon one who has spiritual understanding, and anagogy (*anagogia*), which goes above and beyond even allegory to sacred mysteries not easily comprehended through ordinary uses of language.[37]

While Cassian may or may not have actually read the works of Origen, he clearly read the works of Evagrius Ponticus and may even have learned from him personally. Evagrius had been a monk in Egypt for several years before Cassian arrived. Even though he never mentions Evagrius's name, Cassian borrows liberally from him in his own writings. First, he uses the Evagrian system to outline what Cassian calls the eight principal vices (*octo principalium uitiorum*). Evagrius, writing years before Cassian, calls them the eight thoughts (τῶν ὀκτὼ λογισμῶν). While the word Cassian uses, translated as "vices", may seem more active and participatory than Evagrius's "thoughts" a quick read of Cassian's version shows that every one of the vices is a form of dangerous or tempting thinking, which may or may not lead to bad conduct but will certainly prevent the attainment of ascetic perfection. In addition, in appropriating Evagrius's system of vices, Cassian

---

36. Origen, *On First Principles*, 4.2.4. Idcirco unumquemque sensum exprimat divinis tripliciter in animam suam qui cum ei motus fuerit parum proficere, et redire possunt percipere quam quod sit aliquid animae erit aedificati sermonibus Scripturarum testimoniis innititur et eos, qui sunt ... perfectus sit quod aedificationem ex lege spirituali, quae esider bonum quae sunt umbra futurorum, tamquam a Domini Spiritu. Quemadmodum ergo dicitur consistere in corporis, animae et spiritus, sic quoque non scripturam sacram, liberalitatis divinae, quae cum tibi sive adsalus hominis.

37. John Cassian, *Conferences*, 14.8.2-5.

even uses Evagrius's Greek names for four of them, although he transliterates them into the Latin alphabet.[38] He also makes liberal uses of Evagrius's Greek words, written in Greek in this case, for monastic practice (πρακτική) and mystical contemplation (θεωρητικη).

Evagrius's method of scriptural interpretation follows in the footsteps of Origen and certainly presages that of John Cassian. Unlike Origen and Cassian, however, Evagrius divides scripture into only two categories, literal (αισθητα) and allegorical (αλληγορια). Nevertheless, he still divides his interpretive scheme into three categories like Origen, namely those scriptures that pertain to practice or asceticism (πρακτική), those which pertain to the contemplation of nature or creation (φυσική), and those that pertain to theology or higher contemplation (θεολογική) and this generally corresponds with both Origen's and Cassian's notions of scriptural exegesis.[39]

In addition, Evagrius fully accepted Origen's conviction that God was incorporeal. His writings on contemplation make this abundantly clear. For example, he writes that although many who pray look for visible signs of divinity, this is both ill-advised and ultimately impossible because "God is without quantity and without all outward form."[40] In addition, he cautions praying monks to beware of trying to limit God by placing him within an imagined physical state: "Vainglory is the source of the illusions of your mind. When it exerts its influence on the mind it attempts to enclose the Divinity in form and figure."[41] Both Evagrius and Origen held tightly to an incorporeal God. This explains much in the historical context of Egyptian monasticism at the turn of the fifth century when Cassian and the Tall Brothers would be exiled for espousing this belief. However, it does not explain why Cassian would mention neither Origen nor Evagrius in his own writing.

After Theophilus of Alexandria condemned Origenism, symbolized by his specific condemnation of the notion of an incorporeal deity, it became increasingly dangerous to align oneself with Origen or anyone else, like Evagrius, who had a similarly Origenist theological inclination. Many of

---

38. *Gastrimargia* (γαστριμαργία) for gluttony, *filargyria* (φιλαργυρία) for avarice, *acedia* (ακηδία) for listlessness, *cenodoxia* (κενοδοξία) for vainglory.

39. Cassian, *Conferences*, 14.1.2.

40. Evagrius Ponticus, Ο ΓΝΟΣΤΙΚΟΣ Η ΠΡΟΣ ΤΟΝ ΚΑΤΑΞΙΩΘΕΝΤΑ ΓΝΩΣΕΩΣ, *The Gnostikos*, ed. A. & C. Guillaumont, Évagre le Pontique, Le Gnostique ou A celui qui est devenu digne de la science, Sources Chrétiennes n° 356 (Paris, 1989) 88–193.

41. Evagrius Ponticus, translated by John Eudes Bamberger. *The Praktikos and Chapters on Prayer* (Kalamazoo, MI: Cistercian Publications, 1981), Chapters, 67. ἄποσον δὲ τὸ θεῖον καὶ ἀσχημάτιστον.

Origen's teachings would later be anathematized in 553 CE at the Second Council of Constantinople and anyone else who seemed to follow in his theological footsteps such as Evagrius similarly fell out of favor.[42] Because of the anathematization of his ideas, we do not have the majority of his writings in Greek, "whether by atrophy or by neglect."[43] We do have a number of his writings translated into Latin however, and Ken Parry notes that in these Latin versions, "many of the most eccentric doctrines attributed to him are not to be found."[44] Whether this means that the doctrines were mere fictions created by people determined to rid church orthodoxy of his influence or whether the Latin translator Rufinus excised such doctrines in order to make them more palatable to the orthodox is anyone's guess. Despite all this controversy, Origen continued to have a verifiable influence on theology for centuries. Richard Simon, for example, notes that "most of the Fathers who lived after Origen scarcely did anything but copy his commentaries and other treatises on scripture" and "even those who were opposed to his sentiments could not keep from reading them and profiting from them."[45] However, it is likely for the above political reasons that Cassian, while certainly espousing many of Origen's theological and scriptural notions, prudently avoided mentioning both Origen and the distinctly Origenist Evagrius Ponticus.

Asceticism as Authority

While in the deserts of Egypt, Cassian and his companion Germanus met with a revered monk known as Abba Serapion with whom they discussed the eight principal vices that assaulted any monk trying to attain purity of heart (*puritatem cordis*). For the vices of gluttony and lust, Serapion noted that mere mental vigilance would not suffice. Instead, since these two fundamental vices were carnal in nature (as opposed to more abstract vices such as anger or sadness), physical asceticism was necessary in order to defeat them. According to Serapion, this defeat could only be effected by means of "fasting, vigils, and works of penance, and to these is added living in a remote place, because just as they are generated through the fault of both

---

42. Evagrius Ponticus, *Chapters on Prayer*, 116. Ἀρχὴ πλάνης νοῦ, κενοδοξία, ἐξ ἧς κινούμενος ὁ νοῦς, ἐν σχήματι καὶ μορφαῖς περιγράφειν πειρᾶται τὸ Θεῖον.
43. Ken Parry, ed. *The Wiley Blackwell Companion to Patristics* (Oxford, UK: John Wiley & Sons, Incorporated, 2015), 98.
44. Parry, *The Wiley Blackwell Companion*, 98.
45. Richard Simon, *Histoire Critique du Vieux Testament*, 1.3.1 (1685 edn, p. 403) in vol. 1, p. 212.

soul and body, so they cannot be overcome except by the toil of both."[46] In other words, only ascetic practices would grant the monk sufficient power to be able to overcome the most problematic spiritual obstacles.

Asceticism as a mark of spiritual authority had a long tradition within the history of Christianity and Christian monasticism. As mentioned earlier, Athanasius's *Life of Antony*, despite its questionable veracity as to the details of the famous monk's life, in many ways set the tone for the future monastic way of life. Antony was said to have given up all his possessions and retired to a solitary life in the desert during which he endured demonic temptations and tortures.[47] Since this book was something of an ancient bestseller throughout the Roman Empire, this became the model of a true Egyptian anchoritic life, one in which voluntary deprivations and the stoic endurance of mental anguish, portrayed as demonic attacks, served to transform a normal human being into a saint. Athanasius begins the prologue of the *Life of Antony* by writing to his reader (or patron) "You have entered upon a noble rivalry with the monks of Egypt by your determination either to equal or surpass them in your training in the way of virtue."[48] Athanasius even characterized Antony (and thus Antony's future imitators) as the new martyrs, since Christians were no longer persecuted in the wake of Constantine's acceptance of Christianity.[49] The pursuit of rigorous asceticism, mortifying the body in order to achieve holiness, became a substitute for the willing suffering and death of the earlier Christian martyrs. To further emphasize this point, Antony, in Athanasius' hagiography, actively seeks martyrdom in Alexandria and, failing to attain it, much to his frustration, goes back to his solitary ascetic ways as a worthy alternative.[50]

Athanasius and Antony were hardly the only people in the fourth century or earlier who advocated the ascetic life as indicative of true spiritual authority. Many thinkers, both Christian and pagan, had long characterized the importance and power of the ascetic life before John Cassian would write his own account in the fifth century. What follows is a brief history of

---

46. Cassian, *Conferences*, 5.4.3. Quae ieiuniis, uigiliis et operis contritione perficitur, hisque fuerit remotio localis adiuncta, quia sicut amborum uitio, id est animae et corporis generantur, ita superari nisi utriusque labore non poterunt.

47. Athanasius, *Vita Antonii*, edited and translated by G.J.M. Bartelink, Sources Chrétiennes, 400, Éditions du Cerf, 1994. Translated by Robert C. Gregg, *Athanasius: The Life of Antony and the Letter to Marcellinus* (Mahwah, NJ: Paulist Press, 1980), 2–3.

48. Athanasius, *Vita Antonii*, Prologue. Ἀγαθὴν ἅμιλλαν ἐνεστήσασθε πρὸς τοὺς ἐν Αἰγύπτῳ μοναχοὺς, ἤτοι παρισωθῆναι, ἢ καὶ ὑπερβάλλεσθαι τούτους προελόμενοι τῇ κατ᾽ ἀρετὴν ὑμῶν ἀσκήσει.

49. Athanasius, *Vita Antonii*, 47.

50. Athanasius, *Vita Antonii*, 46–47.

2. Cassian's Context and Asceticism as Basis for Valid Authority   27

the connection between the practices of asceticism and the authority such practices conferred leading up to Cassian's time. Since Cassian would ultimately bring ideas and practices from Eastern Christendom to the West, I also examine here exemplars of both Eastern and Western monasticism in regard to asceticism.

The notion of ascesis as a vital part of the life of the soul had a long history in Greek philosophy before the advent of Christianity. The Greek word ἄσκησις originally connoted physical training, specifically for athletes who would compete in the Olympic games or other such contests.[51] This self-discipline, including methods of physical exercise and diet, was later notionally extended to those who wished to train philosophically by denying themselves hedonistic pleasures in order to train the personal will. Such well-known Greek philosophers as Plotinus and Porphyry, for example, would advocate practicing self-denial as a method of weakening the body in order to strengthen and/or transform the soul.[52] The Cynic philosophers, principally Diogenes of Sinope, advocated giving up every possession unneeded for survival in order to be free of worldly attachments.[53] Even ancient political figures saw ascetic practice as a way to validate both their character and their authority. The Tarantine general Archytas (c. 380–345 BCE), for example, was "[k]nown for his lofty morals, self-control, and rigorous asceticism… [and] greatly admired by Plato and likely served as a model for his philosopher-king."[54] In Virgil's *Aeneid*, the author writes that one only proves oneself worthy of leadership through self-mastery.[55] These early Greek and Roman figures lent a kind of authority to practices of self-denial such that those who practiced them were often seen as fundamentally wise.[56]

In terms of Christian origins, the New Testament described the life of John the Baptist as being particularly ascetic. He was said to have withdrawn alone to the desert, clothed himself in coarse camel hair and eaten

---

51. See, for example, Xenophon, *Memorabilia*, 1.2.24.
52. Plotinus, *Ennead, Volume I: Porphyry on the Life of Plotinus. Ennead I*, Translated by A. H. Armstrong, Loeb Classical Library 440 (Cambridge, MA: Harvard University Press, 1969), 2.
53. Suvák Vladislav, Flachbartová Lívia, and Pavol Sucharek, "The Care of the Self and Diogenes' Ascetic Practices," in *Care of the Self. Ancient Problematizations of Life and Contemporary Thought* (Leiden: Koninklijke Brill NV, 2017), 50–96, 50.
54. Andrea Sterk, *Renouncing the World Yet Leading the Church* (Cambridge, MA: Harvard University Press, 2004), 4.
55. Alison Keith and Leif E. Vaage, "Imperial Asceticism: Discipline of Domination," in Vaage and Wimbush, eds., *Asceticism and the New Testament*, 414–19.
56. See Werner Jaeger, *Early Christianity and Greek Paideia* (Cambridge, MA: Harvard University Press, 1961), 90.

only locusts and wild honey (Mk 1.4-6). Jesus himself had started his ministry with rigorous prayer and fasting and had encouraged followers to give away or sell all their possessions (Mt. 4.1-2, Mt. 19.21). The apostle Paul wrote of how he punished his body to keep it under control and rejected marriage for himself (1 Cor. 9 and 1 Cor. 7.29-35). These seminal figures in the early church set the standard for asceticism as an authoritative praxis for one who "would be perfect (Mt. 19.21)." This notion of asceticism as the correct mode of Christian life, while perhaps not universally accepted in the early years of Christianity, would persist and develop to different extents in the early centuries of the church.

Philip Rousseau writes extensively on the development of ascetic society, especially among the desert fathers of Egypt from whom Cassian would draw the material and ideas for his writings. Rousseau notes, for example, that in the Prologue to the *AP*, "praise is bestowed first on what the text calls 'valiant asceticism—a wondrous way of life'; and only then is reference made to 'the words of those blessed and saintly fathers'."[57] What made these desert monks truly worthy of authority was their austere lifestyles; any words of wisdom they offered could only be seen as wise if they were produced by ascetic practitioners. Initially, feats of asceticism were largely based on hearsay from writings such as the *Life of Antony*. However, eventually "there are," Rousseau explains, "signs... of a change from word to example" in the ascetic literature.[58] In one apothegm, for example, a monk named Isaac becomes frustrated when his master, Cronius, refuses to give him any instructions on how to live. When some other monks approach Cronius, advocating for Isaac and asking Cronius to instruct him more explicitly, Cronius answers "As far as I am concerned, I do not tell him anything, but if he wishes he can do what he sees me doing."[59] What was most significant was not the words or instructions of such monks, important as those were, but rather imitation of their way of life. Lay travelers might travel to the desert and ask for "a word" from one of the venerable monks, but what really mattered was viewing the daily routines of these monks down to the last detail and acting accordingly. It is clearly implied in the early monastic literature from Egypt and Palestine that mere words will not benefit the questioner unless or until he personally puts ascetic principles into practice. One example of such an apothegm referencing Antony in the *AP* is worth quoting in full:

---

57. Philip Rousseau, *Ascetics, Authority, and the Church: in the Age of Jerome and Cassian* (Notre Dame, IN: University of Notre Dame Press, 2010), 39.
58. Rousseau, *Ascetics, Authority, and the Church*, 39.
59. *AP*, Isaac, Priest of the Cells, 2. Ἐγὼ τέως, οὐδὲν λέγω αὐτῷ • ἀλλ' ἐὰν θέλῃ, ὃ βλέπει με ποιοῦντα, ποιήσει χαι αὐτός.

2. Cassian's Context and Asceticism as Basis for Valid Authority

> The brethren came to Abba Anthony and said to him, 'Speak a word; how are we to be saved?' The old man said to them, 'You have heard the Scriptures. That should teach you how.' But they said, 'We want to hear from you too, Father.' Then the old man said to them, 'The Gospel says, "if anyone strikes you on one cheek, turn to him the other also (Matt. 5:39)."' They said, 'We cannot do that.' The old man said, 'If you cannot offer the other cheek, at least allow one cheek to be struck.' 'We cannot do that either,' they said. So he said, 'If you are not able to do that do not return evil for evil,' and they said, 'We cannot do that either.' Then the old man said to his disciple, 'Prepare a little brew of corn for these invalids. If you cannot do this, or that, what can I do for you? What you need is prayers.'[60]

Note that the brethren in this apothegm seem to believe that merely hearing the words of Antony will have some salvific value but are unwilling, or perhaps unable, to put his words, based on the Gospels, into practice. At the end, one can almost hear the exasperation in Antony's voice as he disparagingly calls his interlocuters "invalids," tacitly conveying that only actual ascetic practice, in this case accepting ill treatment without retaliation, will grant them any soteriological value.

Asceticism as a significant marker of authority also had a wide-ranging history in the nascent Christian literary tradition outside of the New Testament long before Cassian wrote his seminal treatises. Prolific second and third century Christian author Tertullian, writing from the Roman-controlled North African city of Carthage, gives us a glimpse of how ascetic practices were used in his early Christian milieu as public penance, which he calls *exomologesis*, transliterating into his native Latin the Greek term meaning repentance, regret, and/or confession. This section from his treatise *On Penitence* (*De paenitentia*) is worth quoting at length:

> And thus *exomologesis* is a discipline for man's prostration and humiliation, enjoining a demeanor calculated to move mercy. With regard also to the very dress and food, it commands (the penitent) to lie in sackcloth and ashes, to cover his body in mourning, to lay his spirit low in sorrows, to exchange for severe treatment the sins which he has committed; moreover, to know no food and drink but such as is plain, not for the stomach's sake, to wit, but the soul's; for the most part, however, to feed prayers on fastings, to groan, to

---

60. *AP*, Antony, 19. Παρέβαλον ἀδελφοὶ τῷ ἀββᾷ Ἀντωνίῳ, χαὶ λέγουσιν αὐτῷ • πῶς σωθῶμεν ; Λέγει αὐτοῖς ὁ γέρον, Ἠχούσατε τὴν γραφήν ; καλῶς ὑμῖν ἔχει. Οἱ δὲ εἶπον • Καὶ παρὰ σοῦ θέλομεν ἀχοῦσαι, Πάτερ. εἶπε δὲ αὐτοῖς ὁ γέρων • Λέγει τὸ Εὐαγγέλιον • Ἐαν τις σε ραπιση εις τὴν δεξιὰν σιαγόνα, στρέψον αὐτῷ καὶ τὴν ἄλλην. Λέγουσιν αὐτῷ • Οὐ δυνάμεθα τοῦτο ποῆσαι. Λέγει αὐτοῖς ὁ γέρον • Εἰ μὲ δὺνασθε στρέψσαι χαὶ τὴν ἄλλην, χὰν τὴν μίαν ὑπομείνατε. Λέγουσιν αὐτῷ • Οὐδὲ τοῦτο δυνάμεθα. Λέγει ὁ γέρον • Εἰ οὐδὲ τοῦτο δὺνασθε μὲ δότε ανθ' οὐ ἐλάβετε. καὶ εἶπον • Οὐδὲ τοῦτο δυνάμεθα. Λέγει οὖν ὁ γέρων τῶν μαθετῇ αὐτοῦ • Ποιησον αὐτοῖς μιχρὰν ἀθήραν • ἀσθενοῦσι γάρ. Ει τοῦτο οὐ δὺνασθε, χὰχεῖνο οὐ θέλετε, τὶ ὑμῖν ποιήσω ; Εὐχῶν χρεία.

weep and make outcries unto the Lord your God; to bow before the feet of the presbyters and kneel to God's dear ones; to enjoin on all the brethren to be ambassadors to bear his deprecatory supplication (before God).[61]

It is significant that many of the practices outlined by Tertullian—fasting, prayer, weeping—would become in later centuries part and parcel of monastic ascetic practice. Even the language of penitence is later used by Egyptian monastics who often speak of frequent weeping "for their sins."[62] The difference, however, is that for Christians in the 2nd and 3rd centuries, those practicing in this way are not leaders, per se, but rather shamed sinners publicly acknowledging their guilt and begging the other members of their communities, as well as God, for forgiveness. Such ascetic practices were designed, as Tertullian puts it, to "move mercy." In other words, they functioned as signs of true repentance before God and thus, if performed sincerely and correctly, evoked God's forgiveness as well as that of their communities. By the time such practices are taken up by desert monks, the goal is not so much divine forgiveness as divine union. While it may not be immediately apparent how such penitential practices in Tertullian's time conferred authority on the repentant sinners, there is a subtle sense in which it does. Tertullian makes it clear that the penitents who accomplish these ascetic practices for the prescribed time are then considered purified, making them worthy of authority and trust within the church. In Tertullian's own words, while this form of physically performed penitence "abases the man, it raises him; while it covers him with squalor, it renders him more clean; while it *ac*cuses, it *ex*cuses; while it condemns, it absolves. The less quarter you give yourself, the more (believe me) will God give you."[63]

Tertullian's Eastern Christian contemporary, Origen of Alexandria, wrote that there were seven practices, all classically ascetic, that would invoke the remission of sins: baptism, martyrdom, almsgiving, forgiveness of the sins

---

61. Tertullian, *De poenitentia*, IX.3–4, in *Patrologia Latina, edited by J.-P. Migne, series 1* (Paris: 1844). Translated by S. Thelwall. From *Ante-Nicene Fathers* Vol. 3. Edited by Alexander Roberts, James Donaldson, and A. Cleveland Coxe. (Buffalo, NY: Christian Literature Publishing Co., 1885). Itaque *exomologesis* prosternendi et humilificandi hominis disciplina est conuersationem iniungens misericordiae inlicem, de ipso quoque habitu atque uictu: mandat sacco et cineri incubare, corpus sordibus obscurare, animum maeroribus deicere, illa quae peccant tristi tractatione mutare; ceterum pastum et potum pura nosse, non uentris scilicet sed animae causa; plerumque uero ieiuniis preces alere, ingemiscere, lacrimari et mugire dies noctesque ad dominum deum tuum.

62. See, for example, *AP*, Antony 33, Arsenius 40 and 41, Gelasius 6. Arsenius is said to have lost all his eyelashes from weeping so much.

63. Tertullian, *De poenetentia*, 9.4. Cum igitur prouoluit hominem, magis releuat; cum squalidum facit, magis emundatum reddit; cum accusat, excusat; cum condemnat, absoluit: in quantum non peperceris tibi, in tantum tibi deus, crede, parcet!

2. Cassian's Context and Asceticism as Basis for Valid Authority

of another, helping a sinner change his ways, charity, and the penitence of tears and confession to a priest.[64] Claudia Rapp notes the significance of these practices which were to become part of daily practice for both cenobitic and eremitic monks. Such penitential exercises were "a spiritual necessity for the individual who felt the burden of his sinfulness, but its effects could radiate beyond its practitioners."[65] Such practices were seen as purificatory, and the purity they invoked conferred a special intercessory power upon those who practiced them. Thus, laypeople would later come to monks who had purified themselves through asceticism and trust these monks to intercede for them with God. This type of authority is part of what would ultimately become problematic for the institutional church as they tried to define the role of monks in relation to the larger church.

One of the ways that asceticism unmistakably conferred authority on the desert monks, at least in the eyes of laypeople, related to the performance of miracles. It is clear in the canonical gospels that Jesus's ability to perform signs and wonders confirmed his status as a spiritual authority. While in the case of Jesus, his power was said to have come from his very identity, in the case of the desert fathers, miraculous power, and thus spiritual authority, could be attained through long and committed ascetic practice. These miracle stories include all within Rudolf Bultmann's typology of Jesus's miracles in the New Testament: exorcisms, healings, nature miracles and the reviving of the dead.[66] Through these stories, the spiritual authority of ascetic monks is tied directly to Christ. Cassian himself acknowledges that such miracles are indeed real, despite his refusal to write about them in either the *Institutes* or the *Conferences*: "Although we have not only heard of many of these and other incredible doings from our elders but have even seen them produced before our very eyes, we are nonetheless omitting all of them: Apart from wonderment they contribute nothing to the reader's instruction in a perfect life."[67] Examples of these miracles abound in early monastic literature.

In one apothegm, Abba Bessarion, a well-known wonder-working monk, is said to refuse to come to any place where he is expected to perform

---

64. Origen, *Homilae en Leviticum* 2.4, in *Patrologia Graeca*, series 12, edited by J.-P. Migne, Paris, 1862. Translated by Gary Wayne Barkley, *Homilies on Leviticus, 1–16* (Washington, DC, Catholic University of America Press, 2010).

65. Claudia Rapp, *Holy Bishops in Late Antiquity: the Nature of Christian Leadership in an Age of Transition* (Berkeley, CA: University of California Press, 2005), 78.

66. Rudolf Bultmann, *The History of the Synoptic Tradition* (trans. John Marshfrom ,1931 German ed.; Oxford: Basil Blackwell, 1972 revised ed.).

67. Cassian, *Institutes*, preface 7. Quae quamvis multa per seniores nostros et incredibilia non solum audierimus, verum etiam sub obtutibus nostris perspexerimus impleta: tamen his omnibus praetermissis, quae legentibus praeter admirationem nihil amplius ad instructionem perfectae vitae conferunt.

miracles. Friends of a demon-possessed man, however, decided to trick the Abba by having the possessed man sleep all night in the church where the Abba would arrive early the next morning. When he arrived, he found the friends praying while the possessed man slept on the church floor. The friends asked the Abba to awaken the man: "The old man said to him, 'Arise and go.' Immediately the devil departed from him and from that hour he was healed."[68] Beyond the fact that Bessarion's power is so formidable that he need not even intend to exorcise the demon in order to effect that exorcism, the following apothegm notes how intensely Bessarion practices asceticism: "Abba Bessarion said, "For 14 days and nights, I have stood upright in the midst of thorn-bushes, without sleeping."[69] His power over the demons is explicitly tied to his ascetic lifestyle.

In another story, a monk named Abba Longinus encounters a woman who has breast cancer and has thus sought him out. She finds him collecting wood by the sea and, not knowing who he is, asks him where she can find Abba Longinus. For humility's sake, the Abba lies and says that the woman should not seek out Abba Longinus, who is an impostor and a deceiver. After asking the woman what is wrong with her that she would need to find Longinus, the woman shows him evidence of her cancer. We are told that Longinus "made the sign of the cross over the sore and sent her away saying, "Go, and God will heal you, for Longinus cannot help you at all."[70] The woman goes away and soon discovers that she has been healed, only later realizing that the man was Abba Longinus himself. Significant here are two points: First, in a previous apothegm we discover the extent of Longinus' ascetic practice when he says, "If ever you are ill, say to your body, 'Be ill and die; if you ask me for food outside the agreed time, I will not bring you even your daily food any more.'"[71] The implication is that asceticism is the source of Longinus's spiritual power. Second, while Longinus correctly displays the humility required of monks by attributing the healing to God rather than himself, it is clear that only a true ascetic could be the vehicle through which such a healing miracle could be wrought.

Nature miracles abound as well in the *AP*. Abba Doulas speaks of Abba Bessarion, in a previously mentioned apothegm: "One day when we were

---

68. *AP*, Bessarion, 5. Καὶ εἶπεν αὐτῷ ὁ γέρων· Ἀνάστα, ἔξελθε ἔξω. Καὶ εὐθέως ἐξῆλθεν ἀπ' αὐτοῦ ὁ δαίμων, καὶ ἰάθη ἀπὸ τῆς ὥρας ἐκείνης.

69. *AP*, Bessarion, 6. Εἶπεν ὁ ἀββᾶς Βισαρίων, ὅτι Τεσσαράκοντα νυ χθήμερα ἔμεινα μέσον ῥάμνων, στήκων, μὴ κοιμώ μενος.

70. *AP*, Longinus, 3. Ἄπελθε, καὶ ὁ Θεός σε θε ραπεύει· Λογγῖνος γὰρ οὐδέν σε δύναται ὠφελῆσαι.

71. *AP*, Longinus, 2. Ἅπαξ κακωθεὶς λέγε, Καὶ κακώθητι, καὶ ἀπόθανον· ἐὰν δὲ ἀπαιτήσῃς με παρὰ καιρὸν φαγεῖν οὐδὲ τὴν καθημερινήν σοι τρο φὴν προσφέρω.

2. Cassian's Context and Asceticism as Basis for Valid Authority

walking beside the sea I was thirsty and I said to Abba Bessarion, 'Father, I am very thirsty.' He said a prayer and said to me, 'Drink some of the sea water.' The water proved sweet when I drank some."[72] Remember that other apothegms involving Abba Bessarion emphasize his years of committed asceticism which made him worthy of such miracles. Futhermore, Bessarion's asceticism also involves trust in God to meet his and his disciple's basic needs. This is illustrated by the end of the above apothegm, again narrated by Abba Doulas: "I even poured some [of the water] into a leather bottle for fear of being thirsty later on. Seeing this, the old man asked me way I was taking some. I said to him, 'Forgive me, it is for fear of being thirsty later on.' Then the old man said, "God is here, God is everywhere."[73] It is noteworthy that while asceticism is the key to the ability of the elder monk to wield divine power over nature, this also involves believing that they will be cared for and sustained by that same divine power.

Finally, asceticism confers upon certain revered monks even the power to resurrect the dead, albeit temporarily. Abba Sisoes tells a pertinent story of his master and teacher, Abba Macarius the Great, one of the best-known and most respected monks in Scetis. In this story, Sisoes tells that he, Macarius, and six other monks go out to work bringing in the harvest for a local farmer. As they are working, they hear a widow weeping nearby. They learn from the owner of the field that the woman is weeping because her husband had received some money from someone who had asked him to keep it safe for him. After hiding it for safekeeping, the husband died suddenly without revealing to anyone where the money was. As a result the owner of the money has threatened to make slaves of the woman and her children to recoup his debt. Macarius summons the woman and asks him to show her where her husband is buried. He sends the widow home, and then, while the other monks pray, Macarius asks the dead body where the deposit had been hidden. "The corpse replied, 'It is hidden in the house, at the foot of the bed.' The old man said, 'Rest again, until the day of resurrection.'"[74] While Macarius goes on in this apothegm to deny any special power of his own after the other monks throw themselves at his feet, other apothegms about him make clear that he lived for a long time as a solitary, is humble

---

72. *AP*, Bessarion, 1. ὅτι Ὁδευόντων ἡμῶν ποτε εἰς ὄχθαν τῆς θαλάσσης, ἐδίψησα, καὶ εἶπον τῷ ἀββᾷ Βισαρίωνι· Ἀββᾶ, διψῶ πάνυ. Καὶ ποιήσας εὐχὴν ὁ γέρων, λέγει μοι· Πίε ἐκ τῆς θαλάσσης. Καὶ ἐγλυκάνθη τὸ ὕδωρ, καὶ ἔπιον.

73. *AP*, Bessarion, 1. Ἐγὼ δὲ ἤντλησα εἰς τὸ ἀγγεῖον, μήποτε παρ᾽ ἐκεῖ διψήσω. Καὶ ἰδὼν ὁ γέρων, λέγει μοι· Διατί ἤντλησας; Λέγω αὐτῷ· Συγχώρησόν μοι, μή ποτε παρ᾽ ἐκεῖ διψήσω. Καὶ εἶπεν ὁ γέρων· Ὁ Θεὸς ὧδε, καὶ πάντη Θεός.

74. *AP*, Macarius the Great, 7. Εἰς τὸν οἶκόν μου κέκρυπται, ὑπὸ τὸν πόδα τῆς κλίνης. Καὶ λέγει αὐτῷ ὁ γέρων· Κοιμῶ πάλιν ἕως τῆς ἡμέρας τῆς ἀναστάσεως.

to the point of allowing himself to suffer accusation and punishment for something he did not do, and made himself suffer deprivation when he had voluntarily received any pleasure.[75] Again, the ability to perform miracles through divine power is the result of long ascetic practice.

Although the performance of miracles was significant in the realm of monasticism and especially monastic hagiography, Christian ascetic practice more generally would develop conceptually in the fourth century and beyond. Fourth-century ascetic theologian and one of the so-called Cappadocian Fathers, Basil of Caesarea, wrote frequently about the value of asceticism for the Christian life. Basil had received a classical education and knew the significance that ancient authorities placed on self-denial. Andrea Sterk notes that Basil's "own strong emphasis on the moral and ascetic virtue of the Christian leader would reflect the ideals of his profane education as well as the influence of his Christian upbringing."[76] In fact, the influences of both Greek philosophy and early Christianity came together, and were not ultimately differentiated, in Basil's ascetic theory.

Sterk notes that Basil had received an extensive classical philosophical education, first studying in Caesarea and Constantinople and then traveling to Athens to study rhetoric.[77] This emphasis on Greek philosophy and rhetoric would certainly have included an emphasis on the value of asceticism, both for the philosopher and good leaders.[78] Sterk writes that for Greco-Roman philosophers, "[p]urification of the soul was attained by such practices as celibacy, austere diet, and other forms of physical denial. The Neoplatonist philosopher Plotinus was known to be particularly severe in his pursuit of these methods of self-purification."[79] In terms of asceticism as the practice of good character for leaders in late antiquity, there were both pagan and Christian rulers known for their austere lifestyles. Among Christian emperors, Theodosius the Younger (401–450 CE) is likely the most salient example.[80] However, the more philosophically minded pagan emperors also

---

75. *AP*, Macarius the Great, 1 and 10.

76. Andrea Sterk, *Renouncing the World Yet Leading the Church: the Monk-Bishop in Late Antiquity* (Cambridge, MA: Harvard University Press, 2004), 39.

77. Sterk, *Renouncing the World*, 38.

78. Robert Kirschner, "The Vocation of Holiness in Late Antiquity," Vigiliae Christianae 38/2 (1984): 105. Kirschner describes this philosophy as "an amalgam of Platonic meta-physics and Pythagorean ascetic piety associated with Neoplatonist succession." On pagan attitudes toward asceticism in the third and fourth centuries see Garth Fowden, "The Pagan Holy Man in Late Antique Society," *JHS* 102 (1982): 33–59.

79. Sterk, *Renouncing*, 38. For descriptions of Plotinus's asceticism, see also Porphyry, *Vita Plotini*, 1–2 and 8.

80. G. F. Chesnut, *The First Christian Histories: Eusebius, Socrates, Sozomen, Theodoret and Evagrius* (Macon, GA: Mercer University Press, 1986), 231–51.

saw asceticism as a necessity for good leadership. There is, for example, the case of the emperor known to Christian history as Julian the Apostate. His ancient biographer, Ammianus Marcellinus, writes that Julian had "no need of choice food, content with a scanty and simple diet" and that he made his bed on the ground when not foregoing sleep altogether, as well as maintaining strict sexual abstinence.[81] Ammanius goes on to explain that in practicing such austerities, Julian was "following the examples of Alexander and Africanus, who avoided such [hedonistic] conduct, lest those showed themselves unwearied by hardships should be unnerved by passion."[82]

All this goes to show the very public value of asceticism for conferring both spiritual/philosophical and temporal authority in the ancient and late antique worlds. Those who demonstrated that they could resist passions through self-denial proved themselves worthy of the authority conferred upon them. It is within this late antique context that Basil writes of the importance of asceticism for the Christian life.

Basil is an excellent exemplar of eastern Christian views on asceticism, views which generally typified those of the monks of his own region of Cappadocia, as well as Syria and Egypt. A look at Basil's views provides us at least part of the context from which Cassian would later feel justified in claiming authority based on asceticism rather than rank (ecclesial or otherwise).

After completing his education in Athens and returning to his native Cappadocia, Basil's first major influence was a monk turned bishop named Eustathius of Sebaste. Although Eustathius would later be condemned for his anti-Nicene views, it was his and his monastic community's commitment to asceticism that originally attracted Basil. In fact, Basil compared them favorably with the fabled monks of Egypt and Syria, noting the austerity and humility of their clothing and diet and later even defending Eustathius (initially) against accusations of heresy.[83]

Basil had journeyed to Syria and Egypt to meet the famed ascetic monks of those regions. He likely gleaned much of his ascetic ideals from the monks of Syria, a region much closer to his native Cappadocia than Egypt. It is important to note, as well, that the monks of Syria were often

---

81. Ammianus Marcellinus, *Res gestae*, LCL (Cambridge, MA: Harvard University Press, 1940), trans. John C. Rolfe, II, 22.9.2 and 25.4.3-4; see also 25.2.2. nullius cibi indigens mundioris, sed paucis contentus et vilibus.

82. Ammianus Marcellinus, *Res gestae*, 24.4.27. Alexandrum imitatus et Africanum, qui haec declinabant, ne frangerentur cupiditate, qui se invictos a laboribus ubique praestiterunt.

83. Basil of Caesarea, Letter 223.2, 3. Compare his own ascetic ideals in Letter 2 (c. 358).

known to practice a more severe type of asceticism than those in Egypt. The most salient and iconic example is Symeon Stylites who lived atop a pillar for almost forty years. However, since Basil did not recommend such extreme asceticism in his writings and Syria did not seem to evoke the same antagonism between monks and clergy as was sometimes present in Egypt and Palestine, Sterk theorizes that it was from his travels in Syria that Basil would later link asceticism and church leadership rather than simply monasticism.[84] While we know that many monks of the era, especially in Egypt, utterly rejected clerical office for themselves, often on the view that bishops were not sufficiently ascetic, Basil seemed to believe that asceticism and a clerical career could and should go hand in hand. Throughout his eventual episcopate, for example, Basil interspersed his clerical duties with periods of contemplative retreat.[85] Sterk also notes that although Basil never explicitly writes of his motivations in accepting church office, two of his earliest influences, third-century bishop Gregory Thaumaturgus and the aforementioned Eustathius of Sebaste, saw no conflict between asceticism and church office.[86] In addition, in his letters Basil never writes of the kind of distrust of bishops often shown in some texts from Egyptian monasticism.[87] This suggests that what granted authority, in Basil's view, was not clerical office as such, as much as ascetic practice within whatever Christian calling one undertook. A monk who was insufficiently ascetic lacked the authority to help others, while a bishop who paid insufficient attention to ascetic practice lessened the authority with which he carried out his clerical duties. Basil actually saw ascetic practice, written upon the body through its physical effects, as a way of marking out those whose purity proved they deserved authority: "Leanness of body and pallor produced by the exercise of continency mark the Christian… making a sparing and frugal use of necessities, ministering to nature [by eating] as if this were a burdensome duty and begrudging the time spent in it."[88] These physical changes wrought upon the ascetic body demonstrated that the Christian was truly pure and

---

84. Sterk, *Renouncing*, 43.
85. See Basil's comments on his retreats to Annesi in Letter 210.1: Courtonne 2, 190.
86. Sterk, *Renouncing*, 43.
87. Sterk, *Renouncing*, 43.
88. Basil, *Ascetical.* In *Patrologia Graeca.* Edited by J.-P. Migne, vol. 3. Paris: 1885. Translated by W.K.L. Clarke. Basil of Caeserea, *The Ascetic Works of St. Basil,*(London: Macmillan, 1925). Question 17, 222 273. ούτω τόν Χριστιανόν τό χατεσχληχός τοũ σώματος χαι η εχ της της έγχρατεĩας επανθοũσα ώχρία χείχνυσιν, οτι αθλητής οντω. … Όσον τό χέρσος, οφθηναι μόνον τον έγχαρτη, μόλις χαι χατά μιχρόν τών αναγκών απτόμενον, χαι ώς λειτουργιων επαχθη ύποτελουντα τη φύσει, και δυσχεραίνοντα μεν τώ καιρώ.

2. Cassian's Context and Asceticism as Basis for Valid Authority

worthy. Note here that Basil designates this ascetic body as that of a Christian generally, rather than a monk, layperson, or bishop. In other words, asceticism was the ideal for all Christians in Basil's thought. While I do not mean to assert that orthodoxy was unimportant for Basil (he was, after all, an enthusiastic supporter of Nicene orthodoxy and clearly had his own struggles with Arians, including Eustathius), orthopraxy, defined primarily as ascetic practice, was at least as important in his theology.[89]

The Desert Fathers of Egypt, those monastic exemplars idealized in Cassian's writings, had a slightly different attitude from Basil's in terms of the connection of asceticism and authority. This is especially clear in the *AP* or *Sayings of the Desert Fathers*. The compiler of this collection of sayings somewhere in Palestine in the fifth century, evidently thought that it was only asceticism that defined authentic spiritual authority rather than ecclesiastic leadership roles or titles. Taken as a whole, the compiler seems to be conveying the notion, as noted by Zachary Smith, that "monks should exist in one sphere of power and authority, while ecclesiastics should exist in another."[90] While there was some crossover between clergy and monks in the *AP*, clergy were only granted a similar authoritative status to monks if they practiced asceticism as well. While monks in the *AP* generally respect the mediatorial function of priests through their administration of the Eucharist, monks' respect for clergy is never based "on their position in the institutional church; instead, monks view seasoned and able ascetics as authoritative and worthy of wielding power in the monastic sphere."[91]

For this reason, monastic progenitor Antony, as depicted in the *AP*, is very different from his portrayal by Athanasius in the *Vita Antonii*. In Athanasius' writing, Antony defers to all bishops and is intensely concerned with orthodoxy, implicitly gaining his authority from it. In the *AP*, however, Antony's vast monastic authority comes from his practice of asceticism. In the very first apothegm in the *AP*, there is a story in which Antony, living in solitude, is tormented by despair and inappropriate thoughts and asks God, "How can I be saved (πῶς σωθῶ)?" In answer, God shows Antony a vision of an exemplar monk who alternates between manual work and prayer. The final line of the apothegm is telling: "He did this and he was saved."[92] For the compiler of the *AP*, salvation is not ultimately a matter of correct belief,

---

89. Basil of Caeserea, *St. Basil: Ascetical Works*, 44–45.
90. Zachary B. Smith, *Philosopher-monks, Episcopal Authority, and the Care of the Self. The 'Apophthegmata Patrum' in fifth-century Palestine* (Turnhout, Belgium: Brepols, 2018), 123.
91. Smith, *Philosopher-monks*, 123.
92. *AP*, Antony 1. Ὁ δὲ τοῦτο ἀχούσας, πολλὴν χαρὰν ἔσχε χαὶ θὰρσος, χαὶ οὕτως ποιῶν ἐσώζετο.

which will automatically keep one from eternal torment, but rather correct ascetic practice, which, while it may also save one from perdition, will also preserve and improve one's self in this life and this body. This ethos is repeated ad nauseum in the *AP*.

In addition, the role of ecclesiastical office is often subtly diminished in the *AP*. As Zachary Smith points out, of the 130 figures whose stories and sayings populate the *AP*, only eight are archbishops or bishops, only nine are priests, and only one is a deacon.[93] Furthermore, all these church hierarchs included by the compiler of the *AP* are ascetic practitioners. These two facts together place emphasis on the fact that for the compiler of the *AP*, mere church office means little while ascetic practice is what confers true authority, regardless of one's status or lack thereof. For this reason, many monks in the *AP* refuse ordination, although in several cases they are forcibly ordained by a less ascetic clergy. While some scholars have interpreted the refusal to be ordained as mere humility on the part of the monks, Smith notes that "the *AP* views ordination as an impediment to ascetic practice," and that "monks do not desire ordination and when it is forced on them, they refuse to serve in their ecclesiastical capacities."[94] If indeed ascetic practice takes authoritative precedence over church office, then being ordained, which is portrayed in the *AP* as a hindrance to the practice of asceticism, can only diminish one's spiritual authority.

This is illustrated in a story in the *AP* about Abba Apphy who when he was a monk "submitted himself to a very severe way of life," but when he had been ordained a bishop "wished to practice the same austerity, even in the world, but he had not the strength to do so." This is presented, not as simply a failure of self-discipline, but also a loss of the intimate relationship with God that Apphy had previously enjoyed. When he asks God if divine "grace has left me because of my episcopate," indicating that this loss of divine grace may be due to his ordination, he receives a revelatory answer: When Apphy was in solitude as a monk, only God was there to help him; however, he is told that "now that you are in the world, it is man."[95] This is representative of the general ideology of asceticism vs. ecclesial authority in the *AP*. As a monk, Apphy practices asceticism and is consequently close to God. As a bishop (we are not told whether or not Apphy was willingly ordained), Apphy is considered to be "in the world," and therefore to have lost much of the intimacy he had before with the divine. Ordination thus represents a loss, both of closeness with God and, more significantly,

---

93. Smith, *Philosopher Monks*, 137–38.
94. Smith, *Philosopher Monks*, 140.
95. *AP*, Apphy 1. νῦν δὲ κόσμος ἐστὶ, καὶ οἱ ἄνθρω ποι ἀντιλαμβάνονταί σου.

2. Cassian's Context and Asceticism as Basis for Valid Authority 39

with the ability to practice asceticism correctly which facilitates that intimacy and in turn grants authority to the ascetic. Note also that a clergyman here is considered to be "in the world" while a monk is both conceptually and geographically outside of it.

Having examined the position on asceticism and authority of Basil and the *AP* as exemplars of eastern Christian and monastic thought, and since Cassian was likely a Latin Christian by birth and was, in the *Institutes* and the *Conferences* writing for a Latin and/or Western audience, I turn here to examine a similarly influential Western exemplar of attitudes toward asceticism, namely Cassian's contemporary Augustine, Bishop of Hippo, in hopes of understanding further Cassian's notions of the deep significance of asceticism and the context in which his writings took place.

Augustine had found himself drawn early on to monastic life and asceticism as the equivalent of the philosophical life idealized in his youth and during his classical education. He had also initially been deeply inspired by hearing of the heroic ascetic struggles in the *Vita Antonii* from a friend, as he notes in the *Confessions*. The *Life of Antony* prompted him, at the point of his conversion, to utter in anguish and shame, "What is wrong with us? What is it that you have heard? People with no education are rising up and seizing heaven, and we, with all our learning, look on! We are entangled in flesh and blood!"[96] Comparing his own spiritual and temporal life which Augustine says involved much self-indulgence and sexual impropriety, with that of Antony as portrayed by Athanasius caused him no little amount of self-loathing. However, more significant here is how Augustine, who ultimately did not choose to retire to a life of desert asceticism as did his contemporary and frequent epistolary interlocutor Jerome, came to see the conflation of asceticism and authority, especially from the perspective of a bishop.

Conrad Leyser notes that "[i]n the Latin West across the fifth and sixth centuries, as the Empire disintegrated, Augustine's crystalline imagination of the eschatological order was increasingly relevant and attractive to Christian ascetics in these parts."[97] Particularly pertinent was Augustine's view of the monastery, with its supposed genealogical connection to the early Christian church depicted as a loving community that held all material possessions in common in Acts 4:32–35, as a prefiguration of the heavenly city that

---

96. Augustine, *Confessions, Volume I: Books 1–8,* Translated by Carolyn J.-B. Hammond, Loeb Classical Library 26 (Cambridge, MA: Harvard University Press, 2014), 8.6–8.
97. Conrad Leyser, *Authority and Asceticism from Augustine to Gregory the Great* (Oxford: Clarendon Press, 2000), 4.

would arrive with the eschaton.[98] However, Augustine's view of the total authority of divine grace minimized, or perhaps even eliminated the role of human agency in one's own salvation.[99] That is, Augustine believed fully that while human beings had free will, that will could not be used intentionally to invoke divine grace or in any way influence the will of God, whose application in human affairs was entirely incomprehensible. He notes, for example, that while the monks to whom he writes in his treatise *On Grace and Free Will (De Gratia et Libero Arbitrio)* maintain sexual continence, they are only able to do so through the gift of divine grace. Their own efforts without God's grace would always be insufficient.[100] This, of course, minimizes, at best, the role that human ascetic effort has in invoking salvation. This argument, later used specifically against the Pelagian heresy, which supposedly stated that since people were granted absolute free will by God that they were entirely responsible for earning salvation, would also be used subsequently by a follower of Augustine's to criticize Cassian and his emphasis on ascetic practice as a necessity for the correct monastic life.[101] Leyser notes that in reading and rereading the writings of Paul, Augustine became convinced that "his confidence in the powers of human reason to fathom the rationality of God's grace was unfounded."[102] These are the ideas of "a man who is axiomatically uncertain of his powers of self-control or his ability to resist temptation: any strength that he has comes from divine grace, and the giving and withholding of that grace is inscrutable."[103] One can see how this idea would come to be seen as being in conflict with Cassian's championing of Egyptian asceticism and its view of ascetic practice as a method of transformation from the mundane human into something divine, or at least on the trajectory to a kind of divine union. In short, any effort toward ascetic prac-

---

98. Augustine. *City of God, Volume I: Books 1–3*. Translated by George E. McCracken. Loeb Classical Library 411. Cambridge, MA: Harvard University Press, 1957, V.15 and also *De Opera Monachorum*, in *Patrologia Latina*, vol. 6, edited by J.-P. Migne (Paris, 1865), Translated by H. Browne. From *Nicene and Post-Nicene Fathers, First Series*, Vol. 3. Edited by Philip Schaff (Buffalo, NY: Christian Literature Publishing Co., 1887), 25.32.

99. Augustine, *De gratia et libero arbitrio,* In *Patrologia Latina*, vol. 44, edited by J.-P. Migne (Paris: 1865). Translated by Peter Holmes and Robert Ernest Wallis, and revised by Benjamin B. Warfield. From *Nicene and Post-Nicene Fathers, First Series*, Vol. 5. Edited by Philip Schaff (Buffalo, NY: Christian Literature Publishing Co., 1887), Chapters 6 and 7.

100. Augustine, *De gratia et libero arbitrio,* Chapter 8.

101. See Prosper of Aquitaine, *Liber contra collatorem*, in *Patrologia Latina*, vol. 51, edited by J.-P. Migne (Paris: 1861).

102. Leyser, *Authority and Asceticism,* 6.

103. Leyser, *Authority and Asceticism,* 7.

2. Cassian's Context and Asceticism as Basis for Valid Authority

tice could hardly confer authority upon anyone, in Augustine's estimation, since it was only through God's unfathomable grace that one was inclined or able to practice asceticism at all.

Likewise for Augustine, not only could asceticism not automatically bestow authority upon its practitioner, but even church office, such as Augustine's own bishopric of Hippo Regius to which he ascribed a rigidly valid authority, brought no guarantees of salvation. Leyser writes that for Augustine, "all those in authority, including bishops and abbots, should eschew illusory certainties about the moral effect of their conduct of power: no one, however powerful, could know whether their actions were in accord with the inscrutable agency of God's grace."[104] For Augustine, one had to follow the commandments from God's word and believe correctly as best as one could, and then hope for the best. But even having done this, salvation was never assured; his own views on predestination precluded any certainty that actions taken on behalf of oneself would have any eternal effects:

> Certainly such an election is of grace, not at all of merits… [T]he election obtained what it obtained gratuitously; there preceded none of those things which they might first give, and it should be given to them again. He saved them for nothing. But to the rest who were blinded, as is there plainly declared, it was done in recompense. All the paths of the Lord are mercy and truth. But His ways are unsearchable. Therefore the mercy by which He freely delivers, and the truth by which He righteously judges, are equally unsearchable.[105]

For this reason, Augustine was wary of Egyptian monasticism and its emphasis on asceticism as a means toward salvation since "the monastic movement threatened to introduce a double standard: a pure Christianity for the few, and a cheapened version for the remainder."[106] Just as those capable of great feats of asceticism had no justification for boasting of their own

---

104. Leyser, *Authority and Asceticism*, 7.
105. Augustine, *De praedestinatione sanctorum*, In *Patrologia Latina*, vol. 44, edited by J.-P. Migne (Paris: 1865). Translated by Peter Holmes and Robert Ernest Wallis, and revised by Benjamin B. Warfield, from *Nicene and Post-Nicene Fathers, First Series*, Vol. 5, edited by Philip Schaff (Buffalo, NY: Christian Literature Publishing Co., 1887), Book 1.11. Electio quippe ista gratiae est, non utique meritorum. superius enim dixerat, sic ergo et in hoc tempore, reliquiae per electionem gratiae saluae factae sunt. Si autem gratia, iam non ex operibus; alioquin gratia iam non est gratia. Gratis ergo consecuta est, quod consecuta est electio: non praecessit eorum aliquid, quod priores darent, et retribueretur illis: pro nihilo saluos fecit eos. caeteris autem qui excaecati sunt, sicut ibi non tacitum est, in retributione factum est. Uniuersae uiae domini misericordia et ueritas. Inuestigabiles sunt autem uiae eius. Inuestigabiles igitur sunt, et misericordia qua gratis liberat, et ueritas qua iuste iudicat.
106. Leyser, *Authority and Asceticism*, 9.

efforts, so non-monastics and regular citizens had no reason for shame. All depended on the mysterious conferral of divine grace; there was no room for second-class citizens in the City of God.

The monastery, for Augustine, was thus a place to perfect the practice of charity rather than to impress with feats of ascetic practice. While, again, charity provided no soteriological guarantees, it was the principal command of Christ and should thus serve as the bedrock guidance for the Christian life (Mt. 22.36-40). While Egyptian monastics may have viewed themselves as directly descended from the original Christian community (Acts 2.44) in that they shared all things in common and ascetically invoked the divine together, Augustine saw the monastery as "a place in which to seek again the *communitas* of the first Christians, in anticipation of the state of the blessed in the heavenly Jerusalem."[107] In addition, he offered a different explanation of the term "monk", usually understood in its original Greek to mean "solitary":

> 'Monos' means 'one', but not 'one' in any fashion. You can be 'one in a crowd': one person with many people can be called one, but they cannot be called 'monos', that is, 'one alone'. 'Monos' means 'one alone'. [Monks] live together as one who make up one person, so that they really are as it is written, 'one heart and one soul'. Many bodies, but not many hearts are rightly called 'monos', that is 'one alone'.[108]

As Leyser puts it, it was not "the monks' seclusion from 'the world' that defined their identity, but rather the transparency of their bond with their fellows."[109] This was a rather massive break with the tradition represented by the *Life of Antony* and other early monastic literature from Egypt and Palestine.

Augustine could not see withdrawal from the world as the Christian ideal. While he had originally wanted to live such a secluded life and had certainly idealized Antony and his spiritual descendants, as a bishop dealing day by day with ordinary citizens and their families, he came to see such a lifestyle

---

107. Leyser, *Authority and Asceticism*, 10.

108. Augustine, *Enarrationes in Psalmos.*, in *Patrologia Latina*, vol. 36, edited by J.-P. Migne (Paris: 1865). Translated by J.E. Tweed. From *Nicene and Post-Nicene Fathers, First Series*, Vol. 8. Edited by Philip Schaff (Buffalo, NY: Christian Literature Publishing Co., 1888), 133. 5 (132.6). Μόνος enim unus dicitur : et non unus quomodocumque ; nam et in turba est unus, sed una cum multis unus dici potest, μόνος non potest, id est, solus : μόνος enim unus solus est. Qui ergo sic vivunt in unum, ut unum hominem faciant, ut sit illis vere quod scriptum est, *una anima et unum cor* ; multa corpora, sed non multae animae ; multa corpora, sed non multa corda; recte dicitur μόνος, id est unus solus.

109. Leyser, *Authority and Asceticism*, 11.

2. Cassian's Context and Asceticism as Basis for Valid Authority

as spiritual elitism, a kind of class system in which ascetics were spiritual aristocrats with householders taking up the space at the bottom of the hierarchy. In a sermon given early in the fifth century, Augustine proposed a system whereby monks could live ascetic lives while still interacting with and not condescending to laypeople and/or clergy: "The community of believers, Augustine proposed, could be divided into three orders: married householders, inmates of monasteries, and the episcopal rulers of the Church. This three-tiered vision of the Church, which seems to have been Augustine's own, became an immediate and enduring standard in the lexicon of Latin ecclesiology."[110] Among other things, this would strip away any vestige of authority based on the merit of human effort. If all depended on God's grace, such human effort deserved no extra award, neither ecclesial authority nor other types of spiritual status. He insisted that "All Christians were equally vulnerable to moral collapse," and "all stood in equal need of peace and charity. There were false monks, and, equally, there were married people who could live in charity on the model of the first Christian community at Jerusalem."[111] He had come to see individual ascetic effort, as championed by Cassian based on his conception of the Egyptian monastic system, as "encouraging individual perfectionism at the expense of the peace of the community as a whole."[112] While the monks were an essential part of the body of Christ, they were not the head.

In addition, Augustine's account of the Fall "turned on the weakness, not of the body, but of the soul."[113] In fact, in Augustine's telling, the Fall happened because of misdirected loves: self-love won out over love of God. This was the original sin, not eating the fruit as such but disobedience and thus a lack of love for the creator who had forbidden eating from the tree.[114] This weakness of soul was not due to bad desires but to pride. This being the case, "to declare war on desire as an ascetic was, in its willful misunderstanding of the human condition, to risk compounding pride with pride."[115] That is, believing that ascetic practice based on human effort of the will was to take the original sin of pride and attempt to root it out with further pride,

---

110. Leyser, *Authority and Asceticism*, 12. See also G. Folliet, 'Les Trois catégories des chrétiens, survie d'un thème augustinien', *L'Année théologique augustinienne* 14 (1954), 81–96.
111. Leyser, *Authority and Ascesticism*, 13.
112. Leyser, *Authority and Ascesticism*, 13.
113. Leyser, *Authority and Ascesticism*, 14.
114. Augustine, *De civitate Dei contra paganos (City of God), Volume I: Books 1–3*. Translated by George E. McCracken. Loeb Classical Library 411. Cambridge, MA: Harvard University Press, 1957. 14. 13–15, 48, 434–38.
115. Leyser, *Authority and Asceticism*, 14.

an endless cycle which Augustine believed would never result in salvation without the intervention of divine grace over which even the most stringent ascetics had no control.

Having established the original sin of pride as the source of human frailty and perdition, Augustine goes on to note that the punishment fit the crime: "God turned body and soul into sites of disobedience, confronting humans with a mirror image of their primal dissension from the divine will. Expelled from paradise, the body was now hopelessly vulnerable to desire in excess of all need, and the fractured will could do nothing about it."[116] People could not effectively use their frail human wills to control their sexual organs.[117] What is significant, though, is that Augustine notes that this lack of control is a punishment for original sin, not the cause. The cause, again, was pride, and ascetics, in Augustine's view continued to compound this sin by asserting that they could heroically battle this errant will themselves, in effect digging themselves into a deeper and deeper hole.

This, in sum, is the major difference between notions of asceticism in the Christian East and West. For Basil, representing the Eastern view, while being a monk may have been the superior form of life, allowing as it did more time for solitude and reflection, there was certainly nothing inherently wrong with accepting a clerical position. What mattered, for maintaining the weight of authority of the clergy, was how ascetic practice remained a commitment despite the arduous nature of clerical duties. For the highly influential Augustine in the Western tradition, however, asceticism, like any other product of the human will, was, first, only possible due to divine grace and second, an inversion of correct priorities. If one believed that one's own efforts invoked salvation, one merely increased the sin of pride from which the corruption of our wills had originated.

It was between these two theological poles that Cassian wrote of the significance of asceticism for the monk. As a Latin-speaking monk who had trained as an ascetic in the East, he was now confronted with translating the Eastern form of life to Western monks. It would be a supreme balancing act and, as mentioned above, he would not be without his detractors.[118]

Cassian's Context: Fifth Century Gaul

Early fifth century Gaul was a turbulent place in which to found a monastery or start a monastic career. Between the years 406 and 413 CE, Rome

---

116. Leyser, *Authority and Asceticism*, 15.
117. Augustine, *Civ. Dei* XIV. 16–20, 438–43.
118. Prosper, *Contra collatorem*, 3.1, *PL* 51.221 and 226.

2. Cassian's Context and Asceticism as Basis for Valid Authority 45

had lost the province to Germanic invaders.[119] The end of almost 500 years of Roman rule in the province created a particular turmoil for the Gallican elite, who, long established as friends of Rome, were suddenly unsure of their positions in relation to the several Germanic kings who had divided Gaul among themselves. It should be observed, however, that while these political changes may have seemed drastic and unforeseen through the eyes of Cassian and other outsiders, the battle for control of Gaul between Germanic tribes and Rome had gone on for centuries.[120] In fact, control by the Germanic tribes was actually a return to the state of Gaul before Rome's conquest of the province. Gaul was well-known by the Romans for supporting usurpers and had done so several times already since Rome's takeover of the province. The fact that the majority of Gallicans could always be counted on to support dissident coups against Rome was a common theme in Roman literature, and authors from Julius Caesar to the fourth century Roman historian Ammianus Marcellinus had written extensively on this topic.[121] When the Germanic tribes invaded and reconquered the province in the year 406 CE, the Roman-friendly elite were apparently of two minds about where their loyalties should lie, as they had been during all such coups in their history.[122] While many hoped that the Empire that had sponsored and protected them from Germanic tribes would continue to do so, others saw the new conquest as a means to gain even more power through participation in the takeover and by seeking roles as courtiers in the new leaders' administrations.

One strategy to ensure their continued wealth and status in the province was for these late-Roman elites to embrace ecclesiastical careers, usually as either monks or bishops.[123] As unusual as this may sound, given the history of monasticism in Europe and its well-known vows of poverty, chastity and obedience, Gallic monasticism had already begun, in the fifth century, to create its own typology of ecclesiastical careers. These religious roles, as Cassian remarked, differed greatly from those of his monastic heroes in Egypt. For this reason, several Gallican ecclesiastical writers, contemporaries of Cassian, would write impassioned rhetoric aimed at convincing these

---

119. Richard J. Goodrich, *Contextualizing Cassian: Aristocrats, Asceticism, and Reformation in Fifth-century Gaul* (Oxford: Oxford University Press, 2007), 9.

120. Raymond Van Dam, 'The Pirenne Thesis and Fifth-Century Gaul,' in *Fifth-Century Gaul: A Crisis of Identity?* Edited by John Drinkwater and Hugh Elton (Cambridge: Cambridge University Press, 1992), 332–3.

121. Ralph Mathisen, *Roman Aristocrats in Barbarian Gaul: Strategies for Survival in an Age of Transition* (Austin, TX: University of Texas Press, 1993), 18.

122. Mathisen, *Roman Aristocrats*, 13–14.

123. Mathisen, *Roman Aristocrats*, 9.

elite men to adopt ecclesiastical careers. Goodrich writes that the foundation of this endeavor was a series of hagiographies of local saints which demonstrated the compatibility of ecclesiastical careers with a patrician style of life:

> hagiographic [w]orks such as the *Vita Martini, Vita Honorati,* and *Vita Germani* were prescriptive as well as descriptive... They advanced the argument that a well-born nobleman would not have to abandon social standing should he accept one of these offices; to the contrary, life as a bishop or monk was simply a continuation of the status into which one had been born.[124]

This point was driven home, for example by the biographer of Martin of Tours, Sulpicius Severus, who, as Goodrich reports, asserted that the "[s]ocial order was preserved in heaven, just as it was on earth; the convert, despite having renounced his claims to an earthly elite status, continued to move among the best men."[125] In his *Dialogi*, Sulpicius makes several instructive references to the subject of his biography, Martin of Tours.

First, he writes that while Martin did not come from the elite classes, becoming a cleric did ennoble him, putting him essentially on equal footing with the privileged. For example, Sulpicius narrates an episode in which Martin, who had just become a bishop, decided to seek an audience with the Emperor Valentinian I. He was refused, but after he spent days in prayer and fasting, divine intervention assured his admission. The Emperor, however, unimpressed with the lowly bishop, refused to stand to greet Martin. Suddenly, Valentinian's throne was engulfed in flames, forcing the Emperor to stand and greet him. From this point on, Sulpicius states that Valentinian was cordial and deferential to Martin.[126] The message is clear: joining the church hierarchy in Gaul, could actually elevate one from one of the great unwashed to the status of nobility. But what of those who were already members of the elite in good standing? Although there was never a guarantee in the unstable political and social world of Gaul that one could keep one's wealth and status, "by seeking a career with God, mortals could become courtiers to the Emperor of Heaven."[127] In other words, the elite would remain elite within the church and in the next world. Well-known

---

124. See Goodrich, *Contextualizing Cassian*, 21–22 and Raymond Van Dam & American Council of Learned Societies, *Leadership and Community in Late Antique Gaul* (Berkeley, CA: University of California Press, 1985), 154.

125. Goodrich, *Contextualizing Cassian*, 24.

126. Sulpicius Severus, *Dialogi*, in *Patrologia Latina*, vol. 20, edited by J.-P. Migne (Paris: 1845). Translated by Alexander Roberts, from *Nicene and Post-Nicene Fathers, Second Series,* Vol. 11, edited by Philip Schaff and Henry Wace (Buffalo, NY: Christian Literature Publishing Co., 1894), 2.5.

127. Goodrich, *Contextualizing Cassian*, 23.

2. Cassian's Context and Asceticism as Basis for Valid Authority

Gallican saint Honoratus (350–429 CE), for example, founded a monastery to which, according to his biographer, Hilary of Arles, nobles and kings would visit. For those visitors, Honoratus, in the middle of the untamed wilderness, somehow provided rich, delicate dishes fit for kings.[128] In addition,

> Honoratus clearly remained enmeshed in the social round, and in the middle sections of Hilary's panegyric, we find him doing the things that any aristocrat would do as a matter of course: constructing buildings, welcoming guests, dispensing patronage in the form of money.[129]

Clearly, Cassian's Egyptian-flavored notions of total renunciation, in which all but the most necessary possessions are given up, did not apply in Gaul. On Honoratus's deathbed, the saint was visited by a profusion of the chief men of the province, as well as the governor. Similarly, at the funeral of Martin of Tours, Sulpicius describes in a letter the great procession, including the entire town and the surrounding countryside.[130] To give his addressee an idea of the grandeur of the funeral procession, he compares it to "an imperial triumph, that most cherished of ancient Roman honors when a victorious general was allowed to parade through the streets of Rome, following his soldiers, captives, and spoils."[131] In Sulpicius's own words,

> Let there be compared with this spectacle, I will not say the worldly pomp of a funeral, but even of a triumph; and what can be reckoned similar to the obsequies of Martin? Let your worldly great men lead before their chariots captives with their hands bound behind their backs. Those accompanied the body of Martin who, under his guidance, had overcome the world. Let madness honor these earthly warriors with the united praises of nations. Martin is praised with the divine psalms, Martin is honored in heavenly hymns. Those worldly men, after their triumphs here are over, shall be thrust into cruel Tartarus, while Martin is joyfully received into the bosom of Abraham. Martin, poor and insignificant on earth, has a rich entrance granted him into heaven.[132]

---

128. Hilary of Arles, *Sermo de Uita S. Honorati*, in *Patrologia Latina*, vol. 50, edited by J.-P. Migne (Paris: 1845). 1215.

129. Goodrich, *Contextualizing Cassian*, 27.

130. Sulpicius Severus, *Epistola tres,* in *Patrologia Latina*, vol. 20, edited by J.-P. Migne (Paris: 1845). Translated by Alexander Roberts, from *Nicene and Post-Nicene Fathers, Second Series*, Vol. 11, edited by Philip Schaff and Henry Wace (Buffalo, NY: Christian Literature Publishing Co., 1894).

131. Hilary of Arles, *Honoratus*, 32.

132. Sulpicius Severus, *Epistola tres,* in *Patrologia Latina*, vol. 20, edited by J.-P. Migne (Paris: 1845). Translated by Alexander Roberts, from *Nicene and Post-Nicene Fathers, Second Series*, Vol. 11, edited by Philip Schaff and Henry Wace (Buffalo, NY: Christian Literature Publishing Co., 1894). Comparetur, si placet, saecularis illa pompa, non dicam funeris, sed triumphi; quid simile Martini exequiis conferatur? Ducant illi prae curribus suis vinctos post terga captivos: Martini corpus hi qui mundum doctu illius

As Goodrich says,

> [w]ith the possible exception of John Cassian, very few fifth-century thinkers would have seen any value in severing connections with the ruling class. It was this very sense of interconnectedness, of being plugged into the network of influential Romans, that made an elite bishop such a great catch for a city or town.[133]

Cassian's notion of total renunciation of position and property would have been a hard sell in Gaul, to say the least.

One subtle technique Cassian employed in his writings, then, was to use the forms of classical literature, the kind with which most educated, elite-born Roman males such as Cassian himself would be entirely familiar, while simultaneously denigrating the value of classical education in comparison with monastic learning. This would allow him to communicate his ideas effectively in a convincing rhetorical style, a kind of Trojan horse into the minds of Gallican monks who were mostly drawn from the ranks of the privileged.

Rebecca Krawiec notes that Cassian structured his *Institutes* and *Conferences* as "monastic equivalents to rhetorical handbooks (the *Institutes*) and works of literary theory (the *Conferences*) [which] are themselves sublime replacements for 'pagan' literature."[134] The point of this rhetorical move on Cassian's part was not to make Gallican monks more comfortable, but rather "to transform his audience through a process analogous to their traditional education."[135] However, the aim here was not simply for the monks to learn by rote the way they had learned in school. Rather, "Cassian taught a new monastic reading culture that valued the Bible and his own works [although] this educational process was no longer limited to producing a skilled speaker but also someone able to experience sublime prayer."[136] To do this, Cassian employed a number of tropes from classical literature and/or rhetorical education, which Krawiec calls an *ars monastica*.[137] This is an apt appellation given the classical definition of *ars* as a "system of instructive rules... for the correct implementation of a perfection-oriented

---

vicerant, prosequuntur; illos confusis plausibus populorum honoret insania: Martino divinis plauditur psalmis: Martinus hymnis coelestibus honoratur, illi post triumphos suos in tartara saeva trudentur: Martinus Abrahae sinu laetus excipitur; Martinus hic pauper et modicus coelem dives ingreditur.

133. Goodrich, *Contextualizing Cassian*, 30.
134. Rebecca Krawiec, "Monastic Literacy in John Cassian: Toward a New Sublimity," *Church History* 81.4 (2012): 765.
135. Krawiec, "Monastic Literacy," 765.
136. Krawiec, "Monastic Literacy," 767.
137. Krawiec, "Monastic Literacy," 767.

repeatable action that does not belong to the naturally inevitable course of events."[138] In other words, Cassian's system of monasticism "imitates traditional education (*paideia*) both in its pedagogical and literary goals. These aimed at creating proper readers, and so speakers, who were formed through the best, or sublime, literature that was used as educational models."[139] Cassian, then, intended his system to include reading in the correct manner which he borrowed in significant ways from the classical *paideia* familiar to the elites making up the majority of Gallican monks. This is a point worth explaining and developing here.

Monasticism has long been known for emphasizing literacy among monks. Most famously, Pachomius, the reputed originator of the cenobitic mode of monasticism, wrote in his rule that every monk must know how to read. In late antiquity, a time when literacy rates were extremely low, this would have meant teaching most people who joined monasteries. Most importantly, reading was seen in Pachomian communities as an indispensable spiritual practice.[140] However, Cassian specifically "posits an analogy between the two processes, literary education, and monastic formation" and thus "his two texts engage the technological process that scholars have examined in equivalent rhetorical works, for example, Quintillian's *Institutio oratoria* and Cicero's *De oratore*."[141] It is important here to note that in addition to a focus on the content of reading, both in scripture and Cassian's own writings—there is an implicit attempt at the formation of a specific type of community through reading. As Krawiec notes, "[l]iteracy, rather than simply a skill, reflects interactions with the acts of reading and writing that create a community identity. The focus is not on who can read and write, but how these activities become expressions of monastic identity."[142] By combining instruction in a precise method of reading with the significance of the content being read, Cassian is forming his own particular community of monks in Gaul based upon the monastic traditions that formed

---

138. Heinrich Lausberg, *Handbook of Literary Rhetoric: A Foundation for Literary Study*, eds. David E. Orton and Dean Andersen, trans. Matthew T. Bliss, Annemiek Jansen, and David E. Orton (Leiden, Netherlands: Brill, 1998), 3.

139. Krawiec, "Monastic Literacy," 767.

140. Douglas Burton-Christie, *The Word in the Desert: Scripture and the Quest for Holiness in Early Christian Monasticism* (New York, NY: Oxford University Press, 1993),18 and 79–81. See also Harry Gamble, *Books and Readers in the Early Church: A History of Early Christian Texts* (New Haven, CT: Yale University Press, 1995), 170, on the formation of monastic libraries, and Guy Stroumsa, "The Scriptural Movement of Late Antiquity and Christian Monasticism," *Journal of Early Christian Studies* 16.1 (2008): 61–77.

141. Krawiec, "Monastic Literacy," 768.

142. Krawiec, "Monastic Literacy,"768.

his own identity. In other words, "Cassian can refashion his aristocratic male audience into monks without renouncing a prominent marker of prestige, literacy and particularly sublimity, even as others, such as wealth, fell by the wayside."[143] Cassian elsewhere in both the *Institutes* and the *Conferences* will insist that renunciation of wealth and social status is a necessary aspect of monastic identity. However, by using familiar literary methods and tropes from classical literature, he softens this blow to the egos of Gallican monks from the elite class, thereby placing monastic identity well within the grasp of educated, privileged males.

Krawiec goes on to note that "[m]onastic formation in Egypt, far from being absent or existing solely to teach illiterate monks to read, was modeled on *paideia*."[144] This philosophical *paideia* upon which monastic training is modeled, is evident in such early monastic documents as the *Letters of St. Antony*, in which an Origenist/Neoplatonic orientation seems clear, indicating that Antony may have been trained in philosophy before becoming a monk. This, of course, is in stark contrast to his portrayal in the *Life* by Athanasius in which Antony is an illiterate peasant.[145] I will address this issue in more detail in a chapter four.

Referring again to practices of literacy in his ideal monasticism, Cassian in the *Institutes* presents copywork, specifically copying of the scriptures, as suitable to fulfill the requirement for manual work in the monastery. He accordingly tells the story of a monk named Symeon who, when he arrives at an Egyptian cenobium, can speak only Latin, which apparently precludes him from doing much of the work of the monastery (perhaps he simply could not understand the instructions given to him in Greek or Coptic). Finally, another monk, seeing that Symeon is becoming idle in his cell and thus vulnerable to temptation, brings him a Latin copy of several of Paul's letters and asks him to copy them in order to send them to someone the monk knows who is in the army. Symeon accepts the opportunity gladly and gets to work enthusiastically. What is noteworthy in this story is that Cassian asserts that the actual final product is for all intents and purposes useless in that area in which Symeon seems to be the only Latin speaker. The value is in doing the work itself, in occupying one's hands and thoughts in order to stave off demonic thoughts and/or temptations.[146] Krawiec writes that "Cassian's story points to the creation of monastic literacy—using writing to conceptualize

---

143. Krawiec, "Monastic Literacy," 768–69.
144. Krawiec, "Monastic Literacy," 769.
145. For more on this contrast, see Samuel Rubenson, *The Letters of Saint Anthony: Monasticism and the Making of a Saint* (Minneapolis, MN: Fortress, 1995).
146. Cassian, *Institutes*, 5.39.

2. Cassian's Context and Asceticism as Basis for Valid Authority 51

monastic identity and define monastic behavior."[147] In other words, by identifying literacy work as monastic, manual work, Cassian effectively identifies those who are literate, specifically the monks drawn from the elite, educated class in Gaul, as monks. Classical education can now be converted into a manual labor worthy of the venerable monastic traditions of Egypt. Thus "Cassian transforms the 'symbolic capital' of regular literacy into the 'symbolic capital' for monastic literacy, since they are the material means now disposed towards the display of monastic virtue."[148] Furthermore, "the figure of Symeon, linguistically lost in Egypt, would resonate with Cassian's audience and so serves as a reminder of the cultural divide between Egypt and Gaul, a divide Cassian is able to bridge with his new monastic literacy."[149] Cassian simultaneously denigrates the classical education he and the monks of Gaul had received and uses its structures to effectively deliver his rhetoric.

Cassian writes that monastic practice consists of "the burden of fasting, intense reading, and the works of mercy, righteousness, piety, and hospitality."[150] It is significant here that in writing for his Gallican audience, Cassian emphasizes reading among the implements crucial to monastic formation, even though in his former Egyptian context, there were clearly many monks for whom reading was not possible. Cassian equates reading, a skill which most Gallican monks had learned as children, with ascetic practice and moral behavior. Thus, for these monks raised and educated to be elite Roman citizens, the "prestige associated with rhetoric now becomes associated with monastic literacy, as defined and taught by Cassian."[151] With such a rhetorical move, Cassian implies that the ability to read, if engaged in the correct manner he teaches, helps to form monks as good as the Desert Fathers of Egypt from whom Cassian claims to have gleaned all the knowledge, rules, and procedures in his writings. Krawiec thus writes that Cassian uses these literary forms and tropes for his own version of *paideia*: "For those monks in Gaul who cannot shed their aristocratic fashioning, Cassian creates a process of re-fashioning that idealized an elite Roman self into an idealized monastic self."[152] In addition, "Cassian's repeated claims to experience, therefore, not only elevate his texts over those written by the less or non-experienced competition. They are also the basis for his authority to teach the monastic literacy he required for his monasticism."[153] In this sense, Cassian can claim

---

147. Krawiec, "Monastic Literacy", 772.
148. Krawiec, "Monastic Literacy," 772.
149. Krawiec, "Monastic Literacy," 772.
150. Cassian, *Conferences*, 1.9.
151. Krawiec, "Monastic Literacy", 773.
152. Krawiec, "Monastic Literacy," 773.
153. Krawiec, "Monastic Literacy," 774.

to be doubly experienced: his own monastic *paideia* in Egypt is further legitimized by his classical education and literacy, placing him firmly in the camp of those Gallican monks who are his primary audience. Like the educational works on rhetoric and oratory written by such literary Roman luminaries as Quintillian and Cicero, Cassian's *Institutes* and *Conferences* "offer a special variety of 'reading lessons' designed to impart specific hermeneutic techniques,"[154] implicitly acknowledging the monks' elite status while redirecting it into monastic training

In addition to the above rhetorical techniques, reframing literacy as worthy of the renunciate, Cassian would also have to argue for the correctness and righteousness of true renunciation of wealth and status. He would have to depend upon establishing authority in an entirely different way, one which would still appeal to those who knew, for example, the famous *Life of Antony* well. With that in mind, I turn to Cassian's notions of asceticism and authority.

Ascetic Validity

Philip Rousseau notes that in the fourth and fifth centuries,

> [a]scetics of all types were convinced, first of all, that their leaders belonged to an historical tradition, to a religious group whose place could be clearly identified, not only in the history of the church, but also in the longer and more general history of God's dealings with mankind.[155]

Indeed, one of Cassian's most explicit arguments for the authority of his ascetic regimen over against that nominal asceticism practiced by monks in Gaul can be found in the *Conferences*: "The cenobitic life came into being at the time of the apostolic preaching."[156] Cassian's mouthpiece in this section, Abba Piamun, goes on to quote from the book of Acts: "There was one heart and one mind among the crowd of believers, nor did anyone claim as his own whatever it was that he possessed, but all things were held in common among them" (Acts 4.32, *NRSV*). The claim to authority here is neither subtle, nor imprecise. Cassian is claiming that the ascetic and monastic way of life, specifically that of renouncing all individual ownership of property, goes back in a direct line to the apostles. This is a startling claim against the authority of the institutional church. Divine authority

---

154. Krawiec, "Monastic Literacy," 774.
155. Philip Rousseau, *Ascetics, Authority, and the Church in the Age of Jerome and Cassian* (2nd ed.) (Notre Dame, IN: University of Notre Dame Press), 22.
156. Cassian, *Conferences*, 18.5. Itaque coenobiotarum disciplina a tempore praedicationis apostolicae sumpsit exordium.

2. Cassian's Context and Asceticism as Basis for Valid Authority 53

was believed to have passed from Jesus to the apostles to the bishops in an unbroken line. The bishop of Rome, for example, was supposed to have gone back in a direct line to the apostle Peter. If instead the monastic way of life were said to go back to the original apostles in Jerusalem, including Peter before he went to Rome, then Cassian was claiming that monastics had a far more direct claim to apostolic authority. This is both a bold claim for the authority of the ascetic way of life and possibly a shot across the bow of the institutional church for any clergy member or hierarch who might have read it. Remember that the clergy in Gaul, as well as the monks, were mostly drawn from the wealthy elite who had lost none of their status or wealth—and had perhaps even gained some—by officially joining the church. For Cassian, as we will see, this refusal of renunciation, this hollow asceticism, is essentially a kind of heresy, especially for those who dare to call themselves monks.

Asceticism for Cassian and his Egyptian teachers has several levels, beginning when one enters a monastery. The ultimate point of all asceticism, in Cassian's thought, is the renunciation of both worldly identity and personal will, to be replaced by a union of the individual soul with God and total surrender to the divine will. He thus writes "the Lord promises an hundredfold in this life to those whose renunciation is perfect… [a]nd therefore our Lord and Savior, to give us an example of giving up our own wills, says: 'I came not to do My own will, but the will of Him that sent Me;' and again: 'Not as I will, but as Thou wilt.'"[157] The progression of this set of renunciations is described in detail by Cassian in the *Institutes*. The first level of disavowals concerns the most superficial level of the monk's appearance. Cassian writes that it is best to begin with the clothing of the monk for "it is proper for a monk always to dress like a soldier of Christ, ever ready for battle, his loins girded."[158] In other words, one must first look like a monk to become a monk. The first step, therefore, to renouncing one's worldly identity is to relinquish one's previous garb and to take on the habit, or robe, of the monk. The reference to the scriptural metaphor of the soldier is apt here (cf. Eph. 6.11-20, 1 Thess. 5.8). The monk, like the soldier, puts on the uniform of his regiment to merge with the unit and to relinquish individuality for a group identity that helps to focus one on the task ahead. As

---

157. Cassian, *Conferences*, 24.26. Proinde etiam illa desideria praemiorum, qua perfecte renuntiantibus in hac uita centuplum dominus repromisit dicens… et idcirco dominus noster atque saluator, ut nobis amputandarum uoluntatum nostrarum formam traderet, non ueni, inquit, facere uoluntatem meam sed uoluntatem eius qui misit ine, et iterum: non sicut ego uolo sed sicut tu.

158. Cassian, *Institutes*, I.1. Itaque monachum ut militem Christi in procinctu semper belli positum accinctis lumbis iugiter oportet incedere.

one modern military author puts it, "There are many psychological implications of military uniforms...[Uniforms] contribute to togetherness, orderliness and discipline, and add to the soldiers' sense of camaraderie, cohesion, and esprit de corps."[159] In addition, Cassian notes that the monk's garb connects him with such biblical and prophetic luminaries as Elijah the Tishbite who was recognized "by his belt and by the hairy and unkempt aspect of his body," and the similarly-attired and hirsute John the Baptist.[160] Cassian also writes that the aspect of communal ownership of garments has a purpose here since

> whatever is arrogated by one or a few within the household of God and is not owned universally by the whole body of the brotherhood is superfluous and overweening and hence must be judged harmful and a token of vanity rather than a display of virtue.[161]

It is abundantly clear that this initial transformation of the bodily appearance aims at the eventual transformation of the soul as well. Cassian goes on to write of the symbolic nature of monastic garb, a rhetoric he borrows from his monastic teacher Evagrius Ponticus.[162] In a later institute, Cassian writes that the clothing removed by the novice is kept by the monastery's bursar until such time as the novice clearly shows adequate spiritual progress. However, "if they notice that he has committed the sin of complaining or is guilty of an act of disobedience, however slight, they strip him of the garb of the monastery... and, dressed once more in what he used to wear... they drive him out."[163] Notable here is the fact that changing clothes is not naively considered a real change of heart or soul. Rather, the novice's previous clothing, his literal, physical tie to a worldly identity, are kept until the novice has proved himself, at which time, the previous clothing is given to the poor.[164] Not only is his clothing initially taken from him, but indeed everything else he possesses as well: "Thus he may know not only that he

---

159. Col. G.P. Krueger, "Psychological Issues in Military Uniform Design." In *Advances in Military Textiles and Personal Equipment*, 64–78 (Philadelphia, PA: Woodhead Publishing, 2012), 64.

160. Cassian, *Institutes*, I.1. Helias Thesbites est, zonae uidelicet indicio et esider incultique corporis specie uirum dei indubitanter agnoscens.

161. Cassian, *Institutes*, 1.2. Quidquid enim inter et dei praesumitur ab uno uel paucis nec catholice per omne corpus fraternitates tonetur, aut suporfluum aut elatem est et ob id noxium iudicandum magisque uauitatis specimen quam uirtutis ostontans.

162. Evagrius Ponticus, R. Sinkewicz, translator, *Evagrius of Pontus the Greek Ascetic Corpus* (Oxford: Oxford University Press), *Prakitkos*, 1–9.

163. Cassian, *Institutes*, 4.6. Sin uero quoddam ex eo murmurationis uitium uel paruae cuiuslibet. Inoboedientiae culpam processisse deprehenderint, exuentes eum monasterii quibus indutus fuerat uestimentis et reuestitum antiquis quae fuerant depellunt.

164. Cassian, *Institutes*, 4.6.

has been despoiled of all his former things but also that he has put off all worldly pride and has stooped to the poverty and want of Christ."[165] The first step of renouncing the old identity and taking on the new is physical, the putting on of different clothing and surrendering all other physical possessions that would tie him either to his previous worldly identity or to the grasping nature of his individual self. Once a novice has proven that he is no fly-by-night convert but is committed to the monastic life, the donation of his previous clothing then bestows upon him the first hints of authority, again based upon his willing renunciation of the primary vestiges of his worldly self.

In examining the renunciation of possessions in the monastic sphere and its ties to a transformation and/or relinquishment of one's worldly identity, a useful hermeneutic notion is the distinction between "ownership" and "use" of things first written about explicitly in the 12th and 13th centuries by another group of monastics, the Franciscans. Although Cassian does not overtly mention this distinction, I believe the notion can be tacitly implied and adds a valuable perspective to his focus on renunciation and the implications for the monastic self. Note, for example, that after one surrenders one's possessions, including clothing, to the monastery, a novice is given use of necessary things—a monastic habit, food, a bed—but that these things belong to the monastery. If one decides to leave the monastery, these things stay behind. One has *use* of the things, but not *ownership*.

Ownership of things, particular items, is deeply tied to modes of identity. Imagine, for example, a carpenter who does not own tools but merely borrows them, a wealthy person who does not own their expensive clothing or mansion, or a scribe who does not own a writing instrument. A skilled carpenter is defined not simply by what he does but by what he owns pertaining to what he does, in this case a particular set of tools. One is defined, at least in part, by owning particular objects relevant to the pertinent identity. Without this aspect of the ownership of tools, one is likely not viewed as a carpenter, but rather a person whose set of skills merely includes carpentry, more a dilletante than a specialist worthy of the name "carpenter". Ownership of the apposite implements, in addition to the repeated, specific activities related to those implements, confers identity upon the owner. If one must borrow tools every time one needs to do carpentry, that is, if one has the use of tools but does not own them, one does not take on the identity of carpenter. Similarly, Cassian demonstrates that when one relinquishes a worldly identity for that of a monk, one relinquishes one's worldly

---

165. Cassian, *Institutes*, 4.5, ut per hoc se non solum uniuersis rebus suis antiquis nouerit spoliatum, uerum etiam omni fastu deposito mundiali ad Christi paupertatem.

possessions, therefore both symbolically and ontologically rejecting that previous identity. However, instead of being given new things to own, one is permanently deprived of the condition of ownership and instead given communal things to use. Not only has one subsumed one's individual identity through this exchange of ownership for use, but in addition one has taken on the communal identity, in that the food, clothing, and shelter one uses at the monastery are merely the property of the community as a whole and never that of any one individual. While one could say that a monk, in this sense takes on a new identity which does not depend upon ownership, I propose that Cassian saw relinquishment of ownership as a move toward kenosis or self-emptying on the part of the monk. Keeping in mind that Cassian's purity of heart (*puritatem cordis*) is his equivalent of Evagrius's word for spiritual perfection, passionlessness (απάθεια), note that at the end of *Institute* IV, Cassian gives this formula, one he says will allow the monk to ascend to the peak of spiritual perfection, which seems to point to such a kenotic reading:

> From the fear of the Lord is born a salutary compunction. From compunction of heart there proceeds renunciation—that is, the being deprived of and the contempt of all possessions. From this deprivation humility is begotten. From humility is generated the dying of desire. When desire has died all the vices are uprooted and wither away. Once the vices have been expelled the virtues bear fruit and grow. When virtue abounds purity of heart is acquired. With purity of heart the perfection of apostolic love is possessed.[166]

It is also worth mentioning that in the original Latin, the condition of renunciation of all possessions is written not as mere deprivation (*privatio*) but as nakedness (*nuditas*), a clear metaphorical picture of emptiness. Given this reading, I discuss below the significance of ownership vs. use in Cassian's writing about renunciation as codified and characterized explicitly by the medieval Franciscans.

Ownership vs. Use

Franciscan monk Hugh of Digne (d. circa 1285 CE) in his treatise *On the Ends of Poverty* (*De finibus paupertatis*) defines poverty as "the voluntary

---

166. Cassian, *Institutes*, XLIII. De timore Domini nascitur conpunctio salutaris. De conpunctione cordis procedit abrenuntiatio, id est nuditas et contemptus omnium facultatum. De nuditate humilitas procreatur. De humilitate generatur mortificatio uoluntatum. Mortificatione uoluntatum exstirpantur atque marcescunt uniuersa uitia. Expulsione uitiorum uirtutes fruticant atque succrescunt. Pullulatione uirtutum puritas cordis adquiritur. Puritate cordis apostolicae caritatis perfectio possidetur.

2. Cassian's Context and Asceticism as Basis for Valid Authority

abdication of ownership for the Lord's sake,"[167] while defining property as "the right of dominion, by which someone is said to be lord of some thing, by which right the thing itself is said to be his, that is proper to the lord."[168] In tying the distinction between use and ownership to identity, Hugh writes that "conserving one's nature does not in fact represent ownership of food and clothing but use; moreover it is possible always and everywhere to renounce ownership, but to renounce use never and nowhere."[169] Similarly, another Franciscan monk, Bonaventure, writes that there are four ways that human beings can relate to temporal objects: ownership, possession, usufruct, and simple use.[170] Bonaventure notes that of these four categories, only one, simple use, is absolutely impossible for human beings to renounce.[171] He uses, as his basis of authority for this position, the papal bull of Gregory IX entitled *Quo elongati*, which states, based on the Franciscan vow of poverty, that "property may be possessed neither individually nor in common" by the Friars Minor (the name Francis of Assisi assigned to the brothers of his order), but that "the brotherhood may have use (*usum habeat*) of equipment or books and such other movable property as it is permitted, and that individual brothers may use these things (*his utantur*)."[172] That is to say, the pope "distinguishes between ownership and use (*proprietatem separavit ab usu*), retaining the former for himself and the Church, while conceding the latter for the needs of the Friars."[173] Note here that the purity of mere use of necessary objects is reserved for monks while ownership is relegated to the church, mirroring the notion of parallel but separate spheres for institutional church and monasticism tacitly included in Cassian's writings. The distinction between use and ownership, therefore,

---

167. Hugh of Digne, *De finibus paupertatis auctore Hugone de Digna*, ed. C. Florovski, in *Archivium Franciscanum Historicum* 5 (1912): 277–90. Spontanea propter Dominum abdicacio proprietatis.

168. Hugh, *De finibus paupertatis*, 2, 283. Ius domini, quo quis rei dominus dicitur esse, quo iure res ipsa dicitur esse sua, id est domini propria.

169. Hugh, *De finibus paupertatis*, 2, 288–89. Haec siquidem, ut earum habeatur usus, sine quibus non conservatur esse nature, sed ut proprietas habeatur, nullatenus compellit.

170. Bonaventure, *Apologia paupertum*, in *Opera omnia*, vol. 14, book 2 (Rome: Citta Nuova, 2005). English translation: *Defense of the Mendicants*, trans. Jse de Vinck and Robert J. Karris (St. Bonaventure, New York, NY: Harper 2005, 366. Cum circa res temporales quatuor sit considerare, scilicet proprietatem, possessionem, usumfructum et simplicem usum.

171. Bonaventure, *Apologia paupertum,* 307–308. Et primis quidem tribus vita mortalium possit carere, ultimo vero tanquam necessario egeat: nulla prorsus potest esse professio omnino temporalium rerum abdicans usum.

172. Bonaventure, *Apologia paupertum*, 368.

173. Bonaventure, *Apologia paupertum*, 308.

pertains to the difference between relinquishing one's very existence, which would happen if one were to surrender use of all necessary things, and relinquishment of a particular identity, which is done in part by the individual renouncing particular possessions pertaining to that identity.

Although, again, Cassian never explicitly uses the terms "use" and "ownership" in this way, evidence of this distinction is especially apparent in the fourth *Institute* which discusses the novice monk's initiation into the monastery. Cassian tells us that when the monk has officially been accepted into the monastery in Egypt, "he is asked with the utmost earnestness if, from his former possessions, the contamination of even a single copper coin clings to him."[174] It is significant that Cassian specifically calls money "contamination" (*contagio*). Money, in many ways, is the ultimate defining possession as it confers power to obtain all other possessions. One who has voluntarily surrendered all money, as is required by monasteries in Egypt according to Cassian, has simultaneously surrendered much of the power to obtain or own anything at all. In addition, Cassian notes that the money taken from a novice monk is merely set aside and "[t]herefore, they do not even agree to accept money from him that would be for the needs of the cenobium."[175] While Cassian writes that the principal reason for this is to prevent the new monk from feeling proud of his contribution to the monastery, he later writes that all the monk's possessions are kept by the bursar of the monastery for a trial period "and kept until, thanks to various trials and tests, he [the novice] has made progress and they clearly recognize the virtue of his life and of his endurance."[176] If, however, the new monk complains or violates the rules of the monastery during this probationary period, Cassian tells us the monks "strip him of the garb of the monastery with which he had been clothed and, dressed once more in what he used to wear, which had been laid aside, they drive him out."[177] If a novice cannot adequately take on the whole identity of a monk by relinquishing every part of his former identity—material possessions, family and civic ties, worldly clothing—he is reintroduced to his former identity via being reclothed in his former garb, given his former possessions, including any money he originally had, and returned to the world.

---

174. Cassian, *Institutes*, 4.3.1. Diligentia summa perquiritur, ne de pristinis suis inhaeserit ei uel unius nummi facultatibus contagio.

175. Cassian, *Institutes*, 4.4. Et ideirco ne usibus quidem coenobii profuturas suscipere ab eo pecunias adquiescunt.

176. Cassian, *Institutes*, 4.6. Donec profectus et conuersationis eius ac tolerantiae uirtutem diuersis temptationibus ac probationibus euidenter agnoscant.

177. Cassian, *Institutes*, 4.6. Exuentes eum monasterii quibus indutus fuerat uestimentis et reuestitum antiquis quae fuerant sequestrata depellunt.

2. Cassian's Context and Asceticism as Basis for Valid Authority   59

Traditions and Regulations

In the second *Institute* Cassian begins to discuss the nuts and bolts, as it were, of correct ascetic practice according to his Egyptian progenitors. After the relinquishment of superficial identity through clothing and possessions, the next renunciation is that of control over one's time and actions. Cassian thus begins the second *Institute* with a discussion of the canonical prayers and psalms; 12 psalms are to be chanted every night because this number is "maintained throughout all of Egypt and the Thebaid."[178] He emphasizes this, as if to make a meta-analysis of his own discourse and its sources, by noting that these particular canonical prayers and psalms and their designated number were "determined in times past in the regions of the East by the holy fathers."[179] Again, observe that Cassian here both instructs the monks of Gaul and models humility for them in that he refuses to take credit for the ordering of canonical prayers and their number and time, attributing them instead to the Egyptian fathers who trained him. This also, parenthetically, ascribes a spiritual and rhetorical weight to Cassian's discourse: he is not inventing these methods as a detached, saintly genius. Rather, he sees himself as simply a minuscule link in a methodological chain going back, as we have seen, to the apostles and, by implication therefore, to Christ himself. This establishes his personal authority in the matter, but also, from the vantage point of history, demonstrates the profound influence a representative of a venerable and longstanding tradition could have.

We know, incidentally, that Cassian's works, whether or not they accomplished what he was attempting to accomplish in his time, did have an enormous influence, principally through Benedict of Nursia's use of Cassian's material for his own highly influential monastic rule.[180] Cassian establishes this historical and authoritative weight again by noting that while some persons—he is undoubtedly referring to the errant Gallican monks here—"have established different models and rules for themselves," he himself is providing readers with "the most ancient constitution of the fathers… in the most time-tried (*antiquissimorum*) customs of the most ancient fathers."[181] Cassian then writes that the number of prayers, "which was set in the

---

178. Cassian, *Institutes*, 2.4. Igitur per uniuersam ut diximus Aegyptum et Thebaidem duodenarius psalmorum numerus.

179. Cassian, *Institutes*, 2.1. Sit in partibus Orientis a sanctis patribus antiquitus statutus.

180. Goodrich, *Contextualizing Cassian*, 1–2.

181. Cassian, *Institutes*, 2.2. Multos namque per alias conperimus pro captu mentis suae, habentes quidem apostolus zelum dei, sed non secundum scientiam, super hac re diuersos typos ac regulas sibimet constituisse… Quapropter necessarium reor antiquissimam patrum proferre in medium constitutionem.

distant past and which is inviolate in the monasteries of those regions even until now," has been established, not merely by "human whim (*arbitrium hominum*), but was given to the fathers from heaven by the teaching of an angel."[182] If there were any doubt about the divine sanction and authority of the methods Cassian describes here, it is surely eliminated by invoking a messenger of God as the revealer of this specific number of canonical prayers. Cassian goes on to tie these canonical prayers to the evangelist Mark, as well, establishing ties not only to the apostles—Mark is traditionally said to have been Peter's interpreter and/or secretary[183]– but to scripture as well. This is further validation of his methods and his rhetoric in general. It is also another clear jab at the institutional church in general, whose sole claim to authority for themselves is that of apostolic succession through the hierarchs. While the apostle Peter is said to have been the first bishop of Rome, Cassian here ties his teachings not to just to eminent monks, as he will in the *Conferences*, but also to older bishops; Mark is also said, in much of Christian tradition, to have been the founder and first bishop of the church at Alexandria.[184] There is an implicit assertion in this connection, that despite its failings now, the church in the past was legitimate, coupled, as are the monks of Egypt, to the prayers and practices established by the apostles and their followers.

Cassian even provides a historically dubious but no doubt rhetorically powerful origin story for the correct liturgy of monks: when "the perfection of the primitive church (*ecclesiae illius primitiuae*) remained inviolate and was still fresh in the memory of succeeding generations," the "venerable fathers, reflecting with unceasing concern (*peruigili cura posteris*) on those who would follow them, came together to discuss what form daily worship

---

182. Cassian, *Institutes*, 2.4. Qui modus antiquitus constitutus idcirco per tot saecula penes cuncta illarum prouinciarum monasteria intemeratus nunc usque perdurat, quia non humana adinuentione statutus a senioribus adfirmatur, sed caelitus angeli magisterio patribus fuisse delatus.

183. Papias, Irenaeus, Justin Martyr, Clement of Alexandria, Eusebius, and Tertullian all identify Mark as Peter's scribe. See, for example, Irenaeus, *Adversus Haereses,* in *Patrologia Graeca* vol. 7, edited by J.-P. Migne (Paris: 1857), translated by Alexander Roberts and William Rambaut. From *Ante-Nicene Fathers*, Vol. 1. Edited by Alexander Roberts, James Donaldson, and A. Cleveland Coxe (Buffalo, NY: Christian Literature Publishing Co., 1885), 3.1, in which Mark is said to have passed Peter's teachings down in written form and Eusebius, *Historia ecclesiastica*, in *Patrologia Graeca*, vol. 20, edited by J.-P. Migne (Paris: 1857), translated by Arthur Cushman McGiffert, from *Nicene and Post-Nicene Fathers, Second Series*, Vol. 1, edited by Philip Schaff and Henry Wace. (Buffalo, NY: Christian Literature Publishing Co., 1890.), 6.14, in which Papias is quoted as saying that Mark had simply written his gospel from Peter's dictation.

184. Eusebius, *Ecclesiastical History*, 2.16.

2. Cassian's Context and Asceticism as Basis for Valid Authority 61

should take throughout the whole body of the brotherhood."[185] Note that the liturgy here is both created and maintained from the "primitive church" not by clergy but rather by the true pious agents of divinity, monks, or at least the apostles designated as proto-monks, for the benefit of true Christians of later generations. Indeed, Cassian specifies with an almost tiresome precision, how the actual number of psalms was finally decided on, a mythology well-planned to appeal to the vanity of monks who would perhaps prefer to see themselves as descended from this early church through the esteemed monks of Egypt. Cassian writes that in a night time service in an earlier age (despite his specificity as to the details of the liturgy, he is vague as to the time period to which he refers), someone stood up to chant the psalms. The cantor,

> sang eleven psalms that were separated by the interposition of prayers, all the verses being pronounced in the same tone of voice. Having finished the twelfth with an Alleluia as a response, he suddenly withdrew from the eyes of all, thus concluding both the discussion and the ceremony.[186]

In case the reader has missed the ultimate point here, Cassian states again that "a universal rule had been established for the groups of the brothers through the teaching of an angel."[187] While divine authority is established through the deity's messenger here, there is also a parallel to the biblical story of the road to Emmaus; the angel, acting in the place of Christ in the gospel story, opens the eyes of the monks to the correct practices, then disappears, his sudden absence leaving no doubt of the approval of the divinity he represented. The clergy, conversely, has dangerously diverged from these methods, leaving only the monks—at least those who practice correctly according to the ancient rule—to practice properly.

Cassian here makes yet another implicit jab at the lax nature of Gallican monasticism, noting that what he calls the first monks, initiated by Mark the Evangelist "went off to quite secluded places on the outskirts of the city and led a strict life of such rigorous abstinence that even those who did not

---

185. Cassian, *Institutes*, 2.5.3. Ea igitur tempestate, cum ecclesiae illius primitiuae perfectio penes suos adhuc recenti memoria inuiolata duraret feruensque paucorum fides necdum in multitudinem dispersa tepuisset, uenerabiles patres peruigili cura posteris consulentes, quinam modus cotidiano cultui per uniuersum fraternitatis corpus decerni deberet.

186. Cassian, *Institutes*, II.4.5. Undecim psalmos orationum interiectione distinctos contiguis uersibus parili pronuntiatione cantasset, duodecimum sub alleluiae responsione cousummans ab uniuersorum oculis repente subtractus quaestioni et caerimoniis finem inposuit.

187. Cassian, *Institutes*, 2.6. Exhinc uenerabilis patrum senatus, intellegens angeli magisterio congregationibus fratrum generalem canonem non sine dispensatione Domini constitutum,

share their religion were astonished at the arduous profession of their way of life."[188] Given what we know of Gallican asceticism at this time, an asceticism that at best belonged in scare quotes for Cassian in that it involved only the slimmest appearance of renunciations and the retention of all one's social status and wealth, this insistence on the true way of life as one of rigorous renunciation and prayer can only be a remonstrance. Remember also that the monasteries of Gaul were initially founded by the local bishop, not a monk. As if to drive this point home, along with his own personal basis for authority in these matters, Cassian notes that in Egypt, "no one is allowed to rule over a community of brothers, or even over himself, unless he not only gets rid of all his possessions but also recognizes that he is in fact not his own master and has no power over himself."[189] Such a description of the devout monk, given the lack of renunciation by Gallican monks and the ostensible leadership of monasteries at this point by the bishop, can only be applied in such rhetoric to Cassian himself.

Continuing his description of how the desert fathers of Egypt conduct their prayers, Cassian makes the first of his many notes about the necessity of moderation. As it turns out, however, the purpose of keeping a moderate number of prayers for the group meetings is simply so that for "those of more ardent faith there might be kept a space of time in which their virtue could run its tireless course without lengthiness also creating tedium for bodies that are exhausted and weary."[190] In other words, the correct procedures strike a balance between group prayer requirements and the space and time required, if a monk is committed enough to forgo large amounts of sleep, to continue in solitary prayer.

Cassian writes that after canonical prayers have finished, each monk returns to his own cell (shared at most by two people) where he can "again celebrate the more eagerly a service of prayers as their own particular sacrifice."[191] Given the earlier reference Cassian makes to people behaving

---

188. Cassian, *Institutes*, 2.5.2. Etenim secedentes in secretiora suburbiorum loca agebant uitam tanto abstinentiae rigore districtam, ut etiam his, qui religionis externi, esset tam ardua conuersationis eorum.

189. Cassian, *Institutes*, 2.3.2. Non enim quisquam conuenticulo fratrum, sed ne sibi quidem ipsi praeesse conceditur, priusquam non solum uniuersis facultatibus suis reddatur externus, sed ne sui quidem ipsius esse se dominum uel potestatem habere cognoscat.

190. Cassian, *Institutes*, 2.12.2. Et idcirco mediocrem canonicarum orationum numerum iudicant diuinitus moderatum, ut ardentioribus fide spatium, quo se uirtutis eorum infatigabilis cursus extenderet, seruaretur, et nihilominus fessis aegrisque corporibus minime gigneretur de nimietate fastidium.

191. Cassian, *Institutes*, 2.12. Idem rursus orationum officium uelut sacrificium studiosius celebrant nec ulterius quisquam eorum in requiem somni resoluitur.

2. Cassian's Context and Asceticism as Basis for Valid Authority

crudely in church,[192] this is likely another upbraiding of the Gallican monks for not only giving scant attention to canonical prayers, but for then rushing back to their beds to catch a few winks. Cassian here emphasizes that both a commitment to the group, displayed in correct behavior at group prayer services (which he calls *synaxis*, transliterating the Greek word into Latin), and a commitment to individual prayer and practice are necessary for the making of a monk. Implicit here is the fact that in the monks of Gaul, Cassian sees neither, or at least insufficient quantities of either. These two commitments are described in the language of theological anthropology when Cassian writes that the monks of Egypt "practice equally the virtues of body and of soul, balancing the profit of the outer man with the gain of the inner."[193] This sentence provides a kind of ideal orientation by which Cassian can judge the conduct of the Gallican monks. It would seem, given the lack of commitment to abandonment of belongings among the monks of Marseilles, that the Gallican monks have been taught to privilege the inner over the outer. While prayer and belief may be important to them, their outer conduct, dress, and manner of speaking is based more upon aristocratic Roman etiquette, in which the elite have free rein to do what they want merely by virtue of their exalted status. As monks, Cassian points out, this is unacceptable. During the communal chanted prayers, for example, Cassian notes that in Egypt, if one of the monks sings louder than he ought, "the cantor is interrupted in mid-course by the elder, who claps his hands from the place where he is seated and makes everyone rise for the prayer."[194] As a monk, one is to blend in during all activities, never intentionally asserting one's individuality. The power of the elder in this example carries with it Cassian's earlier point that only one who has significantly humbled himself is allowed to take charge of a group of monks. One must be obedient first in order to be worthy of the authority of being obeyed.

Yet another aspect of the Egyptian ascetic regimen outlined in Cassian's *Institutes* is the relinquishment of what most would consider a normal social life. This, like the changing of one's garb, is an enormous part of how Cassian and his monastic forebears attempt to annihilate the previous worldly identity of each new monk, leaving them to create a new identity based upon their own Egyptian monastic models. This begins at the very moment when a potential monk arrives at the door of a monastery. Cassian writes

---

192. Cassian, *Institutes*, 2.10.1.
193. Cassian, *Institutes*, 2.14. Nam pariter exercentes corporis animaeque uirtutes exterioris hominis stipendia cum emolumentis interioris exaequant.
194. Cassian, *Institutes*, 2.11.2 Psallentis senioris interciditur plausu, quem dans manu sua in sedili quo sedet cunctos facit ad orationem consurgere, illud omnimodis prouidens, ne quod taedium sedentibus generetur prolixitate psalmorum.

that no one is admitted to a monastery until, "by lying outside [the door] for ten days or more, he has given an indication of his perseverance and desire as well as of his humility and patience."[195] This humility and patience are demonstrated by the novice silently tolerating the disdain of all the other monks for days on end. Cassian writes that "by putting up with taunts [the novice shows] what he will be like in time of trial."[196] Cassian here reiterates that every possession, down to every coin on the novice's person, is then taken away because otherwise "when the first disturbance arose for any reason… [he] would flee the monastery as fast as a whirring slingstone."[197] This acceptance of insults along with the stripping away of all personal possessions is a kind of self-emptying, mirroring that of Christ in the well-known hymn quoted by Paul:

> Let the same mind be in you that was in Christ Jesus, who, though
> he was in the form of God,
> did not regard equality with God
> as something to be exploited, but emptied himself,
> taking the form of a slave,
> being born in human likeness.
> And being found in human form, he humbled himself
> and became obedient to the point of death—
> even death on a cross (Phil. 2.5-8 NRSV).[198]

One who will not defend himself against insults or disdain and who has no personal possessions apart from the other monastics has his identity entirely wrapped up with the other monks. The ceremonial stripping away of his worldly clothing, by the way, is done in front of all the other monks according to Cassian, a solemn and yet poignant ritual emphasizing one's own abject quality apart from those of the monastery who are receiving the novice.[199] However, even at this point, the novice has not yet finished cutting off his previous identity.

---

195. Cassian, *Institutes*, 4.3.1. Igitur ambiens quis intra coenobii recipi disciplinam non ante prorsus admittitur, quam diebus decem uel eo amplius pro foribus excubans indicium perseuerantiae ac desiderii sui pariterque humilitatis ac patientiae demonstrauerit.

196. Cassian, *Institutes*, 4.3.1. Iniuriis quoque et exprobrationibus multis adfectus experimentum dederit constantiae suae, qualisque futurus sit in temptationibus.

197. Cassian, *Institutes*, 4.3.2. Si in conseientia eius pecuniae quantulumeumte latitauerit, sed ubi primum exorta fuerit qualibet oceasione commotio, fiducia stipis illius animatum eontinuo de monasterio uelut funda rotante fugiturum.

198. τοῦτο φρονεῖτε ἐν ὑμῖν ὃ καὶ ἐν Χριστῷ Ἰησοῦ, ὃς ἐν μορφῇ θεοῦ ὑπάρχων οὐχ ἁρπαγμὸν ἡγήσατο τὸ εἶναι ἴσα θεῷ, ἀλλὰ ἑαυτὸν ἐκένωσεν μορφὴν δούλου λαβών, ἐν ὁμοιώματι ἀνθρώπων γενόμενος· καὶ σχήματι εὑρεθεὶς ὡς ἄνθρωπος ἐταπείνωσεν ἑαυτὸν γενόμενος ὑπήκοος μέχρι θανάτου, θανάτου δὲ σταυροῦ.

199. Cassian, *Institutes*, 4.5.

2. *Cassian's Context and Asceticism as Basis for Valid Authority* 65

As a new monk, he is set apart from the others and assigned to an elder who will initially act as his mentor.[200] In this capacity, the novice and his elder will be in charge of hospitality for visitors to the monastery, serving them for one year in order to learn the humility necessary to officially become a monk.[201] After this, if there are no complaints from him or from his elder about him, he is assigned to a different elder along with a small group of other novices.

From the moment the postulant enters the monastery, he is cut off from all his previous social ties, including the family, a drastic move in the ancient world in which, as Peter Brown has noted, one's entire identity was based upon one's family and village ties. Even sexual temptation, often conceived as one of the more difficult temptations to overcome by modern thinkers, was simply "part of a far greater effort to sever the umbilical cord that linked [a monk] to his village."[202] Retreating into the desert was part of physically separating oneself from the elements of that original social identity into which one had been born. Indeed, "the desert was thought of as the… zone of the nonhuman."[203] However, as noted again by Brown, one did not, in "fleeing the world" abandon all social ties but rather one left "a precise social structure for an equally precise and… social alternative."[204]

Rhetorical Authority of the Desert Fathers

Cassian's claim to authority indeed rests on the correct practice of asceticism. However, behind this claim is his other constant and implicit claim: he learned this correct practice from the original ascetic icons, the Desert Fathers of Egypt. Attention to the speakers of Cassian's *Conferences* reveals many of the names famous from other ascetic literature such as the *AP, The Lausiac History*, and *The History of the Monks in Egypt*. What is more, despite all the redactions scholars generally agreed happened before much of this literature was widely published later in the fifth century, the practices and the ethos present within the sayings and stories of Cassian's fabled interlocutors, as well as other revered monks who are discussed but not present as speaking characters in the *Conferences*, seem to be consistent with the stories and quotes by the same figures in the monastic literature.[205]

---

200. Cassian, *Institutes*, IV.7.
201. Cassian, *Institutes*, IV.7.
202. Peter Brown, *The Body and Society: Men, Women, and Sexual Renunciation in Early Christianity* (New York, NY: Columbia University Press, 1988), 214.
203. Brown, *The Body and Society*, 218.
204. Brown, *The Body and Society* 217.
205. Interestingly, Zachary Smith says that the compiler of the *AP*, through his

Below, I demonstrate this congruence for two reasons. First, I intend to show the rhetorical significance of Cassian's use of these illustrious figures, regardless of whether, after 20 years, it was likely that he clearly remembered such conversations in detail. Second, in adding these other voices to Cassian's—or, rather, his to theirs—I show that Cassian was not a lone voice, but was representative of a type of monastic thought, privileging the practice of asceticism, which was pervasive in early monastic circles in Palestine and Egypt. A few cases in point will suffice to demonstrate this.

Cassian focuses through the voice of one monk on the virtue of obedience, also conceived of as renouncing the personal will. One of the monks mentioned as an exemplar of the renunciation of self-will necessary to become a true monk is called Abba John by Cassian. The same story is told of him in the *Conferences* and in the *AP* in which he is called Abba John the Short or, in some translations, Abba John the Dwarf (ἀββᾶ Ἰωάννου τοῦ Κολοβοῦ). In the apothegm, John, as a novice monk is given a task by his master. The master picks up a dry stick and plants it in the ground several miles away from John's cell. He then orders John to water the stick every day until it bears fruit. Cassian notes that elders would often assign such useless and seemingly foolish tasks to novices simply to teach them the value of total obedience (*oboedientia*). In Cassian's version of the story, John accomplishes this arduous and senseless task without complaint for one year after which, since John has clearly proven his compliance, the elder pulls up the stick and throws it away, declaring the task finished.[206] By the time of the earliest version of the *AP*, the story has likely become mythologized: after three years, the elder discovers that the stick has actually begun to bear fruit, after which he takes the fruit to a gathering of the elders and entreats them to "[t]ake and eat the fruit of obedience."[207] Despite the fabled resolution in the *AP*, it is clear the same virtue, total submission, is emphasized in both versions. Abba John is thus referred to reverentially throughout the *Institutes* and *Conferences*.

Cassian's first interlocutor in the *Conferences* is Abba Moses, possibly the well-known monk featured in the *AP*. In the *Conferences,* Moses says the monk's sparse diet has the purpose of

---

rhetorical and redactional choices, presents, among other things, a picture of "monks consistently weaponized by various sides in the heated theological debates of the fourth and fifth centuries." Zachary B. Smith, *Philosopher-Monks, Episcopal Authority, and the Care of the Self: The Apophthegmata Patrum in Fifth-Century Palestine* (Turnhout, Belgium: Brepols Publishers, 2017), 31. This certainly agrees with the portrayals of conflicts between monks and church hierarchs which I will address in chapter three.

206. Cassian, *Institutes*, 4.24.
207. *AP*, John the Short, 1. Λάβετε, φάγετε χαρπὸν ὑπακοῆς.

preserving both body and soul in one and the same condition, and not allowing the mind either to faint through weariness from fasting, nor to be oppressed by over-eating, for it ends in such a sparing diet that sometimes a man neither notices nor remembers in the evening that he has broken his fast.[208]

In the *Lausiac History,* the same Moses is remembered by its author Palladius as practicing "asceticism... zealously, and especially in regard to food. He partook of nothing but dry bread, meanwhile saying fifty prayers daily."[209] The emphasis on asceticism as a necessary set of practices for achieving holiness is stressed in both sources regarding Abba Moses. In the *AP*, there are two apothegms in particular that emphasize Abba Moses's asceticism. The first stresses the importance of solitude when he tells another monk looking for wisdom to "go and sit in your cell and your cell will teach you everything."[210] The second has a person inquire of Abba Moses what benefits long fasts and vigils achieve for a monk, to which Abba Moses replies: "They make the soul humble. For it is written, 'Consider my affliction and my trouble, and forgive all my sins (Ps. 25.18).' So if the soul gives itself all this hardship, God will have mercy on it."[211] As with Abba John above, Moses is portrayed as an ideal monk, one whose practices were learned from eminent monks and subsequently imitated by Moses' monastic descendants.

Conclusion

This chapter examined the monastic culture of Egypt from which Cassian learned his notions of monastic practice and purity. This type of monastic practice included the severe renunciation of a monk's previous identity, including clothing, possessions, and all previous family and social ties. These required renunciations not only aimed at the transformation of each

---

208. Cassian, *Conferences*, 2.23. In uno eodemque statu animam pariter corpusque conseruans, nec ieiunii fatigatione concidere nec grauari mentem saturitate permittens. tanta namque frugalitate finitur, ut interdum se post uesperam nec sentiat aut meminerit refecisse.

209. Palladius, *Lausiac*, Moses, 6 . ...οὐδενὸς ἄλλου μεταλαμβάαων πλὴν ἄρτου ξηροῦ ἐν οὐγχίαις δεχα δύο • πλεῖστον ἐργαζόμενος ἔργον, χαι πεντήχοντα ἐχτελῶν προσευχὰς τὴν ἡμέρας.

210. *AP*, Moses, 6. Ὕπαγε, κάθισον εἰς τὸ κελλίον σου· καὶ τὸ κελλίον σου διδάσκει σε πάντα.

211. *AP*, Moses, 6 (enumerated as instructions given by Abba Moses to Abba Poemen). Αὗται ποιοῦ σι τὴν ψυχὴν ταπεινωθῆναι. Γέγραπται γάρ· Ἰδὲ τὴν ταπείνωσίν μου καὶ τὸν κόπον μου, καὶ ἄφες πάσας τὰς ἁμαρτίας μου. Ἐὰν ἡ ψυχὴ ποιήση τοὺς καρποὺς τούτους, σπλαγχνίζεται ὁ Θεὸς ἐπ' αὐτῇ δι' αὐτῶν. Λέγει ὁ ἀδελφὸς τῷ γέροντι· Τί ποιήσει ἄν θρωπος ἐν παντὶ πειρασμῷ ἐπερχομένῳ ἐπάνω αὐ τοῦ, ἢ ἐν παντὶ λογισμῷ τοῦ ἐχθροῦ.

individual monk, but also at the creation of a group subjectivity, in which all would strive together to meet the monastic ideals presented by Cassian. Since the larger, hierarchical Church did not require such renunciations from each parishioner or even from bishops and clergy, I argue that Cassian is implicitly setting up a duality between Egyptian monasticism as the highest practice of Christianity and Church hierarchs as examples of inferior representatives of a spiritually and ascetically deficient, albeit necessary, institution. Monks clearly were more deserving of authority over themselves than bishops.

In addition, the Gallican monastic system into which Cassian attempted to assert his Egyptian rules was anemic in its asceticism by the measure of those rules. Monastics were not required to surrender any of their wealth or status, and in fact, as the story of Martin of Tours demonstrates, may have even increased in both by joining a monastery. Gallican monasticism was part and parcel of the Gallican church, in which the majority of both monks and clergy were from the upper classes and saw themselves as maintaining their wealth and status in the afterlife. This, of course, would have been entirely unacceptable to Cassian. To correct these errors, Cassian would effectively have to create a new monastic culture with new types of monastic subjects, by separating them from the hierarchical church.

In the next chapter, I turn to Cassian's creation of subjects by analyzing Foucault's notions of subjectivity and its formation and how such notions might effectively apply to Cassian's rhetoric in the *Institutes* and the *Conferences*.

Chapter Three
Foucault, Cassian, and the Creation of Subjects

In the *Conferences*, Cassian explains that the practice of solitude, while not available to everyone since it is a higher practice for those who have eradicated most of their sinful characteristics already, is solely for those monks who have "the desire for greater perfection and a more contemplative route."[1] Such monks, according to Cassian, "long to join in open combat and in clear battles against the demons. They are not afraid to push into the great hiding places of the desert."[2] In suggesting that anchorites or solitary monks are both higher in perfection and more proficient in demonic combat, Cassian creates a consistent scheme of Foucauldian governmentality that I will be investigating in what follows.

The writings of Michel Foucault, specifically his theory of the creation of subjects, provide great help in analyzing the function of the writings of Cassian (and other concurrent monastic literature, as well). A close reading of Cassian's writings through the lens of Foucault reveals that Cassian is a) trying to shape the individual subjectivity of monks and b) trying in turn to form a larger, unified, collective monastic subjectivity which may ultimately rival the authority of the clergy, at least for the monastic sphere. This chapter begins with a discussion of Foucault's theory on the creation of subjects, including the three principal means for the successful deployment of this operation. From there, the chapter proceeds to a definition of the three types of power, among several described by Foucault, which I believe describe methods Cassian uses in attempting to manipulate the subjectivity of monks in Gaul: disciplinary power, pastoral power, and biopower. Finally, I use Cassian's own writings to demonstrate how these types of power are operative within his discourse.

---

1. Cassian, *Conferences*, 18.6. ...sed desiderio sublimioris profectus contemplationisque diuinae solitudinis secreta sectati sunt.
2. Cassian, *Conferences*, 18.6. eo quod nequaquam contenti hac uictoria, qua inter homines occultas insidias diaboli calcauerunt, aperto certamine ac manifesto conflictu daemonibus congredi cupientes uastos heremi recessus penetrare non timeant

Foucault and the Formation of Subjects

Foucault began discussions on the formation of the subject by introducing what he called "governmentality." For Foucault, governmentality is present wherever systems of authority trickle down into an internalized embrace of rules governing an individual's conduct. This makes Foucault an appropriate parallel reading partner with Cassian. Often defined tersely as "the conduct of conduct," governmentality in Foucault's definition is "where the way individuals are driven by others is tied to the way they conduct themselves," a "versatile equilibrium... between techniques which assure coercion and processes through which the self is constructed or modified by himself."[3] Referring to these interweaving processes of external coercion and work on the self or self-formation, Foucault summarized his entire body of work, noting that his overall objective was "to create a history of the different modes by which, in our culture, human beings are made subjects."[4]

The subject, in Foucauldian terms, is not the autonomous actor or agent often idealized in modern, post-Enlightenment thought, an individual whose self is merely the result of her own well or poorly made choices. Instead, Foucault believed the subject to be a social construction whose specific vantage point is the result of the constant interplay of multiple forms of power—including that of the subject themself. He writes

> This form of power applies itself to immediate everyday life which categorizes the individual, marks him by his own individuality, attaches him to his own identity, imposes a law of truth on him which he must recognize and which others have to recognize in him. It is a form of power which makes individuals subjects. There are two meanings of the word "subject": subject to someone else by control and dependence; and tied to his own identity by a conscience or self-knowledge. Both meanings suggest a form of power which subjugates and makes subject to.[5]

What interested Foucault, then, was the specific mechanisms or techniques by which such subjects were formed.

In a 1980 lecture published and translated under the title "Subjectivity and Truth," Foucault notes that the history of the formation of subjects is

---

3. Michel Foucault, Graham Burchell, translator, *About the Beginning of the Hermeneutics of the Self* (University of Chicago Press, 2016), 19–37. Original Publication: *L'origine de l'herméneutique de soi: Conférences prononcées á Dartmouth College* (Librairie Philosophique J. Vrin, 1980).

4. Michel Foucault, "The Subject and Power" In *Michel Foucault: Beyond Structuralism and Hermeneutics*, edited by H. Dreyfus and P. Rabinow (2nd ed. Chicago, IL: The University of Chicago Press, 1983), 208–26. Original Publication: *Le Sujet et le Pouvoir* (Paris: Gallimard, D&E Vol. 4 1982).

5. Foucault, "The Subject and Power," 208.

best undertaken by acknowledging both techniques of domination and techniques of the self. Foucault writes that one who wants to study a genealogy of the subject must "take into account the points where the technologies of domination of individuals over one another have recourse to processes by which the individual acts upon himself. And conversely, he has to take into account the points where the techniques of the self are integrated into structures of coercion or domination."[6] In other words, Foucault saw that the formation of subjectivity was far more complex than a simple heavy-handed exercise of top-down, regulatory power. Rather, it occurred through an intersection of the exercise of domination and the self-construction of potential subjects.

Foucault's ultimate question, then, was how techniques of control, especially those reinforced through discourse, were used to convince subjects to work on themselves in order to form themselves into an ideal which in turn might serve the governing forces.

Foucault's Three Methods for the Creation of Subjects

Foucault identified three means by which subjects are created: First, modes of investigation create subjects as objects of knowledge. Second, practices and procedures divide subjects both from within, and from other subjects according to standards of norm and deviance. Third, practices and procedures of self-management are introduced, by which subjects transform themselves as subjects in order to meet an externally imposed ideal.[7] I find Foucault's analysis useful for investigating Cassian's rhetoric as a process of the creation of certain subjectivities. Indeed, in Cassian's writings, I find all three of Foucault's modes of subjectivation present. This grants great explanatory and analytical power in understanding how Cassian aims at the creation of a very specific type of subjectivity which, if realized at the necessary critical mass of individuals, could result in the realization of Cassian's vision for an ideal, powerful, and separate monastic institution. That is, these individual subjects would ideally form a collective subjectivity as the building blocks of a monasticism outside of the strictures, as well as what Cassian believed were the moral and spiritual failings of the Church.

In fact, Foucault spent time and analysis on Christian monasticism as a particular mode of subjectivity formation, even mentioning Cassian's writings specifically.[8] Foucault writes that

---

6. Foucault, *About the Beginning*, 25.
7. Foucault, "Subject and Power," 208.
8. See for example, Michel Foucault, edited by Henri-Paul Fruchaud, Daniele

[e]very Christian has the duty to know who he is, what is happening in him. He has to know the faults he may have committed: he has to know the temptations to which he is exposed. And, moreover, everyone in Christianity is obliged to say these things to other people and hence to bear witness against himself.[9]

Foucault goes on to talk about the virtue of obedience as the principal framework of subjectivity in which monasticism is contained. Obedience, in short, applies to all aspects of the self because "everything that one does not do on order of one's director, or everything that one does without his permission constitutes a theft."[10] Foucault thus notes that this obedience, far from being the instrumental and thus temporary condition that it was for disciples of pagan philosophers, is a permanent condition for the Christian monk, "a permanent sacrifice of his own will."[11] In constantly and faithfully divulging all his thoughts to another, the monk is performing a sort of externally imposed self-examination of his own thoughts which are liable to deceive him if they are not confessed. Foucault notes that Cassian characterizes this act of confession as a manifestation of truth; the distinction between good and evil thoughts is that evil thoughts can only be spoken of with difficulty and/or shame. Bringing forth an evil thought by verbalization to one's superior makes it "[lose] its power" and in addition the thought "departs as a kind of laughingstock and object of dishonor."[12]

Cassian and Foucault's Three Methods for Creating Subjects

Cassian begins his *Institutes* with the assumption that certain monks in the Egyptian desert, monks with whom Cassian himself lived and studied, live in the correct monastic way. This way includes correct, that is to say, moderate asceticism, as opposed to either luxuriant living or extreme, life-threatening asceticism, both of which must be eschewed. Thus Cassian writes "excessive abstinence trips up a person more disastrously than does thoughtless satiety. For from the latter one can mount to the proper measure of strictness with the help of a salutary compunction, but in the case of the

---

Lorenzini, and Laura Cremonesi. Translated by Graham Burchell, *About the Beginning of the Hermeneutics of the Self: Lectures at Dartmouth College, 1980* (Chicago, IL: University of Chicago Press, 2016), 64–71.
    9. Foucault, *About the Beginning*, 54.
    10. Foucault, *About the Beginning*, 64.
    11. Foucault, *About the Beginning*, 64.
    12. Cassian, *Conferences*, 2.10. ilico namque ut patefacta fuerit cogitatio maligna marcescit… et traductus quodammodo ac dehonestatus abscedit.

former no such thing is possible."[13] It also requires precise daily behaviors, including work, prayer, and study, a schedule which literally accounts for the behavior of each monk during every hour of every day.[14] I argue that Cassian's description of how correct monks behave forms a specific type of knowledge, a kind of standard of correct behaviors by which Cassian, as self-appointed arbiter of proper monasticism, could measure the spiritual progress (or lack of progress) of the monks of Gaul for whom he was writing. Cassian writes as if before his arrival in Gaul, the Gallican monks who make up his intended audience have not had access to the 'science' (*scientia*), or knowledge of living a correct monastic and ascetic life. In his preface to the *Institutes*, for example, he assures his patron that in working toward instituting the Egyptian monastic norms among the Gallican monks, "[i]f I ascertain that something is perhaps not in conformity with the model established by the immemorial contribution of our forebears... you can rely on me to include it or not if it is consistent with the rule."[15] He reiterates this later in the preface, noting that "I do not at all believe that a new constitution in the West, in Gaul, could be more reasonable or indeed more perfect than what has already been instituted" in Egypt.[16] Among other methods, he solidifies this form of knowledge by using well-known and well-respected Egyptian monks as his mouthpieces, in the same way that one could argue that Plato used Socrates in his dialogues: to lend rhetorical authority to his ideas, in this case Cassian's particular formation of monastic subjectivity.

Through the building of this body of knowledge, this 'science' of proper monastic practice, Cassian implicitly forces his audience to choose between only two options: the correct, established methods he outlines or failure to meet these exalted standards. This in turn divides individual monastic subjects within themselves, for if they aspire to become proper monks, they must work on themselves, striving to attain the standard set by Cassian's invocation of the lives of well-known and revered monks. At the same time, the Gallican monks are divided, both from laypeople in that they are set apart and above the lay population, but also from clergy and wayward, or at

---

13. Cassian, *Conferences*, 2.17. Perniciosius continentia inmoderata quam saturitas remissa subplantat. Ab hac namque ad mensuram districtionis intercedente salutari conpunctione conscendi potest, ab illa non potest.

14. Cassian, *Conferences*. See especially Books 2, 3, and 4.

15. Cassian, *Institutes*, preface, 8. [S]i quid forte non secundum typum maiorum antiquissima constitutione fundatum... antiquitus fundatorum fideli sermone uel adiciam uel recidam.

16. Cassian, *Institutes*, preface, 8. Nequaquam credens rationabilius quippiam uel perfectius nouellam constitutionem in occiduis Galliarum partibus repperire potuisse quam illa sunt instituta.

least insufficiently ascetic, monks. True monks, as delimited by Cassian's list of correct behaviors, are established as the norm, implicitly designating all others who fail to reach this lofty standard as deviant.

Finally, as mentioned before, Cassian's list of proper monastic behaviors includes a strict daily routine, control of appetites—both alimentary and sexual—and frequent confession of one's most shameful thoughts to one's spiritual master; in other words, the conduct of conduct.[17] These practices, or "technologies of the self," in Foucauldian parlance, then intersect with Cassian's rhetorical techniques of domination to create a unique form of monastic subjectivity, one which will serve both Cassian's spiritual goal of the achievement of ideal, individual monks and his more political goal of a separate and authoritative monasticism not subject to the whims of non-ascetic bishops.

It now remains to discuss Foucault's notions of the operation of power and to describe which of these modalities of power are involved in Cassian's rhetorical efforts aimed at the Gallican monks. There are four principal modalities of power in Foucault's taxonomy of power: Sovereign power, disciplinary power, pastoral power and biopower. Two principal modes fit Cassian's writings to the monks in Gaul: disciplinary power, pastoral power. A third, biopower, will also be discussed, although this is perhaps less applicable.

Disciplinary Power

Foucault outlines the operation of what he calls disciplinary power most fully in his monograph *Discipline and Punish: The Birth of the Prison.* While the monarchic form of power—sovereign power, in Foucault's idiom—is exercised almost exclusively through explicit punishments and rewards—witness the failed assassin of the king being drawn and quartered quoted at the beginning of Foucault's book[18]—disciplinary power is achieved chiefly through surveillance and the creation of forms of knowledge (Latin: *scientia*). Foucault illustrates the power of surveillance through Jeremy Bentham's design of the panopticon, a prison with a central watchtower from which all prison cells can be seen but whose surveilling agent cannot himself be seen clearly by individual prisoners. While the supervisors and

---

17. Cassian, *Institutes*. See especially Book 2 in which Cassian writes of the necessity of confession and gives very specific instructions on fasting, the correct amount of food, and precise times for eating.

18. Michel Foucault, Sheridan, Alan, translator, *Discipline and Punish*, 3–6, 9. Foucault goes on to note that the spectacle of punishment, in the service of sovereign power, was meant "to equal in savagery of the crime itself."

guards of the prison may certainly watch each prisoner meticulously from the all-seeing watchtower, their actual supervision ultimately becomes unnecessary because of the effect the mere notion of constant surveillance has upon prisoners, according to Bentham. Since the prisoners cannot see their supervisors, it is safest to assume that they are always being watched by the authorities. In fact, guards ultimately need no longer watch prisoners since the prisoners regulate their own behavior under the imagined supervision of the opaque watchtower.[19] This is the very definition of Foucault's disciplinary power: those in power inculcate their surveilling power into the prisoners who then police themselves, as it were, out of fear of the watchful eyes and on behalf of the authorities.

The other principal technique of disciplinary power involves the gathering and/or construction of particular forms of knowledge, principally through the sciences, about potential subjects. In fact, academic forms of knowledge come to be known as "disciplines" precisely because they separate knowledge into discrete domains, which then separates objects studied into equally separate realms based, as Foucault argues, upon what are ultimately arbitrary characteristics. Foucault writes "The fundamental codes of a culture… establish for every man, from the very first, the empirical orders with which he will be dealing and within which he will be at home. At the other extremity of thought, there are the scientific theories or the philosophical interpretations which explain why order exists in general… and why this particular order has been established and not some other."[20] Such academic disciplines construct and then provide standards for the general public by which they may judge what is good or, more to the point, what is "normal." It is on the basis of such norms, for example, that people in modern society exercise regularly, arrive at their places of work or school on time, and complete assignments given to them in those capacities. The disciplines, however, like the implied surveillance above, have a power to coerce individuals to regulate their own behavior.

For example, no overlord need force people to exercise since the knowledge of the benefits of exercise and the norms of public body image are assumed broadly enough to make most people exercise on their own authority. These norms of knowledge, disseminated through mass channels, ensure that most people will fall in line and exercise regularly; or perhaps they will not exercise and will pay the price of feeling "out of step" with or excluded from the world around them, and thus threatened with a punitive isolation.

---

19. Foucault, *Discipline and Punish*, 195–228.
20. Michel Foucault, *The Order of Things: An Archeology of the Human Sciences* (New York, NY: Vintage Books, 1995), xx.

At this point, I must acknowledge that a third aspect of Foucault's disciplinary power, that of production, may not fit as easily within the mode Cassian uses discursively. The entire notion of production and/or commodification was itself a product of a much later age (Foucault locates it in the eighteenth century along with the widespread birth of the prison[21]) and thus it would be anachronistic at best to assume that Cassian had this notion in mind as he created his monastic subjects. However, I would note that Foucault's definition of production within the exercise of disciplinary power leaves some room here for ambiguity. Specifically, he writes that the labor of convicts is "intrinsically useful, not as an activity of production, but by virtue of the effect it has on the human mechanism… [I]t must be of itself, a machine whose convict-workers are both the cogs and the products."[22] Additionally, Foucault notes that if the work of the prison has any real economic effect, "it is by producing individuals mechanized according to the general norms of an industrial society."[23] In this sense, I believe that even the notion of production can at least marginally apply to Cassian's creation of monastic subjects, given that capitalism and even its predecessor mercantilism were not to come for another 1,400 years. Like Foucault's inmates, monks are also constantly occupied as a disciplinary measure. As one writer cited by Foucault puts it, "by occupying the convict, one gives him habits of order and obedience… with time he finds in the regular movement of the prison, in the manual labors to which he is subjected… a certain remedy against the wanderings of his imagination."[24] As in the prison, Cassian's end products were not the baskets woven or any other products crafted but rather the monks themselves, formed according to the ideal they learned and imitated from monastic Egypt.

While monks, in Cassian's ideal formation, are not given a quota for the work they do (as might be done in a piecework factory setting much later in history) the understanding is that any time they are not praying or sleeping, they are performing some type of manual labor. He thus writes that "the fathers throughout Egypt in no way permit monks, and especially the young men, to be idle. They measure the state of their heart and their progress in patience and humility by their eagerness to work."[25] He reinforces the significance of manual labor for monks by quoting several passages from

---

21. Foucault, *Discipline and Punish*, 231–40.
22. Foucault, *Discipline and Punish*, 242.
23. Foucault, *Discipline and Punish*, 242.
24. Cited in Foucault, *Discipline and Punish*, 242.
25. Cassian, *Institututes*, 10.22. Per Aegyptum patres eruditi nullo modo otiosos esse monachos ac praecipue iuuenes sinunt, actum cordis et profectum patientiae et humilitatis sedulitate operis metientes.

the Pauline and Pseudo-Pauline canon, emphasizing the value the apostle placed on the practice of manual work (2 Thess. 3:11, Ephesians 4:28). The point of work in Cassian's scheme was certainly not to produce economic value, although some Egyptian monks clearly wove reed baskets in order sell them and earn money.[26] It was, rather, to produce docile minds and bodies who would obey unquestioningly. This form of production was producing submissive subjects, monks who understood the value of reducing their individual egos in service to the community.

Cassian and Disciplinary Power

One of the principal ways Cassian demonstrates the modality of disciplinary power is through mandating the act of confession to an elder monk. Monks are required to confess their deeds and, more importantly, all their thoughts, becoming, in effect, entirely transparent to another; in this way, Cassian establishes the disciplinary effect of surveillance. In order for monks to achieve the perfection which is defined as salvation for monastics, according to Cassian, they must never hold any thought or past action back from their superior. Through the mouth of Abba Moses Cassian says that

> True discretion is not obtained except by true humility. The first proof of this humility will be if not only everything that is to be done but also everything that is thought of is offered to the inspection of the elders, so that, not trusting in one's own judgment, one may submit in every respect to their understanding and may know how to judge what is good and bad according to what they have handed down.[27]

While no human agent is explicitly outlined as physically watching the monk as in the panopiticon, I argue that the injunction to make one's mind and actions transparent in order to become like the eminent elders of monasticism serves much the same function. With the assumption that each individual monk knows his own thoughts and actions, Cassian sets up a system whereby those who are completely forthcoming about every one of their thoughts and actions are rhetorically placed closer and closer to becoming holy heroes such as Abba Moses. Monks will therefore police their own thoughts and actions in order to reach this high spiritual level, as well as to reach a harbor of safety from demonic forces who are said to attack monks

---

26. See for example, *AP*, John the Short, 30 and 31.
27. Cassian, *Conferences*, 2.10. Uera, inquit, discretio non nisi uera humilitate conquiritur. cuius humilitatis haed erit prima probatio, si uniuersa non solum quae agenda suat, sed etiam quae cogitantur, seniorum reseruentur examinj, ut nihil suo quis iudicio credens illorum per omnia definitionibus adquiescat et quid bonum uel malum debeat iudicare eorum traditione cognoscat.

through their thoughts. To reinforce the absolute necessity of this confession, Cassian writes that "as soon as a wicked thought has been revealed it loses its power... harmful counsels hold sway in us as long as they lie concealed in our heart."[28] This rhetorically establishes each monk as his own policeman, guarding his own mind and actions in order to secure the reward of holiness and salvation promised to the monk who follows obediently the traditions of the renowned elders Cassian uses as his mouthpieces.

To illustrate this point further, Cassian writes of another well-respected monk, Abba Sarapion, who, as a novice, made the ethical error of taking extra bread after each meager monastic meal and concealing it in his cloak to savor later. He emphasizes how the guilt of this infraction burned within him, both compelling him to continue doing it and torturing him with guilt. After Sarapion breaks down and tearfully confesses, an elder monk first tells him that simply bringing this infraction to light has vanquished the devil within him. The more direct and telling result however is told in more colorful language. As soon as the elder has uttered these comforting exhortations, Sarapion says that "a lamp was lighted in my breast and it so filled the cell with its sulphureous smell that its fierce stink barely allowed us to remain."[29] This noxious odor is the physical manifestation of the demonic influence exiting the renewed and sanctified body and soul, expelled by the forced transparency of confession before one's master (and in this case, before other monks as well). Sarapion goes on to note that because of the dangers of hidden thoughts and deeds, "following in the footsteps of the elders, we shall presume neither to do anything new nor to come to any decisions based on our own judgment, but we shall proceed in all things just as their tradition and upright life inform us."[30] The reason for constant self-revelation to one's superior is the fact that the spiritual life, "that which is invisible and hidden, is not seen except by the purest heart."[31] Note first that this confession, long before any institutional church had made this

---

28. Cassian, *Conferences*, 2.10. Uera, inquit, discretio non nisi uera humilitate conquiritur. cuius humilitatis haed erit prima probatio, si uniuersa non solum quae agenda suat, sed etiam quae cogitantur, seniorum reseruentur examinj, ut nihil suo quis iudicio credens illorum per omnia definitionibus adquiescat et quid bonum uel malum debeat iudicare eorum traditione cognoscat.

29. Cassian, *Conferences*, 2.11. Necdum senex haec uerba conpleuerat et ecce lampas accensa de meo sinu procedens ita cellam repleuit odore sulpureo, ut uehementia faetoris ipsius uix in ea nos residere permitteret.

30. Cassian, *Conferences*, 2.11. Ut seniorum uestigia subsequentes neque agere quicquam noui neque discerere nostro iudicio praesumamus, sed quemadmodum nos uel illorum traditio uel uitae probitas informarit, in omnibus gradiamur.

31. Cassian, *Conferences*, 2.11. Quae et inuisibilis et occulta est et quae non nisi corde purissimo peruidetur.

action an official sacrament, renders visible that which is invisible. This necessity of bringing forth all one's thoughts and actions is a kind of surveillance inscribed upon the monk's body and mind. Cassian is able thus to connect this kind of frequent confession to the ideal state of being for which monks strive through asceticism and obedience. By bearing the shame of admitting one's sinfulness through thoughts and deeds, one acquires the humility (*humilitas*) necessary for the conversion of oneself from diabolic to deific. In addition, Cassian surely uses the phrase "purest heart" (*corde purissimo*), akin to his ideal "purity of heart," (*puritatem cordis*) to tie together clearly the purificatory process of purging oneself of sinful thoughts and deeds through willing revelation with that purity of heart associated with Evagrius' ideal *apatheia*, the state in which the passions within are subdued.

The mental geography of the monastic cell also has an undeniably panoptic effect on the conduct of each monk. The monastic space is often characterized as imbued with the authority of older, wiser monks or even God such that staying within the cell's confines constitutes an experience of allowing oneself to be shaped correctly by a divine source. This is a common theme in the monastic literature.

As mentioned earlier, in one apothegm from the *AP*, Abba Moses, coincidentally one of Cassian's mouthpieces in the *Conferences*, tells a struggling monk "Go and sit in your cell, and your cell will teach you everything."[32] This ethos, in which the cell itself watches and teaches the monk who does not transgress its confines, is also found in Cassian's work, especially in the section on acedia (ἀκηδία), perhaps best translated as listlessness or despair. Cassian, following the writings of Evagrius, says that one of the principal symptoms of this form of thought is that it agitates the monk so that he cannot remain in his cell (*cellula*) and convinces him that he is wasting his time by staying within its borders.[33] In addition to manual labor, Cassian writes that the other remedy for this vice is to simply force oneself to remain in the cell as told to him by the same Abba Moses.[34]

The functions of the cell in this case are manifold. First, its borders define the identity of the monk, and one who abandons its boundaries equally abandons his vocation. Second, the cell, if its confines are obeyed, will serve a pedagogical function, teaching the monk endurance of demonic attacks and thus holiness. Third, it plays the panoptic part of God, continuously

---

32. *AP*, Moses, 6. Ὕπαγε, κάθισον εἰς τὸ κελλίον σου· καὶ τὸ κελλίον σου διδάσκει σε πάντα.
33. Cassian, *Institutes*, 10.2.1.
34. Cassian, *Institutes*, 10.25.

watching the monk's conduct. If the monk cannot stay within his cell, he cannot achieve the perfection toward which all monastic practice ultimately aims. In addition, staying inside the monastic cell will ensure that one behaves correctly and thus, through the specific practices taught and then facilitated by the authority of the cell, one becomes an ideal monk.

Cassian also displays that other aspect of Foucault's disciplinary power, that is, the production of a certain form of knowledge. Cassian, for example, has clearly established both the ways and means of the venerable Egyptian monks who function as his ideal, and those of the Gallican monks to whom he is writing, who function as his example of what not to do in order to reach monastic perfection. By contrasting these two groups and their disparate ways of life, Cassian grants himself a rhetorical power over the Gallican monks, noting that they do not meet the ascetic or spiritual standards he establishes through his Egyptian mouthpieces.

In the preface to his *Institutes*, Cassian writes to his patron, Bishop Castor, that his purpose in writing is to "establish in [Castor's] own province, which lacks such things, the institutes of the Eastern and especially the Egyptian cenobia."[35] While Cassian modestly argues that he himself is "wanting in word and knowledge (*scientia*),"[36] he agrees to write about the correct way of monastic life because "the whole of it consists in experience and practice alone."[37] Note first that Foucault's discussion of disciplinary power involves the construction of forms of knowledge, principally the sciences, which is why he argues that this form of power does not come into play until the sixteenth century. However, the very fact that the Latin word for knowledge (*scientia*) is the predecessor to our word science gives a semantic foreshadowing of what Cassian will do in his writings. This includes the rule governing the monks' daily schedule.

The first four books of the *Institutes* give a rudimentary schedule for the cenobitic monks, a rule exemplified later in Benedict's notion that the substance of his rule is *ora et labora* (pray and work). Cassian does not provide us with any information on exactly when the monks are expected to rise in the morning. However, based on later monastic rules influenced by Cassian's writings, we know that they arose very early, likely at sunrise, for their first communal prayer of the day, later known as Matins, although this

---

35. Cassian, *Institutes*, preface, 1.3. In prouincia siquidem coenobiorum experti Orientalium maximeque Aegyptiorum uolens instituta fundari.

36. Cassian, *Institutes*, preface, 1.3. Me quoque elinguem et pauperem sermone atque scientia.

37. Cassian, *Institutes*, preface, 1.4. Totum namque in sola experientia usuque consistit.

word is not used in Cassian's writing.[38] This morning prayer is said to consist of the chanting of three Psalms and prayers.[39] The monks are dismissed after this to return to their cells. Again, Cassian denounces those in Gaul who go back to sleep after Matins, prescribing instead a regimen in the cell of manual work, reading, and unceasing interior prayer.[40] There are three other prescribed communal prayers throughout the daytime hours: Terce, so named because it is at the third hour (9:00 AM), Sext, at the sixth hour (noon), and None, at the ninth hour (3:00).[41] While Cassian does not prescribe a specific mealtime for monks, he does recommend two small loaves of bread per day and the minimum water necessary to maintain health.[42] Other monastic literature from Egypt suggests that this was often taken in one meal every day at the ninth hour.[43] Although Cassian does not mention the type of manual labor in which the monks are supposed to engage, in other monastic literature it is often weaving baskets or plaiting ropes from reeds, the typical type of labor for Egyptian monks who would often sell the baskets and ropes in order to make a living.[44] While self-sufficiency in making a living was important for Egyptian monasticism, the chief function of manual labor was to remain occupied, never allowing the mind or body to give way to distraction. Finally, there is the last communal prayer of the day, in which 12 Psalms are chanted, and there are two scriptural readings, one from the Old Testament and one from the New.[45]

Note that each part of every day is meticulously scheduled, such that only the three or four hours of sleep allowed the monks is unstructured. In terms of disciplinary power, this daily timetable allowed the head monk to maintain control, both through a type of surveillance—each monk had to be seen at scheduled prayers and then return to his cell—and through the discourse which emphasized the rewards of following the schedule faithfully.

It is instructive that while Cassian claims modestly that he is lacking in knowledge, what knowledge he does have has been acquired firsthand by living and practicing with the esteemed monks of Egypt who will henceforth be his models and spokesmen. The very phrase "the whole of it consists in experience and practice alone," gives an indication of the forthcoming

---

38. Benedict of Nursia, Timothy Fry, O.S.B. translator., *The Rule of Saint Benedict* (New York, NY: Vintage, 1998), 16.
39. Cassian, *Institutes*, 3.4.2.
40. Cassian, *Institutes*, 3.4.2.
41. Cassian, *Institutes*, 3.1–2.
42. Cassian, *Institutes*, 12.15.2, 13.6.2.
43. See for example *AP*, Macarius the Great, 3.
44. See *AP* Antony, 1, John the Short, 11, 30, 31.
45. Cassian, *Institutes*, 2.4.

contents of the *Institutes*: through experience living and practicing with the Desert Fathers of Egypt, rather than merely reading hagiographical literature about these venerable monks, Cassian has gathered knowledge of the practices and procedures necessary to achieve a kind of Christian perfection.

Indeed, the *Institutes* will begin with technical descriptions of how the Egyptian monks live, including their dress, prayer times and content (which Psalms and how many are chanted, etc.), food and fasting, and other seeming minutiae. The monks of Gaul to whom Cassian writes can simply copy these ways, whether or not they fully comprehend their significance. Again, this is a knowledge acquired through practice and experience, not reading or deduction.

Finally, in the second half of the *Institutes*, Cassian writes of the eight principal vices (the predecessor notion to the seven deadly sins, borrowed again from Evagrius Ponticus) which all monks who live in the correct manner can expect to confront, and gives simple instructions on how to face such demonic influences. These methods constitute a very specific body of knowledge gathered by Cassian through years of experience among others who had practiced similarly for years. However, it is equally clear that Cassian has formed the contemporary Gallican methods as its own body of knowledge through observation, and will use the body of knowledge gathered from Egyptian monks to mark the discrepancies between the correct practices and methods of the Egyptians and the insufficient practice of the same by the Gallicans. He notes, for example that during silent prayer in Egypt "there is no spitting, no annoying clearing of throats, no noisy coughing, no sleepy yawning emitted from gaping and wide-open mouths, no groans and not even any sighs to disturb those in attendance."[46] This is a clear rebuke of the Gallican monks: there would be no need to so specifically detail such infractions during prayer time had Cassian not seen them in the Gallican monastery. He goes on to say that in Egypt, the prayers are "brief, but frequent,"[47] likely another implicit criticism of the methods in his new province. The concept is clear: Cassian, who learned what he goes on to call the Egyptian Institutes (*Aegyptia Instituta*) through imitation and practice, is now constructing a model of the faults and lacks of Gallican monastic practice through careful comparison with his Egyptian exemplars.

The effect of this would be twofold. First, it provided models and methods for the Gallicans to improve themselves and their practices by

---

46. Cassian, *Institutes*, II.10. In qua non sputus emittitur, nou excreatio obstrepit, non tussis intersonat, non oscitatio somnolenta dissutis malis et hiantibus trahitur, nulli gemitus, nulla suspiria etiam adstantes inpeditura promuntur.
47. Cassian, *Institutes*, 2.10. Quamobrem utilius censent breues quidem orationes sed creberrimas fieri.

comparing themselves with Cassian's outlined knowledge of the Egyptian ideal. Second, it divided the Gallican monks within themselves, breaking them into that which is deficient in correct monastic knowledge (*scientia*) and that which attempts to correct these faults through following the authority of Cassian's experience-derived knowledge.

Pastoral Power

While Cassian makes use of disciplinary power in his rhetorical shaping of monastic subjects, he clearly also makes use of what Foucault terms pastoral power. This modality of power is tied intimately to the rise of Christianity with its notion of a ruler and/or deity as shepherd culled originally from ancient Judaism (cf. "The Lord is my shepherd, I shall not want (Psalm 23:1)"). Foucault points out four ways in which this mode of power differs greatly from that of ancient Greek political thought. "First, the shepherd wields power over a flock rather than over a land."[48] In other words, the ruler or deity does not control a territory and everything within the borders of that territory (people, resources, governance, etc.), but rather is responsible for a flock, or specific group of people, no matter the land within which those people dwell. That is, the relationship between ruler and people is paramount, rather than, in the case of the Greek city-state, for example, the relationship between the ruler and the specific territory. Next, "the shepherd gathers together, guides and leads his flock."[49] Because the shepherd's primary relationship is to his flock or people, he first gathers them together, since without specific ties to a land the flock may be dispersed, then he guides them to right behavior and, more importantly, to whatever resources they need. As their shepherd, the ruler is not simply an overlord, but rather has a responsibility for the well-being of his flock. This leads to the next aspect of pastoral power: "[T]he shepherd's role is to ensure the salvation of his flock."[50] Foucault thus notes that this responsibility entails not simply saving the flock from impending danger. Rather, the shepherd must also constantly monitor the flock, both as a whole and as individuals, and attend to both levels of needs. This last aspect of the individualization of care is where Foucault sees the greatest difference between pastoral power and Greek political thought. While a Greek god, for example, was asked to provide "a fruitful land and abundant crops… he was not asked to foster a flock day by day."[51] Fourth

---

48. Michel Foucault with Jeremy Carrette, translator, *Religion and Culture* (Florence: Taylor and Francis, 2013), 137.
49. Foucault, *Religion and Culture*, 137.
50. Foucault, *Religion and Culture*, 137.
51. Foucault, *Religion and Culture*, 138.

and finally, wielding power is for the shepherd not a privilege, but rather a duty. Foucault notes that "shepherdly kindness is much closer to 'devotedness'."[52] Here, the notion of watching over the flock is important: "First, [the shepherd] acts, he works, he puts himself out, for those he nourishes and who are asleep. Second... he pays attention to them all and scans each one of them. He's got to know his flock as a whole, and in detail."[53] The shepherd is constantly vigilant, both to the needs of the entire flock and those of each individual member. One can begin to see how this notion of leadership, far more than that of the Greek, could be mapped onto the later Christian context of antiquity, despite the many aspects of late antique Christianity culled from Greek sources. We will see that Cassian, while writing instructions for a monastic community—theological and practical –is clearly concerned with both the needs of the community and those of the individual.

In combining most facets of disciplinary power (possibly excluding that of production which, as I mentioned, would have been an economic anachronism in fifth-century Europe)[54] with pastoral power, Cassian sets up a mode of specifically monastic subjectivity in which he, as monks' rhetorical shepherd, is both authoritative guide and watcher and in which individual monks are his concern. However, individual monks also regulate their own behavior out of concern for their own salvation.

Cassian and Pastoral Power

In addition to the displays of disciplinary power in Cassian's rhetoric, we clearly find examples of pastoral power as well. First, the superior monk is responsible for and in charge of his group of monks, rather than a certain land. Monks living in small groups, for example, are often said to have moved about searching for resources and safety from roving gangs of bandits. However, this did not change the responsibility the superior monk had for the well-being and salvation of novice monks. Cassian writes in one *Conference* that novice monks "must with all humility follow whatever you see our Elders do or teach."[55] While this quote exhorts the younger monks

---

52. Foucault, *Religion and Culture*, 138.
53. Foucault, *Religion and Culture*, 138.
54. See especially Foucault, *Discipline and Punish*, in which Foucault notes the increasing formation of "docile bodies" into useful functions and/or production. For example, "by the late eighteenth century, the soldier has become something that can be made; out of formless clay, an inapt body, the machine required can be constructed," 135.
55. Cassian, *Conferences*, 18.3. Quaecumque seniores nostros agere uel tradere uideritis summa humilitate sectamini.

3. Foucault, Cassian, and the Creation of Subjects

to act in accordance with the actions and words of the elders, it also implicitly states that the elders are responsible for providing that good example to their novices, their flock. The elder's responsibility is always to the group of monks within his community, and includes modeling correct practices and behaviors. In addition, Cassian writes that for those individuals who join the larger cenobitic communities

> there is no providing for daily work, no distractions concerning buying or selling, no inescapable worries about the year's supply of food, no concern about the bodily matters that are involved in attending to the needs not only of ourselves but also of our many visitors.[56]

In the larger community, the superior of the monastery is responsible for both the physical and the spiritual needs of his flock.

Next, the shepherd both gathers and leads his flock. In the case of the abbot of a community, the metaphorical shepherd is responsible for keeping the flock together through a litany of collective practices, as well as the assumption of a monastic identity conferred upon each novice as he joins. As Goodrich notes, "those [Gallican monks] who would not submit" to their superiors merely "demonstrated that they had yet to make progress in obedience, a virtue that was a certain prerequisite for progress toward spiritual perfection."[57] Since total obedience was enjoined upon every monk, the superior had the responsibility both to lead by example and to keep the community together.

Third, the leader of the community had to work for the salvation of all monks in his charge. As stated above, the first way an abbot did this was by enforcing total obedience on every member of the community. As Foucault notes, the abbot's responsibilities include the very safety of the community through providing material resources but also "constant, individualized and final kindness."[58] In the case of monks, this meant being ready at all times to hear the individual confessions of the monks' faults in thought, word and deed. As long as monks were diligent in confessing all of their internal evils, their salvation was assured. Finally, the wielding of power in the case of the superior monk was a duty rather than a privilege. Cassian notes this when he writes that

---

56. Cassian, *Conferences*, 19.6. In hac igitur conuersatione diurni operis nulla prouisio, uenditionis uel coemptionis nulla distentio, non annui panis ineuitablis cura, non sollicitudo corporalium rerum, qua non tantum propriis, sed etiam multorum aduenientium usibus necessaria praeparantur.

57. Richard J. Goodrich, *Contextualizing Cassian: Aristocrats, Asceticism, and Reformation in Fifth-Century Gaul* (New York, NY: Oxford University Press, 2007), 60.

58. Foucault, *Religion and Culture*, 138.

Not just anyone is promoted to this rank [that of abbot] because of his own desire or ambition, but he whom the assembly of all the elders considers more excellent and more distinguished than the rest by reason of the prerogative of age and the witness of his faith and virtue.[59]

In addition, Cassian writes that "no one is chosen to rule over a community of brothers unless... he has learned by obedience how he should command those who will be subject to him and has understood from the institutes of the elders what he should pass on to the young."[60] Note in this latter quotation that not only is the leader of a monastery to rule over a community, but also to pass on traditions and knowledge to the young. It is clear here why elder monks would have the name "father" (Ἀββᾶ) attached to them, since, like fatherhood, authority of a community was not taken on as an honored benefit but rather as a sacred duty to continue the unbroken line of correct monasticism. This type of rule entails far more work and far less privilege than that of a typical monarch. It is obligation, not license.

Biopower

Near the end of his life, Foucault introduced yet another term in his typology of power: biopower. While biopower, like disciplinary power, does not fit Cassian's mode of subjectification perfectly, and is less applicable to Cassian's rhetoric than disciplinary and pastoral power, it is possible to read a kind of proto-biopower into his discourse and systematic treatment of ideal monastic life.

Biopower is defined by Foucault as "numerous and diverse techniques for achieving the subjugation of bodies and the control of populations."[61] Principally, Foucault sees the rise of biopower in the 18th century with the appearance of demography and the assessment of the association between resources and people.[62] He goes on to say that biopower consists of "techniques of power... guaranteeing relations of domination and effects of

---

59. Cassian, *Conferences*, 21.1.2. Non enim ad hunc gradum quilibet propria uoluntate aut ambitione prouehitur, sed is quem cunctorum seniorum coetus aetatis praerogativa et fidei atque uirtutum testimonio excellentiorem ombibus sublimioremque censuerit.

60. Cassian, *Institutes*, 2.3.3. Ideoque nullus congregationi fratrum praefuturus eligitur, priusquam idem, qui praeficiendus est, quid obtemperaturis oporteat imperari, oboediendo didicerit, et quid iunioribus tradere debeat, institutis seniorum fuerit adsecutus.

61. Michel Foucault, *The History of Sexuality*, vol. 2, translated from the French by Robert Hurley, 1st Vintage Books ed. (New York, NY: Vintage Books), 140.

62. Foucault, *The History of Sexuality*, 140.

hegemony," specifically by working through institutions such as the military and the schools.[63]

Cassian and Biopower

The notion of biopower might cross into Cassian's territory when one considers again the requirement for all monks to confess all thoughts and deeds that might be considered sinful or otherwise harmful to the soul on a frequent basis. Besides ensuring that monks will watch and regulate their own behavior and even thought patterns, this requirement can also be read as a kind of proto demography, in which each time the monk confesses a wayward thought or deed, the monastic superior has collected data on that monk. How frequently does the monk confess such things? What categories of thoughts and/or deeds does he confess? Have his confessions become more or less frequent recently? In short, while this is certainly not the detailed demography in the modern sense which Foucault documents, I would argue that it is a kind of precursor in which the economy of salvation may be regulated by keeping in mind which monks are experiencing more errant thoughts and committing more errant deeds and which are experiencing fewer in order to provide monks with the requisite spiritual care or even, in the case of a severely wayward monk, to eject him from the community in order to protect the integrity of the whole. Keeping track of such data, even if not in writing, is indeed an exercise of power.

In another sense, the control of the monks' time, with monks required to follow a set daily schedule, recalls Foucault's reference to biopower as "taking charge of life, more than the threat of death, [which] gave power its access to the body."[64] Furthermore, this control, combined with the required confessions, "brought life and its mechanisms into the realm of explicit calculations and made knowledge-power an agent of transformation of human life."[65] The knowledge gathered through these techniques made the monastic superior, the *hegemon*, the controller of the very lives of his subordinate monks. Had Cassian progressed from writing about these techniques to actually practicing them at a working monastery—we have no evidence whether he did or did not—he himself would have become that all-knowing, all-seeing *hegemon* based upon his experience as a monk in Egypt.

Finally, before concluding this chapter, I would like to acknowledge that first, none of these forms of power described by Foucault fits perfectly as

---

63. Foucault, *The History of Sexuality*, 141.
64. Foucault, *The History of Sexuality*, 143.
65. Foucault, *The History of Sexuality*, 143.

an analysis of Cassian's rhetoric. Foucault was, for the most part, analyzing emerging forms of power in what he called "The Classical Age"—roughly 1660 to 1900 CE. While I find his typology of power useful as a tool for analyzing what I believe Cassian is doing with his rhetoric and systematization of the monastic life, one cannot ignore that Foucault is investigating the emergence of capitalism and other modern developments of which Cassian and those of his time could never have dreamed. However, I would argue that using his notions on the creation of subjects and the uses of different types of power helps elucidate what I will argue is Cassian's intention and the outcome of his efforts.

In addition, despite my linear layout of the types of power and their correlations to Cassian's rhetoric and ideas, it must be said that forms of power frequently overlap and, therefore, do not occur in a linear fashion. While I believe that it is accurate to say that Cassian's codification of monastic life can be designated a form of disciplinary power, it is, at the same time, a form of biopower. When Cassian insists that the superior of a monastery must compassionately care for, hear, and reassure the monk confessing disobedient thoughts or actions, this is both an example of pastoral power and disciplinary power. In other words, I see these three forms of power functioning simultaneously, weaving in and out of each other in the interplay of Cassian's writing and the daily operation of the monastery.

Conclusion

In this chapter, Foucault's descriptions of how subjects are created was explained, including the three principal criteria for the successful deployment of this discursive operation. From there, the chapter proceeds to a definition of the three types of power, among several described by Foucault, which I believe Cassian uses in attempting to manipulate the subjectivity of monks in Gaul: disciplinary power, pastoral power, and biopower. Finally, I use Cassian's own writings to demonstrate how these types of power are operative within his discourse.

By comparing Foucault's descriptions of disciplinary power, pastoral power, and biopower with Cassian's own rhetoric in the *Institutes* and the *Conferences*, clear patterns emerge. First, Cassian is attempting to secure his own position as an authority on correct monastic practice. He does this by using eminent, near-legendary monks as his mouthpieces, thus preserving the appearance of the necessary humility personally while simultaneously reinforcing his authority to teach monastic method by placing his own writings within the tradition of the teachings of the venerable fathers of Egypt, monks he personally knew and of whom the monks of Gaul had only heard heroic tales. Second, Cassian establishes a kind of surveillance through mandating the frequent act of confession of thoughts among Gallican monks. By doing so, he effectively talks these monks into submitting themselves to his authority, making their secrets known if indeed they want to reach the spiritual heights of an Abba Antony or Abba Moses. Finally, Cassian makes it clear that one who wants to advance to become head of a community of monks, must first prove that he is humble enough to be completely obedient. The effect of this might be that only he who uncomplainingly does whatever his superior tells him, including following the rules and regulations laid out by Cassian in his writings, would gain the advantage of being named superior of a monastic community. These methods are all clearly evidenced in Cassian's injunctions, as well as in his comparisons of the Egyptian monks to the Gallican. While the Gallicans are kept scrambling to try and meet the high bar of Egyptian monasticism as described by Cassian, Cassian establishes himself as the one who sets the bar.

In the next chapter, I show the conflicts between monastics and church hierarchs in Egypt, verifying that these conflicts were both real and deeply consequential, especially for monks. By so doing, I plan to begin building a case for why Cassian, as an inheritor of Egyptian tradition, might have wanted to separate monasticism from the institutional Church.

Chapter Four

Conflicts Between Monasticism and the Church

In the *Lausiac History* there is a rather unusual story about the well-known monk Macarius the Great (300–391 CE). Macarius had originally been an Egyptian peasant, a camel driver and dealer in niter which was used as a preservative among other uses.[1] Despite these humble beginnings, Macarius, by the time of the story, had become the premier monk and teacher of monks in his area of Scetis in Egypt.

The apothegm says that an Egyptian man fell in love with a married woman and asked a sorcerer for some sort of spell to make her husband throw her out so that she would love him instead. The sorcerer turned the woman into a mare, thinking that no husband could tolerate being married to a horse. The woman's husband, understandably distraught, instead called for the village priests whose spiritual authority could surely counteract such deviltry. However, though the priests came, the woman was not changed back and not only continued as a mare but also refused to eat. At this point, the man brought the mare to the small community of Macarius who, by blessing some water and pouring it on the mare's head, quickly turned her back into a woman. Macarius explained that this drastic transformation into a horse was only possible because the woman had not taken communion for five weeks.[2] Significant here, is the fact that while regular communion, the function and realm of the priests, will keep a person under protection and prevent one from being the victim of sorcery, only the power of an ascetic monk, uneducated though he may be, can save her if she suffers the calamity of an evil spell. This is one of the many demonstrations in early monastic literature of how the asceticism of monks (and even some members of the clergy) is seen as far more effective and important than the mere titles and status of clergy. This would be the basis of many of the conflicts between monastics and clergy in late antique Egypt.

In this chapter, I establish the both the historicity and the monastic perspective of conflicts experienced by Cassian and others between monks and the institutional church as represented by bishops and other clergy. These

1. See *AP*, Macarius, 31.
2. Palladius, *Lausiac History*, Macarius, 6–9.

conflicts were not unique to Cassian and his faction of monks. Indeed, the monastic literature is full of stories of antipathy between monks and bishops. This was a pervasive problem, which sometimes produced disastrous results. While Cassian's writings refer briefly to the conflict he and his fellow monks in the settlement of Scetis had with a bishop, other concurrent monastic discourse (*AP*, *Lausiac History*, etc.), makes abundantly clear that there were many such conflicts and several types of conflict involved. While there was clearly a power differential between monks and clergy, the bitter conflict between Cassian's faction of monks and the bishop of Alexandria actually turned violent and would result in the exile of Cassian and his fellow monks.

While I would argue for the veracity of the conflicts between monks and clergy in early monasticism, it is important to note that these conflicts are written about and rhetorically framed from a particular perspective in the monastic literature. What I hope to establish in this chapter, therefore, is not the bare factuality of these conflictual events, but rather the viewpoint from which monastic writers such as Cassian and the compiler of the *AP* saw these conflicts.

First, this chapter will provide examples of laypeople often viewing monks as wiser and more righteous, indeed as having a more direct line of communication with God, than the clergy.[3] This was repeatedly played out in instances in which bishops and other clergy members were subordinated or even felt pressure to subordinate themselves to the power of monks, as we will see below. Second, I will examine how, in retaliation for this perceived usurpation of power, or simply in order to co-opt the power of monks for the institutional church, clergy would often attempt to forcibly ordain revered monks.[4] While some of these monks reluctantly accepted their ordination, it is clear in the early monastic discourse that many declined ordination, either by escaping to other locations or, in more extreme examples, mutilating themselves in order to make themselves unfit or unable to fulfill ecclesiastic duty. I will discuss some examples of these below and proffer an explanation for this reticence to accept what would, for many, have been considered a great honor.

Third, using Paul Dilley's conceptualization of a monastic theory of mind, I will establish that monks learned to think differently from laypeople

---

3. See for example Peter Brown, "The Rise and Function of the Holy Man in Late Antiquity," *Journal of Roman Studies* 61 (1971): 80–101. Brown notes that in late antiquity, monks were often consulted by laypeople to mediate disputes both personal and legal, to foretell the future, to increase fertility in women, and to bless and curse. Their authority was often more revered than that of either clergy or government officials.

4. See *AP*, Macarius 1, Matoes 9 and especially Palladius, *Lausiac History*, Ammonius 2.

and clergy in late antiquity. Dilley calls monks a cognitive community, in that they learned a system of thought which, along with the appropriate ascetic practices, defined them as monks while simultaneously marking off a boundary between them and all non-monks. I theorize that this conceptual "circling of the wagons" would have drawn an even more substantial wedge between monks and clergy.

Finally, I will demonstrate that there were, in some cases, extreme theological differences between certain groups of monks and the ruling clergy. While redactors of much of monastic literature of the fourth and fifth centuries may have tried to force all Egyptian monastics into the same theological bubble, it nevertheless remains clear that there was a wide variety of practices and beliefs among different factions of Egyptian monks. As Marcella Forlin Patrucco writes, "[T]he story of the relationship between this ascetic milieu and the Church leaders shows a variety of attitudes, alliances and conflicts, as exemplified by the Greek Christian literature flourishing in the fatherland of Eastern asceticism. Essentially normative in their aims, these writings are reliable witnesses of the very difficult and long-term process leading to the incorporation of ascetic practice into the pastoral life of the Church."[5] However, it is equally clear that many of these monks disagreed with the theology and practice of their diocesan clergy. In the case of Cassian, such a disagreement ended with his exile from Egypt and, in a sense, another exile from Constantinople later. While Cassian refers only briefly to the conflict which likely resulted in exile from his beloved desert, other writers refer to this conflict, and others, in much more detail. It is with these writers, particularly those of the *AP* and other collections of sayings and stories that we begin.

Subordination of Clergy to Monks

In the Egypt of the fourth and fifth centuries, "average Christian believers… were encouraged to draw comfort from the expectation that, somewhere… a chosen few of their fellows… had achieved, usually through prolonged ascetic labor, an exceptional degree of closeness to God."[6] Indeed, "the holy man," writes Peter Brown, "was a 'servant of his God'. He was also a 'patron' in that he offered petitions to God on behalf of others."[7] No such power was ascribed to clergy in the lay imagination of the late antique period

---

5. Marcella Forlin Patrucco, "Bishops and Monks in Late Antique Society," *Zeitschrift Für Antikes Christentum* 8.2 (2004): 332–45, 337.
6. Peter Brown, *Authority and the Sacred: Aspects of the Christianisation of the Roman World* (Cambridge: Cambridge University Press, 1997), 57–58.
7. Brown, *Authority*, 73.

4. Conflicts Between Monasticism and the Church

in Egypt and Palestine. Rather, monastic discourse often has bishops, despite their higher status within institutional Christianity, subordinating themselves to the wisdom of monks. Whether or not the historicity of these individual encounters can be ultimately verified, it is important to note that monastic writers of the fourth century and beyond frequently portrayed monks as spiritually superior to clergy. Many of the monks, in turn, displayed a kind of disdain, or at least indifference, toward members of the clergy in this literature.

In one apothegm, an archbishop went with a prominent magistrate to visit a renowned hermit, Arsenius, to ask for a word of wisdom: "after a short silence [Arsenius] answered him, 'Will you put into practice what I say to you?' They promised him this. 'If you hear Arsenius is anywhere, do not go there.'"[8] The audacity of a monk not only denying his wisdom to the premier hierarch in the area but furthermore ordering him to never visit him again displays keenly the power that monks were perceived to have over clergy and even representatives of political power such as magistrates. In another story, a prominent magistrate goes looking for Abba Moses to get a word of wisdom from him. When the magistrate actually stumbles upon Abba Moses in a marsh, he does not recognize him, having never seen him before. In fact, pretending not to be himself, Abba Moses actually tells the magistrate not to search for Abba Moses since he is a fool. The magistrate returns to his village and tells the clergy members what the stranger told him. The clergy, from the magistrate's description are able to recognize that "'It was Abba Moses himself and it was in order not to meet you that he said that,'" as a result of which, we are told, "The magistrate went away greatly edified."[9] Both Abbas Moses and Arsenius feel free to treat the visiting bishops and dignitaries, not with any special deference, but with reluctance and disdain (as Arsenius in fact treats most visitors in his *AP* apothegms).

On the other hand, not only would church hierarchs often defer to monks in terms of spiritual wisdom, but they would also obey the orders of such monks without question. What is also key in these apothegms is the fact that, as Zachary Smith points out, "the *AP's* compiler never indicates that monks viewed bishops or priests as holding special power or authority in monastic communities."[10] In addition, Smith notes that in the *AP*, even the presence of the relatively few ecclesiastical ascetics "depends primarily on their

---

8. *AP*, Aresenius, 7. Μικρὸν δὲ σιωπήσας ὁ γέρων, ἀπεκρίνατο πρὸς αὐ τόν· Καὶ ἐὰν ὑμῖν εἴπω, φυλάσσετε; Οἱ δὲ φυλάσσετε φυλάττειν. Καὶ εἶπεν αὐτοῖς ὁ γέρων· Ὅπου ἐὰν ἀκούσητε Ἀρσένιον, μὴ πλησιάσητε.

9. *AP*, Moses, 8.

10. Zachary B. Smith, *Philosopher-monks, Episcopal Authority, and the Care of the Self. The 'Apophthegmata Patrum' in Fifth-century Palestine* (Turnhout, Belgium: Brepols, 2018), 141.

asceticism, not on their positions in the institutional church."[11] According to Smith, this emphasis on ascetic practice over ecclesial authority implicitly "argues against ecclesial authority over monastic systems."[12] In other words, Cassian's notions of monasticism and the institutional church operating in different spheres was not his own invention but rather an ethos he had adopted from certain factions of monks in the Egyptian and Palestinian deserts.

In another story from the *AP*, a well-respected monk, Abba Gelasius, is approached by a bishop embroiled in theological argument. The bishop pleads with Gelasius to advocate for his side of the argument in order to lend it credence. Gelasius, however, is unimpressed: "If you want to argue about the faith, you have those close to you who will listen to you and answer you; for my part, I have not time to hear you."[13] This condescending dismissal of the bishop causes the bishop at last to order his followers to burn Gelasius at the stake. However, after Gelasius is bound to the stake and surrounded with kindling, the bishop's followers, "seeing that even that did not make [Gelasius] give in nor frighten him and fearing a popular uprising, for [Gelasius] was very celebrated (all this had been given him by Providence from above), they sent our martyr, who had offered himself as a holocaust to Christ, safe and sound away."[14] Note that in this story the bishop is depicted as divisive, if not heretical. Meanwhile Gelasius, the powerful holy man, has received his power "from above" rather than from a title conferred upon him by the institutional church. The ascetic monk was perceived, as Brown notes, as having achieved no less than intimacy with God by which his power far exceeded that of clergy members.[15] In yet another example, Abba Sisoes receives some hungry traveling monks on a designated fast day and sets some food before them of which he also partakes. A bishop arrives, accusing the monk of eating on a fast day. However, when he realizes that Sisoes is providing hospitality to the hungry monks, understood to be a perpetual sacred duty for monks despite the requirement of fasting, "the bishop did penance before [Sisoes] saying, 'Forgive me, Abba,

---

11. Smith, *Philosopher-monks*, 141.
12. Smith, *Philosopher-monks*, 141.
13. *AP*, Gelasius, 4. Ἐὰν περὶ πίστεως θέλῃς διαλεχθῆναι, ἔχεις τοῦτον παρὰ σοῦ ἀκούοντα καὶ διαλεγόμενόν σοι· ἐμοὶ γὰρ οὐ σχολὴ τὰ παρὰ σοῦ ἀκούειν.
14. *AP*, Gelasius, 4. Ὁρῶντες δὲ αὐτὸν μηδὲ οὕτως ἐνδιδόντα, μηδὲ κα ταπτήσσοντα, καὶ εὐλαβούμενοι τὴν τοῦ δήμου ἔγερ σιν, διὰ τὸ περιβόητον εἶναι τὸν ἄνδρα (τὸ ὅλον ἐκ τῆς ἄνωθεν ἦν Προνοίας), ἀπέλυσαν ἀβλαβῆ τὸν μάρ τυρα, τό γε ἐφ᾽ ἑαυτῷ Χριστῷ ὁλοκαυτωθέντα.
15. Brown, *Authority*, 94.

for I reasoned on a human level while you do the work of God'."[16] The bishop's prostration before the monk is a clear physical demonstration of the superior power of the monk over the office of bishop. What is truly striking here, however, is the fact that the bishop acknowledges that while he, as representative of the institutional church, is thinking on a "human level," which certainly includes the honor and authority granted to clergy, Sisoes the monk is doing "the work of God." Not only is the monk superior, but his authority is granted by a superior source. Similarly, when an archbishop visits the monk Pambo and some of the monks in Pambo's community ask him to give a word of wisdom to the archbishop, Pambo refuses, saying "If he is not edified by my silence, he will not be edified by speech."[17]

Of course, in the case of the few ascetic bishops featured in the *AP*, their asceticism takes precedence over their ecclesial positions, granting them authority such that the ecclesial office itself is rendered insignificant in comparison.

Attempts at Forced Ordination of Monks

There are a number of ordained ascetics in the *AP* (18 of the 130 ascetics featured), but as always, their authority in the apothegms is derived from ascetic practice rather than their ecclesiastical positions. When non-ascetic priests, for example, are mentioned in the *AP*, they are generally respected for their duties administering the Eucharist to monks, but sometimes come into conflict with monks as well, usually in the context of taking on more authority over ascetic monks than is appropriate in the compiler's view. For example, in one story, a priest, having heard that a group of monks behaved inappropriately away from their monastic community, angrily defrocks them, severing them from the monastic life. After bringing their monastic habits to the well-known monk Poemen, the priest asks Poemen if defrocking the monks was morally defensible. Poemen tells the priest "you are subject to sin the same way." The priest, suitably chastened and deferring to Poemen's authority, asks the monks' pardon and gives them back their monastic clothing.[18] While there are many stories in the monastic discourse of the fourth and fifth centuries in which members of the clergy, assuming authority over monks, attempt to force ordination upon them, there is no

---

16. *AP*, Sisoes, 15. Καὶ ἤκουσεν αὐτῶν ὁ ἐπίσκοπος, καὶ ἔβαλε μετάνοιαν τῷ γέροντι, λέγων· Συγχώρησόν μοι, ἀββᾶ, ὅτι ἀνθρώπινόν τι ἐλογισάμην· σὺ δὲ τὸ τοῦ Θεοῦ ἐποίησας.
17. *AP*, Theophilus the Archbishop 2. Εἰ οὐκ ὠφελεῖται ἐν τῇ σιωπῇ μου, οὐδὲ ἐν τῷ λόγῳ μου ὠφεληθῆναι ἔχει.
18. *AP*, Poemen 11.

indication that Poemen disrespects the clerical office as such in this story. Neither, however, does Poemen accept the authority of a priest to decide the fate of monks. Poemen's asceticism, as outlined in the other numerous apothegms, grants him authority above and beyond that of the clergy, who apparently should not attempt to claim authority in the monastic realm.[19]

Despite this, there are many stories in the *AP* of the forcible ordination—or attempted ordination—of monks. This seems to be an attempt to co-opt the monks' rhetorical power over the lay population, given the power laypeople seem to have granted monks to intercede for and advise them.[20] What is most interesting in these situations, however, is the fact that monks must generally be forced to accept ordination and often go to extremes to avoid it. Despite the fact that joining the priesthood was a sure means to increased status within towns and villages, David Brakke notes that becoming a clergy member is presented as highly problematic in the monastic literature, since

> ordination to the priesthood provides the quintessential opportunity for vainglory: it appears repeatedly as a problem for the vainglorious monk, often accompanied by scenarios in which admiring laypeople force the "reluctant" monk to accept clerical leadership.[21]

In addition, as we will see below, Cassian sees monastic life, with its separation from the normal, settled life of the populated city or village, as exemplary for the Christian; becoming a bishop or priest necessarily takes one away from the ascetic way of monastic life. A story from the *AP* illustrates this point:

> They used to say of a bishop of Oxyrhynchus, named Abba Apphy, that when he was a monk he submitted himself to a very severe way of life. When he became a bishop, he wished to practice the same austerity, even in the world, but he had not the strength to do so. Therefore he prostrated himself before God saying, 'Has your grace left me because of my episcopate?' Then he was given this revelation, 'No, but when you were in solitude and there was no one else it was God who was your helper. Now that you are in the world, it is man'."[22]

---

19. See for example, *AP*, Poemen 17 and 19 for indications of his asceticism.
20. See for example, *AP*, Arsenius 28, Moses 8.
21. David Brakke, *Demons and the Making of the Monk: Spiritual Combat in Early Christianity* (Cambridge, MA: Harvard University Press, 2006), 67.
22. *AP*, Apphy, 1. Διηγήσαντο περὶ ἐπισκόπου τῆς Ὀξυρύγχου ὀνόματι ἀββᾶ Ἀπφύ· ὅτι ὅτε ἦν μοναχός, πολλὰς σκληραγωγίας ἐποίει· ὅτε δὲ ἐγένετο ἐπίσκοπος, ἠθέλησε χρήσασθαι τῇ αὐτῇ σκληραγωγίᾳ καὶ ἐν τῷ κόσμῳ, καὶ οὐκ ἴσχυσε. Καὶ ἔρριψε ἑαυτὸν ἐνώπιον τοῦ Θεοῦ λέγων· Μὴ ἄρα διὰ τὴν ἐπισκοπὴν ἀπῆλθεν ἡ χάρις ἀπ' ἐμοῦ; Καὶ ἀπεκαλύφθη αὐτῷ, ὅτι Οὐχί· ἀλλὰ τότε ἔρημος ἦν, καὶ μὴ ὄντος ἀνθρώπου, ὁ Θεὸς ἀντελαμβάνετο· νῦν δὲ κόσμος ἐστί, καὶ οἱ ἄνθρωποι ἀντιλαμβάνονταί σου.

Note that what has been lost in the transition from monk to bishop, from ascetic to non-ascetic, is intimacy with God and its attendant dependence upon God alone. Ordination in the *AP*, if it is not accompanied by the requisite asceticism, leads to distance from God.

It seems reasonable to suggest here that the solitary monk, finding greater closeness with God, functions as a kind of synecdoche in Cassian's writing for the separation of monastic realm from that of the institutional church. While Cassian does find the practice of solitude, exemplified by anchorites such as Antony, superior to more communal forms of monastic life, this in no way signifies a vilification of the more cenobitic forms; he is, after all, writing for a cenobitic monastery and recommending practices from the cenobia of Egypt. At the same time, Cassian, by advocating for a separate sphere for monasticism and the institutional church, is not claiming obsolescence for the church. Rather, he is saying that while monastics, through a lifestyle conducive to asceticism, may find a closer relationship to God than lay people or clergy, being a member of the institutional church is still worthy of praise. Monastics as a whole compared with laypeople and clergy, like anchorites compared with cenobites, will through correct ascetic practice both confront their demons and forge a more intimate connection with the divine. Indeed, like solitary monks, Cassian seems to be saying that the monastic profession and its kenotic objectives and tendencies will first tear down the worldly soul of the monk and then build him back up using only divine sources, such as Scripture, prayer, and asceticism. This is clearly preferable, a high objective, in Cassian's writings. However, this does not mean that everyone who is not a monk or does not feel capable of the arduousness of the monastic vocation is unworthy of salvation. Instead, Cassian merely shows that monasticism is a different breed of Christian life, one for which not everyone is suited. If one takes on the mantle of the monk, Cassian writes of the rules and practices that will assure the correct form of life which will lead to the requisite intimacy with God. In other words, Cassian is not writing for clergy or laypeople, and is thus not writing explicitly against such people.

If indeed one comes nearer to God, dependent only upon God when one is alone, perhaps Cassian is suggesting through this praise of solitude that all monks, when allowed not only to practice correct asceticism but also to avoid the theological and practical meddling of the clergy, are also closer to God. While I admit that Cassian never writes this explicitly, his troubled history with non-ascetic bishops, as well as the persecution of the greatly admired ascetic bishop John Chrysostom for whom he advocated with the bishop in Rome may have made Cassian believe that this separation of monastic and ecclesial spheres, like that of the anchorite in his cell, would have been the best thing for all monastics.

In a previously mentioned apothegm, a bishop orders the forced ordination of a monk named Ammonius, one of the Tall Brothers from whom Cassian learned his monastic practice. When the bishop's envoys surround Ammonius, he hurriedly cuts off his left ear in front of them, stating that this makes him ineligible for the priesthood according to Levitical laws. When the envoys return to the bishop empty-handed, the bishop says such laws are only for Jews and that he will still ordain him. The envoys go yet again to ordain Ammonius, who tells them that if they compel him to accept ordination, he will also cut out his tongue.[23] While stories of monastic reluctance to accept ordination abound in the literature, the violence of this one is particularly striking. Why is Ammonius so unwilling to accept holy orders that he will permanently mutilate himself in order to escape it? I contend that in this story and those to follow, monks are unwilling to become part of the established church hierarchy because they see it as spiritually inferior to monasticism principally because fulfilling the ecclesial office makes it more difficult to maintain ascetic practice. If they were to become part of the hierarchy, they would likely lose their ability to practice effective asceticism and therefore lose their own intimacy with God, becoming simply functionaries in a corrupt and inferior system. In his *Church History*, for example, Socrates Scholasticus writes of the Tall Brothers who had been forcibly ordained by the bishop Theophilus, that while in his service, "in process of time, they thought they were being spiritually injured, observing the bishop to be devoted to gain, and greedily intent on the acquisition of wealth, and according to the common saying 'leaving no stone unturned' for the sake of gain, they refused to remain with him any longer."[24]

In further stories of this type, monks simply ran away, often far away, and established solitary cells for themselves in other places when bishops or their lackeys came to ordain them. Isaac, Priest of the Cells is said to have arrived in Egypt after running away from his own land and Macarius the Great arrived at the monastic settlement of Scetis after escaping from forced ordination by the clergy in his region.16 Still other stories portray the monastic view of bishops and clergy as contemptuous, further clarifying why some monks would want to escape ordination. As mentioned before,

---

23. Palladius, *Lausiac History*, Ammonius, 2–3.
24. Socrates Scholasticus, *Historia Ecclesisastica,* In *Patrologia Graeca.* Edited by J.-P. Migne, vol. 3. (Paris: 1864), translated by A.C. Zenos. From *Nicene and Post-Nicene Fathers, Second Series*, Vol. 2. Edited by Philip Schaff and Henry Wace (Buffalo, NY: Christian Literature Publishing Co., 1890), VI.7. ἠνιῶντο δὲ ὅμως, ὅτι μὴ ἐφιλοσόφουν ὡς ἤθελον, τῇ ἀσκήσει προσκείμενοι. Ἐπεὶ δὲ προϊόντος τοῦ χρόνου, καὶ προσβλάπτεσθαι τὴν ψυχὴν ἐνόμιζον, ὁρῶντες τὸν ἐπίσκοπον χρεματιστίκον τε μετερκόμενον βίον, καὶ πολλὴν σπουδὴν περὶ χρεμάτων κτῆσιν τιθέμενον.

the monk Poemen, tells a priest who condemns a few monks for luxuriant behavior, "Look, you are just like the brethren yourself; if you have even a little share of the old Adam, then you are subject to sin in the same way."[25] The priest is thus forced to admit that he himself is ultimately, like the "old Adam," no better than the monks he condemned. Here, the monk Poemen shows himself, as a long-time ascetic practitioner, to be morally and/or spiritually superior to the priest by being both forgiving and non-judgmental with the errant monks, while the priest is presumably protecting or establishing his own reputation for holiness by denouncing them in public. Perhaps this explains Cassian's bold assertion, one he says is common among monks of Egypt, that "a monk ought by all means to flee from women and bishops."[26] The equation of women with bishops is telling, given the sharp devaluation of women in ancient Christian thought. However, the Christian notion of women as temptations makes this equivalence clear. Cassian goes on to say that "neither [women nor bishops] will allow him who has been joined [to them] in familiarity to care any longer for the quiet of his cell or to continue with pure eyes in divine contemplation through his insight into holy things."[27] By forcibly ordaining monks, bishops presented a challenge to the self-negation, also known as humility, toward which the monks were required to aspire. The problem which linked in Cassian's mind the temptations of women and bishops, was the danger of abandoning the monastic and ascetic life and returning to normal social roles, whether husband, father, priest, or bishop.

Zachary Smith notes that there are three categories of apothegms in the *AP* in reference to the ordination of monks: 1) stories about the changes brought about by ordination and/or the lack of aspiration for ordination, 2) stories portraying monks and ordained monks correcting each other, and 3) stories about ordained monks performing miracles.[28] The first category includes the story of Macarius who runs to an entirely new region to avoid ordination.[29] It also includes the stories of Matoes and Theodore of Pherme who are forcibly ordained but refuse to perform their designated priestly functions.[30] Most striking in the stories in this category is that while the

---

25. *AP*, Isaac 1 and Macarius the Great 1.
26. Cassian, *Institutes*, 11.18. Omnimodis monachum fugere debere mulieres et episcopos.
27. Cassian, *Institutes*, 11.18. Neuter enim sinit eum, quem semel suae familiaritati deuinxerit, uel quieti cellae ulterius operam dare uel diuinae theoriae per sanctarum rerum intuitum purissimis oculis inhaerere.
28. Smith, *Philosopher-Monks*, 154.
29. *AP*, Macarius the Great, 1.
30. *AP*, Matoes, 9 and Theodore of Pherme, 25.

monks cannot prevent themselves from being ordained against their wills, they refuse the authority conferred upon them by ordination. This includes but is not limited to the mediatorial authority of administering the eucharist, for example. Monks in these apothegms prefer the authority for which bishops originally wanted to ordain them, namely that attained through asceticism.

The second category includes instances in which ordained monks teach correct ascetic practice to non-ordained monks. In an apothegm in the *AP*, former monk Epiphanius, bishop of Cyprus, for example, teaches one superior of a monastery that while participating faithfully in the canonical prayers is good, "the true monk should have prayer and psalmody continually in his heart."[31] In another story, a monk brags to Epiphanius that he has never taken the luxury of eating meat since he became a monk. Ephiphanius, in turn, tells the monk that since he became a monk, and presumably after he became a bishop as well, "I have not allowed anyone to go to sleep with a complaint against me and I have not gone to rest with a complaint against anyone."[32] Notable in both stories of this ordained monk is that his emphasis is on neither the authority of his church office nor on theology, Nicene or otherwise. Instead, he is teaching monks who believe themselves to be practicing asceticism correctly a better way. Despite the clerical office conferred upon monks like Epiphanius in the *AP*, what truly grants them authority is their ascetic practice.

The third category includes stories about Abba Spyridon, an ordained bishop, and the miracles he performs. Spyridon shows his commitment to asceticism over any power granted by his episcopal status, by continuing to be a literal shepherd even after his ordination, a clear embodiment of humility. When robbers come in the night to steal some of the sheep, the apothegm says that "through an invisible power, the robbers found themselves bound to the sheepfold."[33] What is significant in the portrayal of this incident is that there is no reference to Spyridon's ecclesiastical status in reference to this miracle. Instead, it is clear that the compiler of the *AP* sees the miracle as the result of Spyridon's intimacy with God as a function of his asceticism. In the words of the apothegm, "God, who saves the shepherd, saved the sheep also."[34] In the other apothegm featuring Spyridon, Spyridon's daughter passes away having been in possession of an expensive ornament belonging to someone else. When the owner comes looking

---

31. *AP*, Epiphanius, Bishop of Cyprus, 3.
32. *AP*, Epiphanius, Bishop of Cyprus 4.
33. *AP*, Spyridon 1. οἱ γὰρ κλέπται ἀοράτῳ δυνάμει παρὰ τὴν μάνδραν ἐδέδεντο.
34. *AP*, Spyridon 1. Ὁ δὲ Θεὸς ὁ τὸν ποιμένα σώζων, καὶ τὰ πρόβατα ἔσωζεν.

for the ornament, Spyridon is able, through prayer, to invoke a temporary resurrection of his daughter, who then tells him where the ornament is to be found. Again, there is no mention of his status as a bishop in this apothegm. Instead, his asceticism has granted him the closeness to God to be able to intercede for others and, specifically, to perform miracles. The ethos of the *AP*'s compiler again favors ascetic practice as indicative of holiness and power far above any sort of ecclesiastical position.

Lest we think that only the *AP* features these stories of forced ordination of ascetic monks, indicating that the view of tension between ecclesiastical officials and monks was simply the compiler's unique viewpoint, I offer here similar stories from other monastic sources contemporary with both the compilation of the *AP* and Cassian's works. As Smith notes, "*The Lausiac History* indicates a mutual esteem between ecclesiastics and monks, but this mutual respect does not necessarily imply episcopal control over monks; the exact opposite seems to be the case."[35] Abba Isidore, for example, is said, as a result of his holiness, to be "known to the entire Senate at Rome" and to have traveled with two bishops, Athanasius and Demetrius.[36] There is no hint of Isidore having excessive deference for the two bishops with whom he travels. This suggests a high level of status and respect accorded to the monk, both from secular and ecclesiastical leaders, the source of which, according to the author Palladius, is Isidore's asceticism. Of Isidore's ascetic practices, Palladius says that Isidore, for example, "never wore linen other than a headdress, never took a bath and did not partake of meat."[37] However, tensions are shown to be highest in the story of Ammonios in the *LH* (Called "Ammonius" in the *AP*).

I mentioned this story earlier in the book, but I summarize it again here to emphasize its importance in illustrating depth of the monk's desire to avoid ordination. According to Palladius, a certain city wanted Ammonios, a disciple of the well-known desert monk Pambo, to be their bishop. The bishop of Alexandria, Timothy, thus sent people to bring Ammonios to him for ordination (as usual in these situations in the monastic literature, no one seems to care about Ammonios's own wishes). Ammonios refuses ordination, but when the bishop's people refuse to give up, Palladius writes that Ammonios "took a pair of scissors and sheared off his left ear at the base" telling his would-be captors that he can no longer be ordained according to Levitical laws. Bishop Timothy, dismayed by this reaction when the people return, says to ordain him anyway. Ammonios, whom Palladius describes as

---

35. Smith, *Philosopher-Monks*, 113.
36. *LH*, Isidore 4. οὗτος γνώριμος ὢν τῇ κατὰ Ῥώμην συγκλήτῳ.
37. *LH*, Isidore 2. οὗτος μέχρις αὐτῆς τελευτῆς οὐκ ὀθόνην ἐφόρεσεν ἐκτὸς φακιολίου, οὐ λουτροῦ ἥψατο, οὐ κρεῶν μετέλαβεν.

severely ascetic—he would, for example, apply "a red-hot iron to his members" when the demons attacked him—tells the bishop's people that if they continue to attempt to force him into ordination, he will cut out his tongue.[38] This threat finally ends the siege.[39] Stories of monks attempting to flee from ordination are all but normal in much of the ascetic literature, but this story displays a desperation which makes it unique. Ammonios is unwilling to give up his deeply severe lifestyle, the understanding being that one cannot maintain such rigid asceticism and be a bishop.

No stories or sayings in the *LH* are as strikingly violent as that of Ammonios regarding the relation between monks and clergy, but there are multiple hints of tensions between the two, as well as an emphasis on asceticism over ecclesiastic office in terms of authority. In one story of a monk called Nathanael, several bishops come to visit the monk, who at that point had not left his cell for thirty-seven years. As the bishops are leaving his cell, they expect Nathanael to walk out with them and send them on their way. Nathanael refuses, as the story says "not even a footstep."[40] When a deacon who is also present upbraids Nathanael for his pride in not accompanying the bishops, Nathanael replies "I am dead both to my lords the bishops and to the whole world."[41] Significant here is the fact that the monk equates "the bishops" with "the world". He shows no more deference toward bishops than toward anyone else. Nathanael's authority because of his long ascetic practice is such that he need not defer to bishops or anyone else.

Palladius also writes of Macarius of Alexandria, noting at the beginning of this section that Macarius was the priest of his community at Kellia. However, this is the last mention of his ordination. The entire remainder of the section is dedicated to Macarius's deep asceticism. This includes severe fasting and allowing himself to be bitten by swarms of mosquitos as payment for killing one mosquito. Palladius notes that when Macarius is confronted by demons, they address him as "monk," not "priest." In addition, we are told that Macarius was an expert exorcist but again, no mention is made of his priestly function in this context.[42] Ascetic practice is what both defines Macarius and grants him authority.

Finally, the *LH* writes of Evagrius Ponticus who was almost certainly Cassian's teacher and principal inspiration. What is most interesting about

---

38. *LH.*, Isidore 4. ἀλλὰ σίδηρον ἐκπυρώσας προσετίθε τοῖς ἑαυτοῦ μέλεσιν.

39. *LH*, Ammonios 1–5. βλεπόντων οὖν αὐτῶν λαβὼν ψαλίδα τὸ οὖς αὐτοῦ τὸ ἀριστερὸν ἕως πυθμένος ἐψάλισε.

40. *LH*, Nathanael 3–4. οὐδὲ βῆμα ποδός.

41. *LH*, Nathanael 4. Ἐγὼ καὶ τοῖς κυρίοις μου τοῖς ἐπισκόποις καὶ τω κόσμῳ ὅλω ἀπέθανον.

42. *LH*, Macarius of Alexandria, 1–29.

Evagrius as portrayed by Palladius is that while he starts as an ordained deacon, being granted this church office does not make him a good or admirable person. In fact, it is while he is working as a member of the clergy that he begins his slide into sin and desperation. Palladius tells us that in Constantinople, Evagrius fell in love with a married woman. It is not clear whether the relationship is ever consummated, but eventually Evagrius escapes the city after which he experiences a near-fatal illness, perhaps the physical representation of his sickness of soul.[43] After meeting the eminent ascetic Melania he decides, on her advice, to become a monk and begins to practice asceticism in earnest. This shift from church office to ascetic monk not only heals the illness he had but also helps him to achieve *apatheia*, the Greek equivalent of Cassian's purity of heart. In other words, being an ordained church official, with its increased visibility and status, made Evagrius more susceptible to sin and corruption, quite likely through the temptation of vainglory associated with the office, while ascetic practice healed both his body and soul and made him a better Christian. As the *LH* puts it, "[h]aving purged his mind to the limit for 15 years, he was deemed worthy of the spiritual gift of knowledge, of wisdom, and of the discernment of spirits."[44] This is a good representation of the general ethos of the *LH*: asceticism makes one purer, and thus more authoritative than the mere reception of the title and status of church office.

Finally, I examine another monastic source of the fifth century, the *Historia Monachorum in Aegypto (HM)*, to assess its view of the value of asceticism over that of church authority. The *Historia* was written by an anonymous monk from Palestine and is a kind of travelogue in which the author and six of his fellow monks roam around the Egyptian deserts visiting and learning about many of the best-known ascetics of each region. Like the *AP* and the *LH*, the *HM* describes the virtue and value of asceticism and at least tacitly implies that such practices of self-denial confer greater authority than any ecclesial position alone. One such example can be found in the story of the monk Patermuthius, a former robber and murderer who is converted to Christianity and then spends three years practicing asceticism alone in the desert.[45] After returning to a church, he tells the priests that his three-year training has yielded miraculous results: God has granted him the ability to recite the Scriptures from memory. The author writes that "the

---

43. *LH*, Evagrius Ponticus, 9.
44. *LH*, Evagrius Ponticus, 10. ἐντὸς οὖν δεκαπέντε ἐτῶν καθαρεύσας εἰς ἄκρον τὸν νοῦν κατηξιώθη χαρίσματος γνώσεως καὶ σοφίας καὶ διακρίσεως πνευμάτων.
45. *Historia Monachorum*, translated into Latin by Rufinus of Aquilea, in *Patrologia Graeca*, vol. 21, edited by Migne (Paris, 1849), translated by Norman Russell as *The Lives of the Desert Fathers* (Trappist, KY: Cistercian Publications, 1980). On Copres, 6.

priests were once again astonished at him for having attained the highest degree of ascesis."[46] Implicit here is that Patermuthius, despite his sordid past, has in three years of asceticism made himself spiritually superior to the priests. For this reason, when the priests beg Patermuthius to stay with them he departs again for the desert solitude in which he had previously lived. Having found the way of life he believed to be best, he was loth to abandon it for life with (or as) clergy.

Other stories in the *HM* indicate that asceticism confers spiritual power upon the practitioner that mere church position does not. Abba Helle, for example, a monk who had been an ascetic since childhood, according to the author, performed a miracle to bring a priest from the other side of a river to the monks' weekly mass or *synaxis*. The author tells us the problem was not the river itself but a huge crocodile who had already devoured several people. Since there is no ferry, Abba Helle calls the attention of the dangerous animal who instead of attempting to eat him offers his back as a raft across the raging waters. The monk climbs aboard the beast and asks the priest to do likewise but the priest is too afraid. Subsequently, Abba Helle rides the beast to the other side and then tells it, "it is better for you to die and make restitution for all the lives you have taken." The beast obeys and dies, allowing the priest to cross.[47] Significant here is the power of Abba Helle, whose source is his longstanding ascetic practice, which allows him to accomplish feats that the priest would not even attempt.

Hagiography as Rhetorical Weapon

One of the first sources explaining Egyptian asceticism and monasticism to the world in Greek was the hagiography of Antony, ostensibly the father of Christian monasticism.[48] Written by the bishop of Alexandria, Athana-

---

46. *Historia Monachorum*, On Copres, 7. Presbyteri vero mirabantur, quod subito conversus, acerrimam statim ingerit sibi abstinentiam.
47. *HM*, On Abba Helle, 7–9. Melior est tibi mors, quam tot scelerum et tot homicidiorum involvi reatu.
48. For a dissenting opinion, arguing that the *Life of Antony* was originally written in Coptic, rather than the Greek of Athanasius' version, by a close disciple of Antony's, see T.D. Barnes, "Angel of Light or Mystic Initiate? The Problem of the Life of Antony", *Journal of Theological Studies*, xxxvii (1986), 353–68. Barnes's argument in short is that first, the language describing Antony after his emergence from his long sojourn in the tomb is not characteristic of Athanasius, and second, that Athanasius would never have been so modest as to avoid mentioning his own part in the events described in the *Life*. I must admit, I am unconvinced by these arguments, especially given the zealous, anti-Arian theology of the *Life* which at the very least suggests the strong possibility of Athanasian authorship.

sius, this biography, *The Life of Antony (Vita Antonii)* although certainly not a biography in the modern sense, became an international bestseller in its time. In his *Confessions*, for example, Augustine of Hippo in north Africa just before his dramatic conversion experience, discusses the *Life* with his friend Ponticianus, comparing himself and his learned friends unfavorably with the unlettered and pious depiction of Antony.[49]

In some ways, the *Life of Antony* reads more like an adventure story than a biography, with Antony as the action hero. After defeating the demons and achieving perfection, Antony becomes livid about the heresies of the day, heresies against which coincidentally Athanasius himself was fighting tooth and nail in the wake of the Council of Nicea. Several scholars have made the case that the entire purpose of the hagiography was for Athanasius to be able to claim Antony's not-inconsiderable authority for his own Nicene position. I agree wholeheartedly with this suggestion about the *Life of Antony's* rhetorical purpose. As Samuel Rubenson writes, "the aim of the *Vita* [*Antonii*] was less to propagate the ideals of the Egyptian monks, than to correct them and enlist the support of the monks for the author's ecclesiastical policy."[50]

In the book, Antony, an illiterate, orphaned peasant, goes into the desert alone, fights against hordes of demons, often physically, and eventually defeats them, living a life of deprivation and solitude that is difficult to imagine as real, and finally, like Athanasius himself, becomes a zealous heresy fighter. While Athanasius' story certainly fired the imagination of many at the time and made a case for the highly-revered Antony as being on his side in the many theological conflicts of the day, there is good reason to believe that much of Athanasius' portrait of Antony is a rhetorically useful fiction.

To counter this portrayal of Antony, it is highly useful to look at the letters ostensibly written by Antony himself. While there are never ironclad guarantees of authenticity in scholarship on ancient documents, I remain

---

49. Augustine, and Henry Chadwick, translator, *Confessions* (Oxford: Oxford University Press, 2008), 8.15. The portrayal of Antony as an unlettered peasant puts Augustine, an educated rhetor, to shame, and he exclaims to his friend Alypius "What is wrong with us? What is this that you have heard? Uneducated people are rising up and capturing heaven, and we with our high culture without any heart—see where we roll in the mud of flesh and blood."

50. Samuel Rubenson, *The Letters of St. Antony: Monasticism and the Making of a Saint* (Minneapolis, MN: Fortress Press, 1997), 131. See also B. Brennan, "Athanasius' Vita Antonii: A Sociological Interpretation," *Vigiliae Christianae,* 39 (3), 209–27; M. Williams, "*The Life of Antony* and the Domestication of Charismatic Wisdom," in *Charisma and Sacred Biography*, Journal of the American Academy of Religion, Thematic Studies Series, 48:3 (Chico, CA: Scholars Press, 1982), 23–45; R. Gregg and D. Groh, *Early Arianism—a View of Salvation* (Philadelphia, PA: Fortress Press, 1981), 142–53.

convinced of the letters' authenticity by Samuel Rubenson's vital study. Rubenson shows that the letters are well-attested in other sources, that the originals were most likely written in Coptic, and that said originals can be reliably dated to the first two decades of the fourth century, placing them well within the lifetime of the historical Antony. In addition, having established with a reasonable degree of certainty that the letters can authentically be traced back to the historical Antony, Rubenson makes clear how the Antony of the letters is vastly different from the image of him as portrayed in the *Life of Antony*: "The letters show that the purpose of the *Vita* was neither to 'humanize' a charismatic teacher nor to 'elevate' a simple monk, but to use the influence of Antony to depict the victory of Orthodoxy over pagans and heretics, the victory of the cross over the demons, of *gnosis* by faith over *gnosis* by education, of the 'man taught by God', the *theodidaktos*, over the philosophers (emphasis added)."[51]

There are several key points in the letters of Antony that set him apart from his depiction in the *Vita*. First, it is highly unlikely that Antony was illiterate. William Harmless notes that many ancient sources cite Antony as a writer of epistles.[52] Jerome, for example, counted Antony as one of the luminaries of Christian thought in his *On Illustrious Men* and comments that Antony wrote seven letters in Coptic and that these had been translated into Greek.[53] In fact, while there is a general tendency after the *Life of Antony* becomes popular to assume that most, if not all, Egyptian monks are from illiterate peasant stock, Harmless and others have shown the folly of this assumption.[54] In addition, there are several versions of the letters, including versions in Coptic, Syriac, Georgian, Latin, Arabic, and Greek. It is thus certainly plausible that Jerome's assumption of a Coptic original is correct. However, Athanasius might have more easily portrayed his Antony as humble and unassuming (and particularly deferential toward himself and other clergy) by portraying him as illiterate and therefore low-status.

Second, Antony seems to have a very Platonic or Neoplatonic view of the importance of knowing oneself in order to know God: "Truly, my beloved, I write to you 'as to wise men' (1 Cor. 10.15), who are able to

---

51. See Rubenson, *The Letters of St. Antony*, 187.
52. Rubenson, *The Letters of St. Antony*, 187.
53. Jerome, *Liber de Viris illustribus,* In *Patrologia Latina*, vol. 23. Edited by J.-P. Migne (Paris: 1845) translated by Thomas P. Halton as *On Illustrious Men,* translated by Thomas P. Halton (Fathers of the Church; v. 100) (Washington, DC: Catholic University of America Press, 1999), LXXXVIII.1.
54. Harmless, *Desert Christians,* 78. See also Pachomius, *Regula et Praecepta* 139 (Boon, 49–50; trans. Veilleux, CS 46:166), in which cenobitic monks who are illiterate must go three times a day to a literate monk to learn to read scripture.

4. Conflicts Between Monasticism and the Church

know themselves. I know that he who knows himself knows God and his dispensations for his creatures."[55] "A wise man has first to know himself, so that he may then know what is of God, and all his grace which he has always bestowed upon us and then to know that every sin and every accusation is alien to the nature of our spiritual essence."[56] Compare this notion with the Neoplatonic writing of Plotinus, for example:

> How then can you see the sort of beauty a good soul has? Go back into yourself and look; and if you do not yet see yourself beautiful, then, just as someone making a statue which has to be beautiful cuts away here and polishes there and makes one part smooth and clears another till he has given his statue a beautiful face, so you too must cut away excess and straighten the crooked and clear the dark and make it bright, and never stop "working on your statue" till the divine glory of virtue shines out on you, till you see self-mastery enthroned upon its holy seat.[57]

In both cases, self-knowledge, or soul knowledge, is necessary for the ethical and spiritual development of the soul. Self-knowledge reveals what is divine and/or beautiful in the soul, allowing oneself to "cut away" or separate from all that is not divine and/or beautiful.

Third, Antony seems to draw directly from the writings of Origen, although Origen is never explicitly mentioned in the letters, for his cosmology and other ideas, including the pre-existence of souls (or minds):

> As for those rational beings in whom the law of promise grew cold and whose faculties of the mind thus died, so that they can no longer know themselves after their first formation, they have all become irrational and serve the creatures instead of the Creator.[58]

---

55. Samuel Rubenson and Anthony, *The Letters of St. Antony: Monasticism and the Making of a Saint* (Minneapolis, MN: Fortress Press, 1997), Ep. 3: 39–40.

56. Rubenson, *The Letters of St. Antony*, Ep. 7: 58.

57. Plotinus, translated by A.H. Armstrong, *Ennead, Volume I: Porphyry on the Life of Plotinus*, Loeb Classical Library, 440 (Cambridge, MA: Harvard University Press, 1969). 1.6.9. Πῶς ἂν οὖν ἴδοις ψυχὴν ἀγαθὴν οἷον τὸ κάλλος ἔχει; Ἄναγε ἐπὶ σαυτὸν καὶ ἴδε· κἂν μήπω σαυτὸν ἴδῃς καλόν, οἷα ποιητὴς ἀγάλματος, ὃ δεῖ καλὸν γενέσθαι, τὸ μὲν ἀφαιρεῖ, 10τὸ δὲ ἀπέξεσε, τὸ δὲ λεῖον, τὸ δὲ καθαρὸν ἐποίησεν, ἕως ἔδειξε καλὸν ἐπὶ τῷ ἀγάλματι πρόσωπον, οὕτω καὶ σὺ ἀφαίρει ὅσα περιττὰ καὶ ἀπεύθυνε ὅσα σκολιά, ὅσα σκοτεινὰ καθαίρων ἐργάζου εἶναι λαμπρὰ καὶ μὴ παύσῃ τεκταίνων τὸ σὸν ἄγαλμα, ἕως ἂν ἐκλάμψειέ σοι τῆς ἀρετῆς ἡ 15θεοειδὴς ἀγλαΐα, ἕως ἂν ἴδῃς σωφροσύνην ἐν ἁγνῷ βεβῶσαν βάθρῳ.

58. Samuel Rubenson, *The Letters of St. Antony*, Ep. II.4–5. The letters of St. Antony are preserved in fragments in Coptic, Syriac, Georgian, Latin and Arabic. For this reason, as well as my lack of expertise in four of those languages, I don't include any original or older translations of the letters. Instead I defer to the scholarly pedigree and English translations of Rubenson, who writes on page 34 that "even if the Arabic and Latin versions are translations of texts closer to the original than the Georgian and the

Antony's view is Neoplatonic in that its cosmology and worldview include, like that of Origen, the preexistence of souls who had fallen away from God or the One and into incarnation.[59] The end or *telos* of human life was to return to the unity from which souls had originally come. This was done through contemplation and self-knowledge.[60]

Third, asceticism was considered a key step for the Neoplatonist in effecting the ascent of the soul to the One.[61] In fact, the soul had only two possibilities of movement: ascent toward the One and descent away from the One. According to Plotinus, the descent of souls into bodies occurs when the attention of the individual soul is turned toward the physical world. This includes the pursuit of bodily comfort and pleasure, something the monastics always mistrusted. Note for example the apothegm of Abba Daniel in the *AP* which says, "The body prospers in the measure in which the soul is weakened, and the soul prospers in the measure in which the body is weakened."[62] The antidote to this descent into bodies is for the soul to ascend toward unity with the One. Ascent, the highest purpose of the soul according to Plotinus, involves turning the attention away from the physical, including pleasure and comfort, and toward "the beauties of soul, virtues and kinds of knowledge and ways of life and laws," finally arriving at "the ultimate, which is the first, which is beautiful of itself."[63] Plotinus writes of this as "invoking God himself, not in spoken words, but stretching ourselves out with our soul into prayer to him, able in this way to pray alone to him alone."[64] Thus when Antony writes that a person must "know himself," he refers not to knowing the personality, but rather to knowing and/or turn-

---

Syriac versions, this does not make them more reliable. The Arabic version is a very free translation and the Latin is often confused, probably due to a poor source. Although the Syriac version of Letter I is not only the one preserved in the oldest extant manuscripts, but, no doubt, the oldest preserved translation, it does not present the most reliable text. In a number of passages and in important expressions the accord between the three other versions shows that the Syriac translator was less accurate than has been supposed. Except for the parts preserved in Coptic, the best witness to the original text is no doubt the Georgian version. Only when at least two of the other versions agree against the Georgian should we be obliged to reject its readings."

59. Plotinus, *Enneads*, 4.7.
60. Plotinus, *Enneads*, I4.9.6.
61. William Turner, "Neo-Platonism," in *The Catholic Encyclopedia* (New York, NY: Robert Appleton Company, 1911). Retrieved May 17, 2019) from New Advent: http://www.newadvent.org/cathen/10742b.htm
62. *AP*, Daniel, 4. ὅτι ὅσον τὸ σῶμα θάλλει, τοσοῦτον ἡ ψυχὴ λεπτύνεται· καὶ ὅσον τὸ σῶμα λεπτύνεται, τοσοῦτον ἡ ψυχὴ θάλλει.
63. Plotinus, *Enneads*, 5.9.2. τῆς ψυχῆς κάλλη, ἀρετὰς καὶ ἐπιστήμας καὶ ἐπιτηδεύματα καὶ νόμους, ἕως ἐπ' ἔσχατον ἥκῃ τὸ πρῶτον, ὃ παρ' αὑτοῦ καλόν.
64. Plotinus, *Enneads*, 5.I.6. ὧδε οὖν λεγέσθω θεὸν αὐτὸν ἐπικαλεσαμένοις οὐ λόγῳ

ing the attention to one's deepest essence, the soul (ψυχῇ). When one turns away from the world and toward the soul, the soul begins to ascend, ultimately attaining union with the One/God.

Fourth, while Athanasius's Antony establishes the great monk as both a fighter and classifier of demons, many of whom he physically battles in his early days, Antony's demonology, one in which incorporeal demons need human bodies through which to manifest themselves, is quite different in the letters:

> Truly, my children, [the demons] are jealous of us at all times with their evil counsel, their secret persecution, their subtle malice, their spirits of seduction, their fraudulent thoughts, their faithlessness which they sow in our hearts every day, their hardness of heart and their numbness. And if you seek, you will find [the demons'] sins and iniquities revealed bodily, for they are not visible bodily. But you should know that we are their bodies, and that our soul receives their wickedness.[65]

Finally, in discussing the heresy of Arius against which Athanasius's Antony fought so zealously,[66] Antony's letters, while they do disagree with Arius' position, take a very different, and much more compassionate tack, one that views Arius not as a contemptible heretic but rather as an unfortunate ignoramus:

> As for Arius, who stood up in Alexandria, he spoke strange words about the Only-begotten: to him who has no beginning, he gave a beginning, to him who is ineffable among men he gave an end, and to the immovable he gave movement. That man has begun a great task, an unhealable wound. If he had known himself, his tongue would not have spoken about what he did not know. It is, however, manifest that he did not know himself.[67]

These letters portray Antony very differently from the popular depiction of him in the *Life*. I would argue that the portrayal in the *Life* was done intentionally because Athanasius, like the bishops who forced ordination upon revered monks, wanted to co-opt the popularity and the perceived wisdom of Antony for the institutional church and his own theological position. Such rhetorical choices, designed to make monks and bishops appear to be completely aligned with the episcopate despite the complexity and variety of monastic beliefs and practices, would build into a critical mass that

---

γεγωνῷ, ἀλλὰ τῇ ψυχῇ ἐκτείνασιν ἑαυτοὺς εἰς εὐχὴν πρὸς ἐκεῖνον, εὔχεσθαι τοῦτον τὸν τρόπον δυναμένους μόνους πρὸς μόνον.

65. Rubenson, *Letters of St. Antony*, Ep. 6.23, 27–32, 50–51.

66. For those unfamiliar with the tenets of Arianism and especially its Christology, see Rowan Williams, *Arius: Heresy and Tradition* (London: SCM Press, 2005).

67. Samuel Rubenson and Anthony, *The Letters of St. Antony*, Ep. IV.7–18.

would ultimately result in violent incidents between monks and clergy such as the Origenist Controversy to which I turn next.

The Origenist Controversy

The historical lesson of the Origenist Controversy, so named because the monks who did not anthropomorphize the deity were associated by their enemies with Origen who likewise did not believe in God's corporeality, was that in the fourth and fifth centuries, theological debates, far from being merely conceptual, could have severe real-world consequences. The particular incident involving Cassian would end with the destruction of the small settlement of monks in which he and his cohort lived, and with the exile of Cassian and other prominent monks from Egypt. However, the controversy had more historical and theological debates at its root. The complicated nature of these debates warrants a bit of background information, if only to demonstrate that it exemplified the type of theological issues raging in the Christianity of the late fourth and early fifth centuries.

In many ways, the controversy had its origins in the pre-Nicene era and its references to the resurrection of the body, as well as orthodox reactions against the devaluation of materiality in Gnosticism.[68] In this era, there was a concern in some congregations that persecutors of Christians could destroy the body, thus making the resurrection of the body impossible. Orthodox presbyters assured their congregations that while the body could be killed by persecutors, it could not be destroyed.[69] These concerns around the value or lack of value of materiality and/or the body would be reenacted in debates around the significance of asceticism, especially among fourth century monks in the Egyptian desert.

For ascetics, the self could be transformed by an ascetic re-fashioning of the body. Opponents of this approach, including Augustine of Hippo whom I will discuss in a later chapter, decried an exclusivity they perceived in this approach since not all Christians were capable of rigorous ascetic practice and thus were precluded from the spiritual heights claimed by desert monks.[70] This focus on the body also sparked debates on the nature of the deity, including the meaning of "the image" with which humans were said to be created by God (Gen 1.26). Did this image signify a body, such that God was, like human beings, embodied? Or did it signify instead a noncorporeal

---

68. Elizabeth A. Clark, *Origenist Controversy* (Princeton, NJ: Princeton University Pres, 1992), 3–4.
69. Clark, *Origenist Controversy*, 3.
70. Clark, *Origenist Controversy*, 6.

4. Conflicts Between Monasticism and the Church   111

essence which nevertheless connected humans in some way to God, despite the Fall? These debates led eventually to the violent confrontation between Theophilus and the monks of Scetis.

Cassian alludes to the beginning of this controversy in the *Conferences*. As usual, the bishop of Alexandria, Theophilus, had sent Easter letters to all churches, cities and monasteries in his diocese. In this festal letter, Theophilus had decried the heresy of the anthropomorphizing of God. However, Cassian makes it clear that many monks were sent into severe distress by this denunciation. In Cassian's words, "this was received with such great bitterness by nearly all the various sorts of monks who were living throughout the province of Egypt."[71] This remark about the "simplicity" of many of the monks is likely an indication of an implicit class system among the monks based on previous education or lack thereof. Cassian viewed the majority of Egyptian monks as being of uneducated backgrounds while his teachers Evagrius and the Tall Brothers, as well as Cassian himself, were all classically well-educated. Cassian also writes that one unlettered monk, Serapion, cried out in anguish, "They have taken my God away from me. I have no one to hold on to, and I don't know whom to adore or to address."[72] Cassian writes that another educated monk, Abba Isaac, explained to him that this error was due to the simplicity of Serapion and monks like him which caused them to incorrectly interpret the image in which scripture says humans were created.[73] Socrates Scholasticus, in his fifth-century church history, notes that the more educated monks believed the opposite: God, as an unlimited being, could not be circumscribed by a body or subject to the passions unfailingly associated with bodies. However, when many of the anthropomorphite monks arrived at the bishop's residence to protest this view, their anger convinced Theophilus that he had been wrong (or perhaps that it was merely safer to agree with an angry mob). Theophilus then sent out another letter asserting the opposite: God indeed had a physical body.

Socrates goes on to say that Theophilus's letter kindled a violent feud between the two monastic factions. The end to the conflict came when Theophilus, having armed the uneducated monks for use as his henchmen, marched with them out to Nitria, the monastic settlement of the Tall Brothers and their faction in the Egyptian desert, and forcibly evicted them from the area.[74]

---

71. Cassian, *Conferences*, 10.2.2. Quod tanta est amaritudine ab uniuerso propemodum genere monachorum, qui per totam prouinciam Aegypti.
72. Cassian, *Conferences*, 10.3. Tulerunt a me deum meum, et quem nunc teneam non habeo uel quem adorem aut interpellem iam nescio.
73. Cassian, *Conferences*, 10.5.
74. Socrates, *Ecclesiastical History*, 6.7.

The next time we see Cassian emerging from the dark depths of history, he is in Constantinople under the protection of the ill-fated ascetic bishop John Chrysostom. Church historian Socrates Scholasticus writes that when bishop John "proceeded to rebuke many of those in public office also with immoderate vehemence, the tide of unpopularity began to set against him with far greater impetus."[75] John specifically was said to have insulted Eudoxia, wife of the current Roman emperor Flavius Arcadius, for erecting a large silver statue of herself near the church of Constantinople.[76] For John, whose principal focus in regard to the laity was encouraging them to give alms to the poor, this was an unpardonable display of opulence in a city with tremendous poverty. For the offense of insulting the empress, John, who had already been exiled once and allowed to return, was exiled a second and final time.

In addition to the empress, attacks upon Chrysostom are, according to the writings of church historian Sozomen, initiated by the very same bishop, Theophilus, who had expelled Cassian and his cohort from Egypt. Thus, Cassian twice experienced the malice and vengeance of church politics. In fact, before Chrysostom's ultimate exile and death, Cassian is one of those who goes to Rome to advocate for the beleaguered bishop of Constantinople.[77] First exiled from his Egyptian idyll with his teachers and monastic models, then representing the exiled Chrysostom to the bishop of Rome, Cassian experienced firsthand the potential wrath and horror of the powers of the institutional church. It seems reasonable, therefore, to surmise that he may have felt a certain antipathy toward, if not an outright fear of the intrusive powers of bishops and a corresponding idealization of Egyptian monasticism, often attacked by the wide-reaching powers of bishops and other representatives of the church in any region.

Monasticism as Cognitive Community

Another sense in which monks and clergy may have been in conflict involves differences in cognition and/or cognitive training between the two. In *Monasteries and the Care of Souls in Late Antique Christianity*, Paul Dilley shows the ways in which cenobitic monasticism in particular trains monks in a way of thinking which differs markedly from that of laypeople or clergy of the late antique period. While this may not be a "conflict" per se, it is a way in which differences in cognitive discipline and character may have contributed

---

75. Socrates, *EH*, 6.5. Επειδή δε και πολλούς των εν τέλει πέρα του προσήκοντος εξελέγχειν επειράτο , τηνικαύτα και ο κατ᾿ αυτού φθόνος πλείων εξήπτετο.
76. Socrates, *EH*, 6.18.
77. Sozomen, *Ecclesiastical History*, 8.26.

to driving a wedge between ascetically oriented monks and non-ascetic bishops and clergy. In short, Dilley designates these early monasteries as "cognitive communities" with a common system of monitoring, evaluating, and regulating thought. Transformation of the pre-monastic self involves not only the traditional daily rules and discipline of the cenobium "but also the exercise of free choice, and in particular active participation in the disciplining of thoughts and emotions… based on metacognition."[78] Dilley's analysis thus identifies a precise summary of a monastic theory of mind which views the mind/heart as permeable, believes that one's thoughts can come from beings other than oneself, creates thoughts which are morally as meaningful as actions, believes the mind is able to be fashioned and controlled intentionally by the mind itself, is sensitive to sensory input, particularly auditory, and is at least partially legible to others, particularly God and some ascetic saints who are able to know the thoughts of others. In what follows, I will give a brief overview of Dilley's monastic theory of mind and its relevance to the conflicts between monastics and the institutional church.

Dilley notes that among the most prevalent spiritual practices used in the original Pachomian cenobia was meditation on Scripture. Unlike traditional literary training in the Roman world, however, the goal of this meditation was not the advancement of one's status or profession. The point was rather "the memorization of passages that could be repeated throughout the day, whether carrying out a labor assignment, participating in collective prayer, or negotiating a temptation through interior dialogue."[79] This had the dual purpose of fashioning one's mind in accordance with the messages of holy Scriptures while also maintaining thoughts that were morally pure and excluding those that were impure. Thus "progress in virtue was marked by the acquisition of a more generalized scriptural speech."[80] Noted fourth-century ascetic theologian and Cappadocian father Basil of Caesarea wrote that "there is a tone of voice and a symmetry of speech and a fittingness of occasion and a particular vocabulary which are fitting for and distinctive of the pious, which is impossible to learn without having unlearned his former habits."[81] In order to unlearn these former habits, one had to change the mind (μετάνοια). Frequent memorization and vocal repetition of scriptural phrases

---

78. Paul Dilley, *Monasteries and the Care of Souls in Late Antique Christianity: Cognition and Discipline* (Cambridge, London: Cambridge University Press, 2017), 293.
79. Dilley, *Monasteries,* 111.
80. Dilley, *Monasteries,* 111.
81. Basil of Caesarea, *Longer Responses,* 13 (PG 31: 949). Est enim et vocis contentio, et sermonis modus, et opportunitas temporis, et verborum proprietas, quae pietas cultoribus propria sit et peculiaris: quam fieri non potest ut discat qui consueta non dedidicerit.

was believed to have this effect. The rest of the time, monks were encouraged to keep silence in order to avoid affecting those around them or, worse, reinforcing one's own worldly tendencies. Dilley notes that "[b]asic needs, for instance communication at the dinner table, could be expressed through gestures, further eliminating the need for non-biblical speech."[82] While this practice was certainly respected by both laypeople and clergy in late antiquity, there is no evidence to suggest that any non-monastics widely performed or even encouraged others to engage in such a practice. This was a specifically monastic practice. The recognition that the mind was impressionable and thus required constant input from holy sources set monastics apart.

In addition to this type of meditation on scripture, monks were taught other methods of taking in scripture, such as "learning how to transcribe and interpret passages; listening intently to their recitation, in disciplinary, liturgical, and meditative contexts; and discussing their meaning with other members of the monastic house after group catechesis."[83] The result of all these methods was that scripture was "'written on the heart,' playing a key role in the new monastic theory of mind: disciples could draw on them during internal deliberations, identifying a particular verse as spoken by God to themselves... and adopting others as their own voice."[84] This was a powerful mode of transformation exclusive to monks who attempted through their various approaches to scripture to literally replace their former minds with thoughts formed only according to scripture. The evidence for its effectiveness is in the monastic literature, in which monks constantly refer to scripture rather than merely giving out advice or opinions based on their own personalities.[85]

In addition, the importance granted to scriptural exercises in the cenobium is further verified by the emphasis placed on near-universal literacy in Pachomian monasteries. One of Pachomius's precepts states that "there will be no one at all in the monastery who will not learn letters and will not retain anything from the Scriptures: at a minimum the New Testament and the Psalter."[86] While memorization was key in this process of transforming the mind, reading was apparently considered just as significant. Furthermore, Cassian's implicit references to classical education are mirrored in Pachomian references to monastic literacy instruction which Dilley notes parallels Graeco-Roman educational practices: "Literacy instruction consisted of roughly

---

82. Dilley, *Monasteries*, 111.
83. Dilley, *Monasteries*, 113.
84. Dilley, *Monasteries*, 113.
85. Examples of these are too numerous to mention, but from the *AP* alone see Antony 3, Epiphanius 6, 7, and 9, and Poemen, 71.
86. Pachomius, *Praecepta*, 140.

three stages: preliminary, grammatical, and rhetorical. While the latter two provided access to elite culture, the first was more practical, and might be pursued, for example, by workers in low-status professions for record-keeping."[87] Rafaella Cribiore notes that there is written evidence for a similar educational method in several late antique Egyptian monastic sites.[88] The monastery at Phoibammon, for example, has several Greek alphabets written on several of its walls, which Dilley notes may have been used for beginning instruction in letters.[89] After learning basic lettering, students of both classical and monastic literacy moved on to syllables. When these were deemed proficient, the students moved on to word lists, examples of which have been found at the monastery of Epiphanius as well as at Phoibammon.[90] Precept 139 in the Pachomian rule also refers to models written out by teachers for students to copy. Such practices are well-attested in Egyptian monasteries where, for example, a papyrus of Psalm 109:1 written proficiently, likely by the teacher, and copied four times by other, less proficient hands.[91] Cassian's emphasis on reading is thus not only an implicit appeal to the educated monks of Gaul, but also part of the vast tradition of monastic Egypt upon which his writings draw.

In addition to reading, writing, and memorization of scriptural passages, there were other methods by which monks learned to shape their own thoughts such that they would be pleasing to God. Dilley writes that monks were taught to fear God through judicious input from superior monks. In one of the *Lives* of Pachomius, for example, we are told that the cenobitic founder "was always meditating on the fear of God, the remembrance of the judgments, and the torments of the eternal flame."[92]

Dilley notes that the assumption of clairvoyance in God and certain saints was an inextricable part of the early monastic theory of mind. This had a moral component, as inculcating monks with the "fear of God… extends the notion of what is shameful from sins committed in public to acts and even thoughts, which are not visible to others."[93] The fact that thoughts, rather than simply acts, are considered to have moral weight, means that cognitive

---

87. Dilley, *Monasteries*, 115.
88. Rafaella Cribiore, *Gymnastics of the Mind: Greek Education in Hellenistic and Roman Egypt* (Princeton, NJ: Princeton University Press), 24–25.
89. Dilley, *Monasteries*, 115.
90. Dilley, *Monasteries*, 116.
91. Crum and Bell, *Wadi Sarga: Coptic and Greek Texts* (Gyldendal, Nordisk Forlag: Copenhagen, 1922), no. 5.
92. Johannes Vahlen, ed., *Corpus Scriptorum Ecclesiasticorum Latinorum* (Imperial Academy of Sciences: Vienna, 1866), 26: 208.
93. Dilley, *Monasteries*, 158–59.

strategies become necessary to avoid immoral thoughts while cultivating those which are morally upright. This begins with the assumption that God sees and judges every private thought, whether it is revealed to others voluntarily or not. Thus, for example, "the divine panopticon was reinforced through monastic difference in several ways, including the surveillance network, which placed monks under the constant watch of their superiors and colleagues."[94] The knowledge that God as well as other monks were constantly keeping track of any revelations of private thoughts, meant that a monk could never let down his guard. He must be constantly and consistently attentive to the trajectory of his mind and make constant effort to cultivate moral thoughts through prayer and the reading and contemplation of scripture. In addition, some monastic leaders claimed clairvoyance, a spiritual gift which allowed them to read the hearts/minds of others. This ability again re-emphasized the lack of mental privacy assumed in the monastic context: the deity or one of the clairvoyant saints/elders always knew what monks were truly thinking. Among other things, this spurred monks on to reveal their every thought to the monastic superior for, as Cassian says, an evil thought revealed loses its power.[95] In other words, while not all saints are said to be clairvoyant, it is incumbent upon all monks to make their minds as transparent as possible to an elder monk. This transparency, whether voluntary or at the hand of God or a mind-reading superior, allows no space in the mind in which evil thoughts can abide. Again, this sort of transparency in the late antique era in which confession is neither seen as mandatory nor a sacrament for the laity or clergy, demonstrates another clear cognitive difference between monks and everyone else.

Furthermore, monks were individually responsible for not allowing evil thoughts to enter their minds or remain there once such thoughts had entered. Thus the entire project of the care of souls in monasteries was based on "*metacognition*, that is 'one's knowledge concerning one's own cognitive processes and outcomes and anything related to them.'"[96] This assumed a high degree of free will and control of mental processes for each individual monk. Thus Pachomius is quoted as saying that each "person has the freedom to gain control over the passion by fighting against it."[97] In the same hagiography of Pachomius, the author writes that in Pachomius's early days as an anchorite, "he did not allow a foul thought to enter into his

---

94. Dilley, *Monasteries*, 159.
95. Cassian, *Conferences*, 2.10.
96. J.H. Flavell, "Metacognitive Aspects of Problem Solving", in *The Nature of Intelligence*, edited by L. B. Resnick, Hillsdale (Hillsdale, NJ: Laurence Earlbaum, 1976, 231–35. Quoted in Dilley, *Monasteries,* 9.
97. *V. Pach. SBo* 107 (CSCO 89:142).

heart to dwell in it."[98] Monks were responsible for ensuring that the input from outside their minds would correspond to the holiness toward which they aspired, including established prayers and meditation on scripture. For exogenous thoughts, however, the monk was believed to be able to either assent to or reject thoughts based on their own free choice, having learned from their monastic vocation what sort of thoughts were morally acceptable. The difference this sort of monastic mindset would have made between monks and lay people or clergy is evident in a story from the Syriac version of the *AP* in which some philosophers visit a group of monks. The philosophers insist that they, like the monks, live ascetic lives. However, a monk replies that "We keep watch over our minds." The philosophers reply that they are unable to do this.[99] One thing that clearly defines monks, then, is that they are vigilant with their thoughts and are expected to have greater control over their minds than non-monks.

In addition, believing that the mind was extremely sensitive and vulnerable to outside input, monks in the cenobium were carefully given only sensory input which lead to moral and holy thoughts. As mentioned earlier, the fear of God was considered by Pachomius and his followers to be one of the most essential traits of a monk. Without this, monks would not feel pressure to watch their thoughts and actions for fear of eternal punishment. One of the most common ways to inculcate this into individual monks was through homilies or even admonitions to individuals given by the superiors of the monastery. In one case, for example, the superior Theodore is observed reprimanding another monk, asking him "Why do you not have the fear of God before your eyes (Ps. 7:10)? Do you not know that God tries the hearts and innards (Rev. 2:23)?... Know therefore that if you do not repent... [the Lord] will condemn you to eternal fire."[100] Dilley notes that "by referring to appropriate scriptural texts in their rebuke of sinful disciples, monastic teachers imitated the divine voice of blame so frequently invoked in descriptions of the last judgment."[101] Similar rhetorical methods are found in the homilies of superiors like Pachomius:

> Go out to the tombs and see the condition of humans, that it is nothing... therefore let us weep for ourselves while we have the opportunity, lest, when the hour of our departure arrives, we be found requesting God for more time

---

98. *V. Pach. G1* 18 (Halkin: 11).
99. E.A.W. Budge, *The Wit and Wisdom of the Christian Fathers of Egypt: The Syriac Version of the Apophthegmata Patrum* (London: Oxford University Press, 1934), 53.
100. *Epistles of Ammon* 20 (Goehring, *Epistula Ammonis* 137).
101. Dilley, *Monasteries*, 166.

to repent… therefore let us strive with our whole heart, keeping death before our eyes at every hour, and at every hour imagining the fearful punishment.[102]

It is important to note that both the admonition and the homily are spoken out loud and thus physically heard. Hearing remains the principal type of sensory input given to monks to organize their thoughts around what is most important in the transformation of their mental life. Cassian's *Conferences*, for example, is organized not so much as a travelogue, although that is certainly a constitutive element, but rather as a series of conversations or dialogues with venerated elder monks. In fact, to call them dialogues is to virtually ignore the fact that they are principally orations by the elders, lectures on asceticism, practice, and theology. Despite any doubts modern readers may have in the historical veracity of the words or the apparently impressive memory of Cassian, it is noteworthy that in these written orations, Cassian uses the same rhetorical methods listed by Dilley, using scriptural quotations to imitate God's voice rather than that of an individual elder, no matter how well-respected. Thus, we find passages such as this one, attributed to Paphnutius, frequently in the *Conferences*:

> The blessed Apostle declares thus that all the endurance by which we are able to put up with the trials that afflict us comes not from our own strength but from the mercy and guidance of God: 'No trial has seized you except what is common to humanity. But God is faithful, who will not permit you to be tried beyond your capacity. But with the trial he will also provide a way out, so that you may be able to endure (1 Cor. 10.13).'[103]

Note that while most of this passage is taken up by the quotation of the actual verse being used, even the introduction to the quotation is merely a paraphrase of its contents. In other words, a venerable elder should use scriptural content far more often than his or her own words. The paraphrase here summarizes the content which is then followed by the validation of the actual scriptural quotation. All authority then, even in the most respected of monks, is referred back to the divine through scripture. This is one measure of progress in the monk, the ability to rely more on scripture in conversation than upon one's own self-generated ideas.

Although it is not mentioned in Dilley's monograph, there is one other significant way in which monasticism in Egypt, at least as conceived by works such as the *AP* and the *LH*, constitutes a cognitive community with

---

102. *Paralipomena* from the *Life of Pachomius*, edited by F. Halkin, 19–20 (Halkin: 144–45).
103. Cassian, *Conferences*, 3.17. Beatus apostolus ita pronontiat : temptatio uos non adprehendit nisi humana, fidelis autem deus, qui non permittet uos temptari super id quod potestis, sed faciet cum temptatione etiam exitum, ut sustinere possitis.

defined boundaries that set it apart from both the institutional church and lay society. While the Bible clearly commands "Do not judge, so that you may not be judged (Mt. 7.1)," judging others for their sins seems part and parcel of much ancient Christian writing. From Paul judging both Christians who disagreed with him and pagans, to Tertullian, Athanasius, and Epiphanius of Salamis, to name a few, judging those who do not live up to the moral ideals of one's own Christian life is a frequent source of rhetoric in ancient and late ancient Christianity. In this sense, the Egyptian monks' refusal to judge even the worst of sinners seems not only odd but radical. I would therefore argue that this refusal to judge, the embodiment of humility in the monastic literature, truly sets monks apart. What follows are some examples of this, demonstrating how different from normal social relations this attitude was.

Abba Agathon, for example, "whenever his thoughts urged him to pass judgment on something which he saw, he would say to himself, 'Agathon, it is not your business to do that.' Thus his spirit was always recollected."[104] This apothegm implies that not judging is more than a moral injunction. Instead, it literally helps to keep the monk's spirit recollected or unified, a necessity when one is attempting resist temptations and distractions. When Abba Moses is summoned to a monastic council about what to do with a monk who had committed a fault, he first refuses to go. When the priest convening the meeting will not give up asking him to attend, Moses finally agrees to go. However, "[Moses] took a leaking jug, filled it with water and carried it with him. The others came out to meet him and said to him, 'What is this, Father?' The old man said to them, 'My sins run out behind me, and I do not see them, and today I am coming to judge the errors of another.' When they heard that they said no more to the brother but forgave him."[105] As if to reinforce this point, there is a set of instructions in the *AP* which Moses gave to his disciple Abba Poemen, the first of which is the following: "The monk must die to his neighbor and never judge him at all, in any way whatsoever."[106] Implicit in the first apothegm is the fact that even the perfect practice of asceticism, as Moses is said to have achieved, does not

---

104. *AP*, Agathon, 18. Ὁ αὐτὸς ὅτε ἔβλεπε πρᾶγμα, καὶ ἤθελεν ὁ λογισμὸς αὐτοῦ κρῖναι, ἔλεγεν ἑαυτῷ· Ἀγάθων, μὴ ποιήσῃς αὐτὸ σύ. Καὶ οὕτος ὁ λογισμὸς αὐτοῦ ἡσύχαζεν.

105. *AP*, Moses, 2. Καὶ λαβὼν σπυρίδα τετρημ μένην, καὶ γεμίσας ἄμμου, ἐβάστασεν. Οἱ δὲ ἐξελ θόντες εἰς ἀπάντησιν αὐτοῦ, λέγουσιν αὐτῷ· Τί ἐστι τοῦτο, Πάτερ; Εἶπε δὲ αὐτοῖς ὁ γέρων· Αἱ ἁμαρτίαι [284] μού εἰσιν ὀπίσω μου καταρρέουσαι, καὶ οὐ βλέπω αὐτάς· καὶ ἦλθον ἐγὼ σήμερον, ἁμαρτήματα ἀλλό τρια κρῖναι. Οἱ δὲ ἀκούσαντες, οὐδὲν ἐλάλησαν τῷ ἀδελφῷ· ἀλλὰ συνεχώρησαν αὐτῷ.

106. *AP*, Moses, seven instructions, 1. Εἶπεν ὁ ἀββᾶς Μωϋσῆς, ὅτι ὀφείλει ἄν θρωπος ἀποθανεῖν ἀπὸ τοῦ ἑταίρου αὐτοῦ, τοῦ μὴ κρίνειν αὐτὸν ἕν τινι.

grant the right to judge. The second apothegm notes first that one must "die to one's neighbor." This can only mean that one must relinquish one's personal will in order not to offend or harm another person. This potential harm could include judging one's neighbor, and the absoluteness of the phrase "in any way whatsoever" demonstrates that there are no exceptions: no one may be judged by a monk, no matter how grave the sin, according to Moses. Otherwise, the monk's humility, the *sine qua non* of monastic identity, will be compromised. This dying to one's neighbor is a frequent reference in the *AP*, and is further clarified in yet another apothegm attributed to Abba Moses: "Do no harm to anyone, do not think anything bad in your heart towards anyone, do not scorn the man who does evil, do not put confidence in him who does wrong to his neighbor, do not rejoice with him who injures his neighbor. This is what dying to one's neighbor means."[107] A final example of this humility is evident in an apothegm attributed to Abba Xanthias, who is quoted as saying, "A dog is better than I am, for he has love and he does not judge."[108] Considering how lowly was the status of animals compared with humans in the late antique Roman world, the way in which Xanthias willingly grants himself a status even lower than a dog is telling.[109] However, the reason he feels this to be appropriate is that unlike humans, dogs are faithful despite any maltreatment and seem to lack the mental faculties which allow humans to judge one another. Monks, the saying implies, must entirely abandon that faculty relating to anyone but oneself.

---

107. *AP*, Moses, 7. Μὴ ποιήσῃς κακὸν μηδενὶ ἀνθρώπῳ, μηδὲ λογίζου πονηρὸν ἐν τῇ καρδίᾳ σου εἴς τινα· μηδὲ ἐξουδενώσῃς τινὰ ποιοῦν τα κακόν· μηδὲ πεισθῇς τῷ κακοποιοῦντι τὸν πλησίον αὐτοῦ, μηδὲ χαῖρε μετὰ τοῦ ποιοῦντος κακὸν τῷ πλησίον αὐτοῦ.

108. *AP*, Xanthias, 3. Ὁ κύων κρείσσων μού ἐστι· διότι καὶ ἀγάπην ἔχει, καὶ εἰς κρίσιν οὐκ ἔρ χεται.

109. Aristotle, *On the Soul, Parva Naturalia. On Breath*, Translated by W. S. Hett. Loeb Classical Library 288 (Cambridge, MA: Harvard University Press, 1957), 2.3. Aristotle's view of the soul was still highly influential for both Christians and pagans in the late antique Mediterranean world. In short, he believed that every living thing, including plants and animals had a soul. However, the type of body one had—plant, animal, human—determined the type of soul one had: "In addition to these senses some [living creatures] also possess the power of movement in space, and others again—viz., man, and any other being similar or superior to him—have the power of thinking and intelligence." (ἑτέροις δὲ καὶ τὸ διανοητικόν τε καὶ νοῦς, οἷον ἀνθρώποις καὶ εἴ τι τοιοῦτον ἕτερόν ἐστιν ἢ καὶ τιμιώτερον.) Animals had what Aristotle called sensible souls while only humans possessed a rational soul. This made them far superior to animals, as well as separating them from animals categorically.

Conclusion

The significance of these conflicts for Cassian's thought cannot be understated. The monastic corpus of writings shows that monks and bishops often disagreed. Bishops, in order to co-opt the popularity of the monks as arbiters of wisdom, would often forcibly ordain monks. Monks, in turn, did everything in their power to escape this fate in order to maintain their ascetic regimens. In addition the lives of monks were often rhetorically coopted as well in an effort to claim the power and popularity of monks for the clergy.

Moreover, Cassian himself also experienced the violence of disagreement between monks and clergy, finally being ousted from his beloved Egyptian desert because of a theological disagreement. In this chapter, I have established that conflicts between monks and clergy are well-attested. Such conflicts, I believe, formed the basis for Cassian's rhetorical attempt years later to separate monasticism from the authority of the institutional church. Indeed, his likely distrust of the authority of the clergy probably helped him to surreptitiously form a plan to make those monks who followed, like him, the dictates of the Egyptian Institutes, part of a more autonomous entity.

Several of the above conflictual episodes might fall under what Foucault would term sovereign power. According to Foucault, sovereign power is power exercised through visible, dominant agents, usually some type of ruler.[110] This is certainly the case with forced ordination, in which monks were often physically coerced, at the behest of bishops (Greek: επίσκοπος or "overseer"), into accepting positions of authority on behalf of the institutional church. Similarly, the theological decree of Theophilus, which ended with the expulsion of Cassian and others from Egypt, was the exercise of sovereign power.

The tacit subordination of clergy to monks and the rhetorical manipulation of Antony's subjectivity, however, falls squarely under the banner of disciplinary power. One plausible reading, for example, is that by subordinating themselves to the superior power of monks, bishops were merely attempting, in a subtle way, to convince the monks (and perhaps laypeople as well) that they and the monks were united with a single ethos and purpose. The creation of a specific form of subjectivity in the *Life of Antony*,

---

110. Michel Foucault, and Robert Hurley, *The History of Sexuality: An Introduction* (New York, NY: Vintage Books, 1990), 136. "[Sovereign] power in this instance was essentially a right of seizure: of things, time, bodies, and ultimately life itself; it culminated in the privilege to seize hold of life in order to suppress it." In the case of Gelasius above, the bishop claimed the right to take Gelasius's life for refusing to take his side in a dispute. In the case of forced ordination, monks' bodies were often seized and certain rites performed over them to co-opt their power for the clergy.

meanwhile, can be read as an attempt by Athanasius both to shore up his own theological position with the help of Antony's mighty reputation and to shape the subjectivity of future monks, such that they, too, would be strident advocates for the Nicene position.

While I cannot argue for total certainty behind these theories, I do contend that such a reading may have influenced Cassian in his attempts to shape monastic subjectivity later on. First, he would choose what Foucault would call a disciplinary approach as both more effective than sovereign power and more in line with the monastic way of training under which he had learned. Second, while the bishops can be said to have employed a disciplinary approach as well, it was key for Cassian that the subjectivity of present and future monks be shaped not by outsiders to monasticism, but rather by what he considered to be the truest insiders: the desert fathers of Egypt.

In addition, with the help of Paul Dilley's work we can identify monastics as a "cognitive community," that is, a community set apart from the rest of society by a distinct way of thinking. The cognitive assumptions underlying this way of thinking, or monastic theory of mind, include that the mind is porous, with thoughts able to be inserted into one's mind by outside forces, that thoughts, not just actions, are morally significant and must therefore be constantly observed and guarded, that thoughts can be shaped by the mind itself, putting responsibility for maintaining good thoughts and rejecting evil thoughts upon the individual monk himself, that thoughts are highly susceptible to sensory input, particularly auditory input, and that one's thoughts are not private in that they can be discerned and read by both the deity and certain clairvoyant saints. This monastic theory of mind would in many ways have set monks apart from both laity and clergy, thus increasing the plausibility that there would be conflicts between the powerful clergy and the increasingly powerful monks.

In the next chapter, I examine evidence that Cassian truly advocated for monasticism and the Church to function in separate spheres. This evidence will demonstrate that he wanted more autonomy for monastic theology and practice, a separate sphere in which monks could be entirely unhindered by bishops or other clergy members.

Chapter Five

Cassian's Rhetorical Attempts to Separate Monasticism from the Church

In the *Institutes*, Cassian tells an anecdote which clearly demonstrates his view of the perils of monks becoming clergy:

> I remember a certain old man from the time when I was living in the desert of Skete. He was going to a certain brother's cell in order to pay him a visit, and when he got near the door he heard him inside muttering something. Wanting to know what he was reading from Scripture or what, as the custom is, he was going over by memory, he stood still for a little while. And when this most devout interloper focused his hearing and listened more carefully, he discovered that he was so much at the mercy of this spirit's onslaught as to believe that he was in a church and exhorting a congregation with a sermon. And when the old man, still standing near, heard him finish his discourse and then, changing his role, announce the dismissal of the catechumens as if he were a deacon, he at once knocked on the door. The man came out, greeting the old man with the customary reverence and bringing him in. Since the realization of what had been in his mind was troubling him, he asked how long ago he had come, in case he were scandalized had he been standing at the door for a long time. The old man replied in a pleasantly amused manner: "I only arrived," he said, "when you were announcing the dismissal of the catechumens."[1]

It is instructive that this anecdote is included in the section of the *Institutes* on combating vainglory. The solitary monk, alone in his cell, and even the cenobitic monk, dressed and behaving the same as everyone else in the monastery, has little hope of individual glory. For this reason, the monk in

---

1. John Cassian, *Institutes*, 11.16. Memini cuiusdam senis, cum in heremo Soiti commorarer. qui cum ad cellam cuiusdam fratris gratia uisitationis adueniens ostio proximasset audissetque eum quiddam obmurmurantem intrinsecus, paululum substitit, cognoscere uolens quidnam de scripturis legeret uel, sicut est moris, operans memoriter recenseret. cumque piissimus explorator aure diligenter adplicita curiosius auscultaret, ita eum repperit huius spiritus inpugnatione pellectum, ut in ecclesia facere se crederet exhortatorium plebi sermonem. cumque subsistens senex audisset eum finisse tractatum et mutato rursus officio celebrare uelut diaconum catechumenis missam, tum demum pulsauit ostium. qui egressus occurrensque seni ueneratione solita introducensque eum, quam olim uenerit, cogitationum suarum conscientia remordente perquirit, ne scilicet diutius ad ostium stans iniuriam pertulisset. ioculariter senex grateque respondit: modo, inquiens, ueni, quando tu missam catechumenis celebrabas.

the apothegm imagines the grandeur and fame of being a priest or bishop, giving an edifying sermon to large, adoring crowds, and then sees himself as a deacon with the power and authority to dismiss the catechumens and others at the end of the service. This desire for power and glory, tenacious as it is, must be struggled against in Cassian's assessment and ultimately renounced if one is to be a true monk. He thus writes that vainglory "suggests clerical rank and a desire for the priesthood or the diaconate [to the monk]. It makes out that, even if a person has achieved this unwillingly, he will be filled with such holiness and strictness as even to be able to offer examples of holiness to other priests."[2] Note here that Cassian acknowledges that many monks are ordained "unwillingly," subtly reinforcing the common conflicts between clergy and monks in Egypt.

By the time John Cassian started writing *The Institutes* and *The Conferences*, he had completed a long journey, both physically and theologically. As a novice, he had learned the ways of cenobitic monasticism from his first Palestinian monastery and endured the trials and tribulations of living with a group of men under strict rules and regulations. Believing that he had exhausted the possibilities of this type of monastic life in the three years he was there, and that the discipline in that monastery was deficient, he had then gone on to travel to Egypt to meet the legendary Desert Fathers, learning from them about solitude, ascetic practice, and the theological implications of both. While many of these notions may have been based upon the writings of Origen, Cassian never acknowledges this debt and in fact, may have been completely unaware that his type of monasticism was so heavily indebted to Origen.[3]

However, he had also learned that this so-called Origenist way of life was not universally practiced or accepted, even among monastic communities in Egypt, as shown by the mob of angry monks who threatened Theophilus of Alexandria when he first asserted that God was incorporeal. His expulsion from the Thebaid, forced him to look for shelter in the massive cultural center of Constantinople with John Chrysostom.

---

2. John Cassian, *Institutes*, 11.14. Nonnumquam uero clericatus gradum et desiderium presbyterii uel diaconatus inmittit, quem si uel inuitus fuisset indeptus, tanta expleturum sanctitate ac rigore depingit, ut, ceteris quoque sacerdotibus praebere potuerit sanctitatis exempla,

3. Cassian's teacher, Evagrius Ponticus, also makes no explicit mention of Origen. I would suggest that this might signify that Origen's influence on monastic theology and practice had become so pervasive by the end of the fourth century that many were unaware of its original source. The other possibility, of course, is that even by Evagrius' time, Origen's doctrines were becoming controversial and that one was better off espousing doctrines without explicitly referencing their source.

5. Cassian's Attempts to Separate Monasticism from the Church 125

Becoming ordained as a deacon there, he surely learned the basics of formal liturgy and perhaps even pastoral care, although this may have been done, at least in part, so that Chrysostom could grant him and the Tall Brothers protection. Nevertheless, by the time Cassian arrived in Gaul, his final destination whether or not that was his intention, he had clearly prioritized his collected knowledge. While he could easily have fulfilled the duties of a member of the clergy in Marseilles, he chose instead to inspect and write about the monastic practices he had learned in Egypt as a young man. While much of this included what the layperson might see as tedious minutiae, it also included, surreptitiously perhaps, his view that the clergy, at least those who did not also practice asceticism, had little or nothing to offer monks who practiced correctly. For this reason, I argue that he sought a very real separation between clergy and monastics such that monastics could be their own authority, free of both theological and practical meddling by bishops.

In this chapter I argue that in the *Institutes* and *Conferences*, Cassian is advocating for a separation between the spheres of monasticism and the institutional church. As noted before, Cassian writes provocatively that "a monk ought by all means to flee from women and bishops."[4] This is indeed an odd comment for Cassian to include in his writings, though he claims it is a common saying among monks and not his own, if he does not intend to set up bishops, the ultimate authorities within the institutional church in his time, as a sort of adversary. At the end of the chapter, I address one possible objection to the notion of monks living without the services of clergy: administration of the Eucharist.

Returning to the Origenist Controversy, we must remember that Cassian was expelled from his beloved Egyptian paradise because of the Church's meddling in the theological affairs of the monks, principally the Tall Brothers whom Cassian revered. As mentioned above, the next time we see Cassian emerging from obscurity, under the protection of the ill-fated John Chrysostom, he again witnesses the dark side of clerical power. The attacks upon Chrysostom are, according to the evidence available, initiated by the very same bishop Theophilus who expelled Cassian and his cohort from Egypt. Thus, Cassian twice experiences the malice and vengeance of church politics. In fact, before Chrysostom's ultimate exile and death, Cassian is one of those chosen to go to Rome to advocate for the beleaguered bishop of Constantinople.[5] First exiled with his teachers and monastic models, then

---

4. Cassian, *Institutes*, 11.18. Omnimodis monachum fugere debere mulieres et episcopos.
5. Sozomen's *EH* reproduces a letter from Innocent, bishop of Rome, affirming that two people, "Germanus the presbyter and Cassianus the deacon" came to Rome to apprise the bishop of John Chrysostom's persecution. Sozomen, *EH*, 8.26.

representing an ascetic bishop unjustly deposed, Cassian has experienced firsthand the destructive potential of the powers of the church.

In the *Conferences*, Cassian writes "Whoever lives not by his own judgment but by the example of our forebears (*maiorum*) will never be deceived."[6] As usual in his writings, Cassian invokes the authority of elder monks, rather than bishops. Indeed, bishops and the clergy begin to seem almost obsolete, superseded, even, in Cassian's total omission of them in the context of gaining the wisdom of discernment as a monastic. I argue that given the above context of the Church in Roman Gaul of the fifth century, such an exclusion cannot be a mere oversight on Cassian's part.

Accordingly, this chapter will examine Cassian's monastic writings, the *Institutes* and the *Conferences*, for evidence that he truly wanted monasticism and the institutional church to operate in separate spheres. As noted above, The *Institutes* were written about and for cenobitic communities. They were, in general, a manual for correct monastic practice within communities based on what Cassian had learned as a monk in Egypt. The *Conferences,* on the other hand, are more inner-focused and theological in scope, aimed at solitaries or small groups of monks. I separate the evidence here into three distinct categories. First, Cassian presents several monastic exemplars, including prophets, apostles, and even Christ himself. I argue that Cassian's intention with this category is to show not only that monks are the rightful spiritual heirs of these revered biblical figures, but also that monks, rather than bishops and clergy, are contemporary versions of these figures. Second, Cassian makes repeated appeals to distinct monastic traditions. Through this category, Cassian intends to show how truly holy figures should behave by codifying correct monastic practice and emphasizing the vast importance of asceticism in this quest for holiness. Implicitly, he makes clear that most bishops and clergy, especially when compared with monastics, do not follow the correct way of life. Third, Cassian writes subtle denigrations of Church hierarchs or their theological heroes, especially those who write of monasticism with only hearsay as a source. While on the one hand Cassian shows how monks behave correctly through ascetic practices, he also delicately disparages bishops, clergy, and some of their theological champions for not measuring up to the monastic and ascetic standards he defines.

In addition, this chapter will provide an analysis of how all three categories of evidence intersect with Foucault's notions of disciplinary power and pastoral power. In this sense, Cassian's writings create a specific type of monastic subjectivity, one in which monks are both shepherded as a

---

6. Cassian, *Conferences*, 2.10.2. Nullatenus enim decipi poterit, quisque non suo iudicio, sed maiorum so uiuit exemplo.

group by Cassian and taught to police themselves regarding correct monastic practice.

In all three categories of evidence presented, I argue that Cassian is not only drawing a clear, bold line between monastics and bishops, but also that the line he draws is meant not merely to separate the two, but rather to exclude bishops and clergy from the sphere of monasticism. He is not merely defining "us" vs. "them", but more accurately circling the wagons. In this way, he creates a closed system in which monastics, are to be informed and led only by other monastics, past and present. This is true, regardless of how far he must stretch the definition of monastics rhetorically, as we see below.

Cassian and Castor

Before introducing the evidence, I must address the elephant in the room: the relationship between Cassian and Castor. How could Cassian, in advocating for separate spheres for monasticism and the institutional church, be on such seemingly good terms with Castor, bishop of Apta Julia? Castor seems to have requested that Cassian write the *Institutes* and *Conferences* and I do not find, in Cassian's writings, any explicit evidence that Cassian either resented Castor himself nor that he had any resistance to fulfilling that request. However, I believe that the relationship was more complicated than Cassian's ancient and educated notions of humility and politeness would have allowed him to demonstrate.

First, I see no reason to believe that Cassian had a personal grudge against all bishops. Indeed, he both accepted the protection of and then advocated for the bishop John Chrysostom of Constantinople after he had been exiled from Egypt by another bishop, Theophilus of Alexandria. What I find, instead, in Cassian's writings is not a general antipathy toward all bishops, but rather the notion that bishops generally are ill- equipped to both found and advise monasteries, unless these bishops value and practice asceticism, the real basis for authority in Cassian's oeuvre. Cassian says as much when, in the preface to his *Institutes*, he says that Castor's province lacks anything resembling the holy cenobia of Egypt and that despite his prodigious virtues, Castor needs Cassian to teach Gallican monks the sacred ways of Egyptian monasticism.[7] In other words, there is nothing wrong with what the bishop himself does *within his own realm*. The problem comes when, like Theophilus, a bishop, dares to overstep his authority by presuming to tell monks how to live, believe, or worship. In Cassian's view, monks are not inherently superior to bishops except that, unlike bishops, they know

---

7. Cassian, *Institutes*, preface, 2–3.

correct monastic practice. There is little reason, therefore, for bishops to cross the line into polemicizing monastic belief or praxis. In this sense, Cassian likely views Castor as both a good bishop and a good patron in that he seems to entrust Cassian completely with instructing monks while he himself merely facilitates this process of learning by bringing in an experienced monk as leader and teacher.

Second, even if Cassian had felt a general aversion to bishops because of his exile, he was surely not stupid. Having already experienced a violent expulsion at the hands of bishop Theophilus, Cassian certainly had no doubts about either the power or the malice of some bishops. Had he explicitly insulted a bishop at whose request he was writing, he might not only have been similarly treated, but might also have lost the opportunity to train Gallican monks in the ways of Egyptian monasticism. His mission was not to insult or conquer bishops, but rather to encourage and maintain correct monastic practice. He could best do this by treating bishops respectfully and yet, to the extent possible, excluding them from the monastic realm.

Monastic Exemplars: Prophets and Apostles

Having suffered exile at the hands of a bishop and watched as John Chrysostom fell victim to a similar fate, Cassian would no doubt be wary of overtly confronting the hierarchs of his time and region. However, as Zachary B. Smith notes, there was, among Cassian's idealized monks of Egypt, a definite ethos, displayed prominently in the *AP*, for example, of separating monasticism from the institutional church. According to this notion, questions of both monastic theology and practice should be made only on the basis of the authority of fellow monastics. As Smith says, "The violent realities of monk-bishop and monk-monk relationships in Egypt with Theophilus and Cyril, and in Palestine after Chalcedon, do not appear in the *AP*. Instead, the compiler offers tacit suggestions that bishops and monks should operate in two largely separate spheres of concern and authority."[8] The references to this separation are thus subtly and cleverly inscribed in Cassian's writings, as well.

Cassian begins his preface to the *Institutes*, addressed to Castor, the bishop of Apta Julia in Gaul, by alluding to the Hebrew Bible. He notes that Solomon, the king of Israel renowned for his wisdom, nevertheless took on

---

8. Zachary B. Smith, *Philosopher-monks, Episcopal Authority, and the Care of the Self: The Apophthegmata Patrum in Fifth-century Palestine* (Turnhout: Brepols, 2017), 46.

5. Cassian's Attempts to Separate Monasticism from the Church   129

a poor foreigner, Hiram of Tyre, as proxy in overseeing the building of the Temple. Cassian thus compares himself and his role to that of Hiram:

> If, therefore, the princedom that was loftier than all the kingdoms of the earth, and the noble and excellent scion of the Israelite race, and the divinely inspired wisdom that surpassed the skills and institutes of all the people of the East and all the Egyptians by no means disdained the advice of a poor foreigner, rightly also do you, most blessed Pope Castor,[9] instructed by these examples, deign to summon me in my utter want and poverty to collaborate in your great work. You are setting out to construct a true and spirited temple for God not out of unfeeling stones but out of a community of holy men.[10]

Note here how Cassian uses the Hebrew Bible reference to assert his own significance in building "the Temple" of a new monastery. Hiram in the story of Solomon's construction of the Temple, is the intermediary between Solomon's admittedly significant idea to build the magnificent Temple and the men and processes of actually building it (1 Kgs 5.1-18). While Hiram is not a prophet as such, he is crucial to the construction of Solomon's Temple, acting as an agent without whom the Temple could not be properly built. This seems to hint at Cassian's notion of his own role as well as the role of monks in general: monks are those who show the way, who actively build the edifice of Christian life through ascetic practice while bishops, represented by Solomon, simply wield power passively. Given that Cassian directly addresses Bishop Castor in this preface, this characterization of bishops must include Castor as well.

Entitled *The Garb of the Monks*, Book 1 of the *Institutes* indeed begins with a description of how monks should dress and the spiritual reasons and implications of this type of clothing. While this could be read simply as a rote description or instruction on how to dress in proper monastic fashion, it is notable how differently a monk and a priest or bishop dressed in fourth and fifth century Roman provinces such as Gaul. Ecclesiastical dress had just begun to be somewhat standardized in the Western church at the time of Cassian's writings. Priestly vestments included the *alba*, a long flowing

---

9. The term "pope", which Cassian uses to address Castor the Bishop of Apta Julia in Gaul (*Ad Castorem Pontifecem*) can be misleading for modern readers. While this is indeed the term that developed later into the word now used for the bishop of Rome alone, it was, at the time of Cassian's writing, simply another honorific term in Latin for bishop. See for example Tertullian, *De Pudicitia*, 13.

10. Cassian, *Institutes*, preface, 2. Si ergo illo uniuersis regnis terrae sublimior principatus ot Israheletici generis nobilior excellentiorque progenies illaque sapientia diuinitus inspirata, quae cunctorum Orientalium et Aegyptiorum disciplinas ot instituta superabat, nequaquam pauperis atque alienigenae uiri consilium dedignatur, recte otiam tu his eruditus exemplis, beatissime papa Castor, uerum ac rationabile deo templum non lapidibus insensibilibus, sed sanctorum uirorum congregatione.

robe of white linen, the *orarium*, a long scarf worn around the neck, the *planeta*, an outer cloak that covered the torso and would later develop into the more elaborate chasuble.[11] The richness of clerical dress was in stark contrast to the intentional poverty of monastic clothing.

The monk, like the priest, had to look the part. Unlike the priest or bishop, however, the monk was not expected to reflect, through merely liturgical garments, the very glory of God. Instead, he was to express the humility of Moses, the prophets, and even Christ himself. Thus "it is proper for a monk always to dress like a soldier of Christ, ever ready for battle."[12] A soldier dresses like his compatriots in arms, trying not only to fit in but to literally blend in with both the purpose and the esprit de corps of his fellow combatants. One had to look like a monk in order to become a monk. Cassian states that beginning his discussion with the "outward appearance… we shall then be able to discuss, in logical sequence, [monk's] inner worship."[13] While Cassian may very well privilege the inner being, the outer was significant to the inner's identity and development.

Cassian goes on in this section to compare monks' garb with that of the prophets of the Hebrew Bible, writing that those "responsible for the beginning of this profession, namely Elijah and Elisha, went about dressed in this way."[14] In addition he writes in the *Conferences* that "some people are completely set upon the remoteness of the desert and on purity of heart, as we know Elijah and Elisha were in times past and the blessed Antony and others were in our own day."[15] Here, by invoking and connecting biblical prophets and the legendary father of Christian monasticism, Antony, Cassian has converted the celebrated prophets into monastic progenitors, granting authority both to the prophets themselves in this role and to their successor monks as a continuation of prophetic roles. In addition, he writes that in relation to prophetic dress, "the leaders and authors of the New Testament—namely John, Peter, and Paul and other men of the same caliber—behaved likewise."[16] In addition, solitary desert monks lived their lives

---

11. Robert Alexander Stewart Macalister, *Ecclesiastical Vestments: Their Development and History* (Charleston, SC: Nabu Press,1896), 37–45.

12. Cassian, *Institutes*, 1.1. Itaque monachum ut militem Christi in procinctu semper belli positum accinctis lumbis iugiter oportet incedere.

13. Cassian, *Institutes*, 1.1.1. Quorum interiorem cultum consequenter tuuc poterimus exponere, cum exteriorem ornatum sub oculorum depinxerimus obtutibus.

14. Cassian, *Institutes*, 1.1.2. Hoc enim habitu etiam illos ambulasse, qui in ueteri testamento professionis huius fundauere primordia, Heliam scilicet et Helisaeum.

15. Cassian, *Conferences*, 14.4.1. Quidam enim summam intentionis suae erga heremi secreta et cordis constituunt puritatem, ut in praeteritis Heliam et Helisaeum nostrisque temporibus beatum Antonium aliosque.

16. Cassian, *Institutes*, 1.1.2. Ac deinceps principes auctoresque testamenti noui,

in imitation of John the Baptist, who spent his whole life in the desert, and of Elijah and Elisha and the others whom the Apostle recalls thus: 'They went about in sheepskin and in goatskin, in distress, afflicted, needy, the world unworthy of them, wandering in deserts and mountains and caves and caverns of the earth'.[17]

Not only are monks the legitimate heirs of a type of apostolic succession, as asserted earlier, but they are also inextricably interwoven with the writings of sacred scripture.

I will hereafter call this form of authority identified by Cassian "apostolic praxis", based as it is upon correct practice interpreted through the stories of biblical figures over mere institutional authority or belief. The very fact that Cassian implies this biblical connection to those of his own profession and not to bishops or clergy leaves little doubt about who has the authority to sanction correct practice. It is important to Cassian that monks be recognizable *qua* monks, not simply through their behaviors, but also by their dress and personal habits. He thus tells the story of how King Ahaziah recognized Elijah by a simple description of his hirsuteness and leather belt (2 Kgs 1.1-8), comparing descriptions of John the Baptist to this ideal as well. Bishops and laypeople must quickly be able to recognize a monk when they see him, as the king recognized Elijah, and therefore know that this is a dedicated soldier of Christ. In other words, a monk must never be mistaken for a bishop or clergy member, and the ascetic nature of the monk's appearance is key to recognizing his asceticism, humility and wisdom.

In Books 2 and 3 of the *Institutes*, Cassian, once again invoking the authority of the Egyptian fathers, discusses prayers and how they are to be conducted. Without going into too much unnecessary detail, Cassian prescribes the number of prayers to be said, the number of Psalms to be sung or chanted, and the frequency on different days during which these should be accomplished. As he attempts to shape monastic subjectivity to his ideal, he delineates correct prayer practices, excluding those he has already seen in Gaul which do not conform with what he saw and learned in Egypt. In this way, he creates a definite line between true monks as those who follow Egyptian practices, and false or non-monks who do not. These inadequate monks of Gaul are endorsed primarily by regional bishops rather than the

---

Iohannem uidelicet, Petrum et Paulum ceterosque eiusdem ordinis uiros taliter incessisse cognoscimus.

17. Cassian, *Conferences*, 18.6.2. Citing Heb. 11.37-38. Ad imitationem scilicet Iohannis Baptistae, qui in heremo tota aetate permansit, Heliae quoque et Helisaei atque illorum de quibus apostolus ita memorat: circumierunt in melotis et in pellibus caprinis angustiati, adflicti, egentes, quibus dignus non erat mundus, in solitudinibus errantes et montibus et speluncis et in cauernis terrae.

monks or traditions of Egyptian monastics. To define genuine monks, and thus establish his ideal, Cassian will once again go beyond simply invoking his precious desert fathers by also tying their traditions to the authority of biblical figures.

Cassian writes, for example, that while there are formal prayer and chanting services for the monks, outside of these the monks "almost never omit meditating on the psalms and on other parts of Scripture, and to this they add entreaties and prayers at every moment."[18] Why is this significant in contrast to the way bishops and clergy might practice? Cassian says, in reference to the monks' constant meditation, that "what is unceasingly offered is greater than what is rendered at particular moments, and a voluntary service is more pleasing than functions that are carried out by canonical obligation."[19] While Cassian appreciates the liturgical forms of both the church and monasteries, different though they may be, he honors monks for voluntarily and on an individual basis following Paul the Apostle's injunction to "pray without ceasing" (1 Thess. 5.17, ἀδιαλείπτως προσεύχεσθε). This is clearly understood as an obligation for monks, outside of their group worship and prayer, while such is not the case, or at least not explicitly, for the bishop or priest.

As for prayer and worship at the end of the week, Cassian once again ties monks explicitly to Christ's original apostles and the primitive church:

> In the time of the apostolic preaching, when the Christian religion and faith was founded, it was determined throughout the Orient that a vigil should be celebrated at the start of Saturday, because when our Lord and Savior was crucified on a Friday… his disciples stayed awake the whole night and gave no repose at all to their eyes. Hence from that time on a vigil service has been assigned to this night, and up to the present day it is observed in similar fashion throughout the Orient.[20]

As historically dubious as this explanation may be, Cassian's concern lies elsewhere. As before, while the practice—in this case the Saturday night

---

18. Cassian, *Institutes*, 3.2. Ut psalmorum quoque uel ceterarum scripturarum meditatio numquani penitus omittatur, cui preces et orationes per singula momenta miscentes in his officiis.

19. Cassian, *Institutes*, 3.2. Plus enim est id quod incessanter offertur quam quod per temporis interualla persoluitur, et gratius uoluntarium munusquam functiones quae canonica compulsione redduntur.

20. Cassian, *Institutes*, III.9.1. Quas a tempore praedicationis apostolicae, quo religio ac fides Christiana fundata est, per uniuersum Orientem idcirco statutum est inluscescente sabbato debere celebrari, quod domino ac saluatore nostro sexta sabbati crucifixo discipuli adhuc recenti eius passione perculsi peruigiles tota nocte manserunt, nullatenus quietis somnum suis oculis indulgentes. quamobrem ex illo tempore huic nocti deputata uigiliarum sollemnitas usque in hodiernum diem per uniuersum Orientem similiter obseruatur.

5. Cassian's Attempts to Separate Monasticism from the Church 133

vigil—is important, what is more essential is the link to a mythical primitive church, a connection implicitly superseding that of the institutional church of Cassian's day. Perhaps many of the church's teachings have been passed down along with bishops, but again these dogmas go largely unmentioned by Cassian.

Instead, he simply notes that since the original Christians practiced this way, monks continue to do so. In asserting this, Cassian continues to invest monks with more authority than bishops. In the *Conferences*, he makes this claim even clearer: "The discipline of the cenobites took its rise at the time of the apostolic preaching."[21] Thus the entire system of cenobitic traditions and practices are generally connected to the authority of the apostles and the primitive community, where "the multitude of believers had one heart and one soul, and none of them said that what he possessed was his own, but all things were common to them (Acts 4:.32)."[22]

Here I would like to revisit Foucault's notions of subjectivity and power and briefly analyze the intersection of these notions with Cassian's monastic exemplars above.

The purpose of this analysis is to elucidate my theory, namely that Cassian was advocating for a separation of authority between monastics and the institutional church by rhetorically creating a specific type of monastic subjectivity. Remember that Foucault outlines three methods by which subjects are created. First, modes of investigation create subjects as objects of knowledge. Second, practices and procedures divide subjects both from within, and from other subjects according to standards of norm and deviance. Third, practices and procedures of self-management are introduced, by which subjects transform themselves as subjects to meet an externally imposed ideal.

First, Cassian creates monastics as objects of knowledge by creating a monastic history, beginning with the prophets of the Hebrew Bible, continuing through the apostles and the primitive church, and ending with the monks of Egypt whom he repeatedly idealizes in his rhetoric. In doing this, Cassian draws a line around those he sees as monks, circumscribing them through their practices, procedures, dress, schedules, forms of prayer, and work. He then turns this edifying history upon the monks of Gaul, implicitly asking whether in comparison with his definition they can indeed be called

---

21. Cassian, *Conferences*, 18.5.1. Itaque coenobiotarum disciplina a tempore praedicationis apostolicae sumpsit exordium

22. Cited in Cassian, *Conferences*, 18.5.1. Multitudinis autem credentium erat cor et anima una, nec quisquam eorum quae possidebat aliquid suum esse dicebat, sed erant illis omnia communia.

monks and specifically whether they, through their own practices, fit within his circle of true monastics.

Second, this definition of true monks divides the monks from within. Every virtue Cassian identifies in Elijah, the apostles, and the monks of Egypt implicitly points at faults in the monks of Gaul. The Gallican monks are thus divided within as they are encouraged to work on themselves, becoming more and more like these monks of old. In other words, the highest part of each monk works on the lower, less adequate part in order to bring it up to Cassian's lofty standard.

Third, this transformation is understood to be accomplished by frequent comparisons with the monastic ideals Cassian outlines. Cassian's rhetoric provides the ideal practices of true monks. With these practices so well-defined, the monks of Gaul can police their own practices, comparing themselves with the ideal Cassian provides and changing or eliminating behaviors that do not fit with this ideal (or alternatively, leaving monastic life altogether). Thus Cassian, with his well-established role as arbiter of correct practice, shapes the monastic subjects of Gaul into his ideal.

Appeals to Distinct Monastic Traditions

The second category of evidence Cassian employs concerns monastic rituals and customs. While strictly outlining the nuts and bolts of these ascetic traditions, Cassian never says explicitly that these customs are only applicable to monastic practice. Instead, he uses them to delineate between monks and those of the institutional church who generally do not cultivate ascetic habits in the way he describes. Those who do practice asceticism, even if they are clergy or laity, would also meet with Cassian's approval. Remember, for example, how Cassian worked with and advocated for the ascetic bishop John Chrysostom. It would thus seem that Cassian, while not explicitly denying the institutional church's link to the authority of apostolic succession through bishops, draws a different line of succession to monastics, one of apostolic praxis. The bishops may have inherited position and authority in one sphere, but only monastics of the Egyptian variety model Christian practice correctly.

Cassian therefore writes of "the method of the canonical prayers and Psalms [which] was determined in times past in the regions of the East by the holy fathers."[23] Significantly, and characteristically, the number and type of prayers and Psalms are traced not to any figure in the institutional

---

23. Cassian, *Institutes*, 2.1. Qui modus canonicarum orationum psalmorumque sit in partibus Orientis a sanctis patribus antiquitus statutus, agnoscat.

5. Cassian's Attempts to Separate Monasticism from the Church 135

church, but rather to the desert fathers of the past. After establishing this as the measure of correct prayer practice, Cassian, using the commanding "royal we", says "we know that in this way different canons have been established in different places, and we have seen nearly as many models and rules being used as we have seen monasteries and cells."[24] Having just noted the existence of one correct canonical method of prayer, this disparagement of the lack of accurate prayer rules can only be a slight against the monks of Gaul, a sign that they have yet to connect their lives and practices to the venerable fathers of the past. This is significant because although Cassian himself is writing these instructions, it is at the behest of a bishop. It seems too farfetched to be coincidence that the monastery organized and instituted by a bishop is, according to Cassian, doing almost nothing correctly according to the monastic traditions of Egypt. Cassian's entire purpose, as an inheritor of these rituals and customs, is to correct such errors. He writes that he thinks it

> necessary to lay out the most ancient constitution of the fathers, which is being observed by the servants of God even until now throughout Egypt, so that the uninstructed infancy in Christ of your new monastery may be initiated in the most time-tried customs of the most ancient fathers.[25]

Not only was the correct prayer rule created long ago by the ancient desert fathers, according to Cassian, but it continues to be practiced today in an unbroken line of tradition, such that any monk who went to Egypt in Cassian's time would find a uniform practice among all monks. This, of course, is a highly unlikely claim, but once again feeds directly into Cassian's rhetorical method. In addition, Cassian conspicuously calls the Gallican monks "uninstructed" and implies that they are mere "infants" in the faith. This is a matter of authority: who has sufficient authority to set up the rules and regulations of a proper monastery, a bishop or a monk properly trained in Egypt? Cassian's answer is clear.

In addition to the regular prayer and chanting prescribed by Cassian, frequent meditation upon scripture is also paramount. As usual, Cassian explicitly connects this practice to biblical authority, using metaphors referring to well-known biblical stories and symbols. For example, in encouraging each monk to meditate continually on scripture, Cassian says a monk

---

24. Cassian, *Institutes*, 2.2. Atque in hunc modum diuersis in locis diuersum canonem cognouimus institutum totque propemodum typos ac regulas uidimus usurpatas, quot etiam monasteria cellasque conspeximus.

25. Cassian, *Institutes*, 2.2.2. Quapropter necessarium reor antiquissimam patrum proferre in medium constitutionem, quae nunc usque per totam Aegyptum a dei famulis custoditur, quo nouelli monasterii in Christo rudis infantia antiquissimorum potius patrum uetustissimis institutionibus inbuatur.

should "do this until continual meditation fills your mind and as it were forms it in its likeness, making of it a kind of ark of the covenant."[26] The ark is said to have contained the stone tablets of Moses, which Cassian compares to the Old and New Testaments, a golden jar, which he compares to the monk's memory of scripture, and manna, which he compares to the spiritual understanding of scripture.[27] In other words, this continual meditation upon scripture forms the monk's mind into a spiritual treasure chest, something intimately connected with God, much like scripture itself.

While the ideal monastery of which Cassian writes is not entirely without hierarchy, Cassian writes that the leader of a monastery is not "allowed to rule over a community of brothers, or even over himself, unless he not only gets rid of all his possessions but also recognizes that he is in fact that he is not his own master and has no power over himself."[28] Furthermore,

> He should be obedient to all as one who realizes that, in the words of the Lord, he must return to his former infancy and claim nothing for himself out of consideration for his age or on account of his many years, which he reckons as lost because they were foolishly wasted in the world.[29]

First, in speaking of this humble, ideal *hegemon*, Cassian can only be describing himself. Having seen the monasteries of Gaul and clearly judged them deficient in comparison with those of Egypt, Cassian here tacitly sets himself up as the ideal monastic leader. Second, Cassian implicitly differentiates between the monastery, where the *hegemon* can only become a leader by first serving all and being humble, and the institutional church, where one can be promoted to a bishopric simply at the whim of political and social forces. For example, in an article on Origen and the election of bishops, Everett Ferguson writes that bishops generally chose their own successors, based upon whatever criteria seemed valid to them. These successors were then approved or disapproved by priests and other prominent people: "From the fourth century, there comes definite evidence of bishops choosing and ordaining their own successors. Theodoret records that at Alexandria itself

---

26. Cassian, *Conferences*, 14.10.2. Donec continua meditatio inbuat mentem tuam et quasi in similitudinem sui formet, arcam quodammodo ex ea faciens testamenti.

27. Cassian, *Conferences*, 14.10.2.

28. Cassian, *Institutes*, 2.3. Non enim quisquam conuenticulo fratrum, sed ne sibi quidem ipsi praeesse conceditur, priusquam non solum uniuersis facultatibus suis reddatur externus, sed ne sui quidem ipsius esse se dominum uel potestatem habere cognoscat.

29. Cassian, *Institutes*, 2.3. Sic oboedire cunctis, ut redeundum sibi secundum sententiam domini ad infantiam pristinam nouerit, nihil sibi consideratione aeui uel annorum numerositate praesumens, quam in saeculo inaniter consumptam se reputat perdidisse,

5. Cassian's Attempts to Separate Monasticism from the Church 137

Athanasius chose Peter II as his successor."[30] The leader of a monastery, then, as depicted by Cassian, is clearly the superior moral subject.

As important as it is for Cassian to enumerate the correct number of Psalms and prayers for monastic worship, it is equally important that each monk comport himself correctly during worship. He writes, therefore, that during the worship services in Egypt "everyone is so silent that, even though such a large number of brothers has gathered, one would easily believe that no one was present apart from the person who stands to sing the psalm in their midst."[31] One wonders if this silence is the opposite, not only of monastic services Cassian has witnessed in Gaul, but also of services for laypeople presided over by bishops. In the case of monastic worship, the head monk, or even simply the monk whose turn it is to chant the psalms, has greater authority than a bishop in that he commands the silence apposite to worship. As usual, however, both the silence of the monks and their superior authority derive from their asceticism. Cassian writes that the monks keep the worship service purposely brief and perform the majority of it seated as opposed to the lay practice of standing during worship "for they are so worn out from fasting and from working the whole day and night that, if they were standing and were not helped by this kind of rest, they would in fact be unable to get through the number [of prayers] in question."[32] Asceticism's authority derives from the monk emptying himself of all worldly and sinful things, because "unless the vessel of our heart has first been cleansed of every foul-smelling vice it will not deserve to receive the oil of blessing."[33] This reference to the cleansing of the heart is, of course, in accordance with Cassian's all-important and oft-repeated notion of "purity of heart," the only state in which union with God can occur. Since bishops and clergy are not required to practice such rigid asceticism, ridding themselves of impurity, monks who practice correctly are clearly more authoritative and even closer to God.

---

30. Everett Ferguson, "Origen and the Election of Bishops," *Church History: Studies in Christianity and Culture* 43(1): (1974), 27.

31. Cassian, *Institutes*, 2.10.1. Tantum praebetur a cunctis silentium, ut, cum in unum tam numerosa fratrum multitudo conueniat, praeter illum, qui consurgens psalmum decantat in medio, nullus hominum penitus adesse credatur, ac praecipue cum consummatur oratio.

32. Cassian, *Institutes*, 2.12.1. Ita namque ieiuniis et operatione totius diei noctisque lassescunt, ut, nisi huiuscemodi refectione adiuuentur, ne hunc quidem numerum stantes explere praeualeant.

33. Cassian, *Conferences*, 14.14.2. Ita igitur et uas pectoris nostri, nisi prius fuerit ab omni faetidissima uitiorum contagione purgatum, non merebitur suscipere illud benedictionis unguentum.

Finally, Cassian writes that this silent discipline is not merely a function of the group context in which the monks worship. In fact, after worship:

> none of them dares to linger or to chat for a while with anyone else... Once they have gone outside they accomplish [manual labor] in such a way that hardly any conversation is carried on among them, but each one does his assigned task while going over a psalm or some scriptural text by memory.[34]

Manual labor is essential for monastic practice because monks follow the example of Paul, who "although he should rightly have been provided for because he was laboring for the sake of the Gospel, nonetheless... preferred to work day and night in order to earn his daily bread."[35] For Cassian, the fact that the monks individually practice this silent work and prayer is far more indicative of their ascetic authority. By contrast, lay congregations, perhaps less impressed by their less than ascetic bishops than monks by their hegemon, seem often to have viewed the commands of their bishops as mere suggestions often trumped by tradition, secular or at least non-Christian though it may have been. In one of his homilies, for example, Cassian's contemporary, Augustine, quoted one of his parishioners as pleading in reference to taking a concubine "'Surely I can do what I like in my own house?' I tell you, no: you cannot. People who do this go straight to Hell."[36] While the bishop played an important role within lay society, some laymen clearly felt free to choose their own behavior regardless of the bishop's injunction. This, Cassian may be implying, is a function of the clergyman's lack of authority earned through correct practice. The monk, however, had no such split between private and public life. He was to surrender and submit himself completely to the authority of the head monk even when he was entirely alone. The *hegemon* had vastly more authority simply by having proved himself to be a successful practicing ascetic.

Cassian, in describing the attainment of this ascetic authority, thus refers to a verse from the New Testament: "In watching, in fasting, in chastity, in

---

34. Cassian, *Institutes*, 2.15.1. Absoluta nullus eorum uel ad modicum subsistere aut sermocinari audet cum altero... Quod ita explent foras egressi, ut nulla inter eos sermocinatio penitus conseratur: sed sic unusquisque opus exsequitur iniunctum, ut psalmum uel scripturam quamlibet memoriter.

35. Cassian, *Institutes*, 18.11.3. Quod ne apostolus Paulus incideret et quidem cum ei in euangelio laboranti haec praebitio merito deberetur, diebus tamen ac noctibus maluit operari, ut cotidianum uictum uel sibi uel his qui eidem ministrantes opus exercere non poterant suis manibus praepararet.

36. Augustine, *Sermones de Tempore*, in *Patrologia Latina*, vol. 38, edited by J.-P. Migne (Paris: 1865). Translated by R.G. MacMullen. From *Nicene and Post-Nicene Fathers, First Series*, Vol. 6. Edited by Philip Schaff (Buffalo, NY: Christian Literature Publishing Co., 1888), 224.3.

5. Cassian's Attempts to Separate Monasticism from the Church 139

knowledge, in long-suffering, in gentleness, in the Holy Spirit, in unfeigned love (2 Cor 6.5-6)." Cassian interprets this verse as both instruction and description of the order in which ascetic virtues are correctly acquired. He writes that the monk "proceeds from watching and fasting to chastity, from chastity to knowledge, from knowledge to long-suffering, from long-suffering to gentleness, from gentleness to the Holy Spirit, and from the Holy Spirit to the reward of unfeigned love."[37] It is significant that Cassian invokes the authority of scripture to undergird the authority of asceticism. By proceeding through these successive levels of ascetic virtue, one ultimately arrives at love, which is God (1 John 4.8).

Book 4 of the *Institutes* concerns mainly the novice's entrance to the monastery and all the various renunciations involved. Cassian takes special pains to remind his readers that "whoever seeks to be received into the discipline of the cenobium is never admitted until, by lying outside for ten days or more, he has given an indication of his perseverance and desire as well as of his humility and patience."[38] As harsh as this may sound to modern ears, it is only the beginning of the process of being allowed to become a monk. The potential novice must prove, by tireless striving and a conspicuous show of utter humility, not to say abjection, that he is ready to commit to the arduous life of a monk. This is yet another example of Cassian's implicit jabs at the Gallican monks who, remember, joined various clerical and monastic offices principally because renunciation of wealth and status was not required. For Cassian, however, the monk joining a monastery should gain neither honor nor status from his new affiliation. Rather, unlike the newly ordained bishop of a city or village, whose status as such would increase powerfully, the monk should become nobody, losing all public esteem and fortune merely for the sake of following the godly way of life.

Once the monk has withstood the initial period of apparent rejection, he is now asked "if, from his former possessions, the contamination of even a single copper coin clings to him" because if so, it is feared that "when the first disturbance arose for any reason whatsoever, he would be encouraged by the security of that sum and would fell the monastery as fast as a whirring slingstone."[39] In addition to stripping the new monk of all money,

---

37. Cassian, *Conferences*, 14.16.8. Qua coniugatione uirtutum euidentis sime nos uoluit erudire de uigiliis atque ieiuniis ad castitatem, de castitate ad scientiam, de scientia ad longanimitatem, de longanimitate ad suauitatem, de suauitate ad spiritum sanctum, de spiritu sancto ad caritatis non fictae praemia perueniri.

38. Cassian, *Institutes*, 4.3.1. Igitur ambiens quis intra coenobii recipi disciplinam non ante prorsus admittitur, quam diebus decem uel eo amplius pro foribus excubans indicium perseuerantiae ac desiderii sui pariterque humilitatis ac patientiae demonstrauerit.

39. Cassian, *Institutes*, 4.3.2. Ne de pristinis facultatibus suis inhaeserit ei uel unius

Cassian tells us that "all his former possessions are removed from him, such that he is not even permitted to have the clothing that he wore."[40] The significance of depriving the novice of all belongings, including his clothing which will be replaced by a standard monastic robe or habit, is found in discarding the monk's worldly identity. A person's identity does not solely consist of thoughts and beliefs but is also often built upon the foundation of clothing and possessions, signals of one's social status in the ancient world as now. Furthermore, this act is symbolic of the stripping away of all self-reliance, and the resulting total dependence on God for one's needs. Thus, Cassian writes that the new monk,

> knowing that he will be clothed and fed from [the monastery] ... will learn both to possess nothing and never to be worried about the morrow, according to the words of the Gospel, and he will not be ashamed to be on a par with the poor... among whom Christ was not ashamed to be numbered and whose brother he did not blush to call himself.[41]

It is notable here that Cassian first sees monks in solidarity with the poor of the world, although obviously in the case of monks the poverty is voluntary. However, it is significant as well that this voluntary poverty tacitly opposes them to bishops, for whom poverty was not only not required, but who could, in Cassian's time, expect to have a significant amount of money because of their status. To illustrate this, it is important to note the relation between wealth and the bishop as representative of the church in Cassian's time.

Within the Roman Empire of Constantine's time, specifically in 321 CE, a law had been written which was included in the Theodosian Code stating, "at death, people shall have the right to leave property to the Church."[42] While this legal permission for wealthy individuals to bequeath money would

---

nummi contagio... si in conseientia eius pecuniae quantulumeumque latitauerit, sed ubi primum exorta fuerit qualibet occasione commotio, fiducia stipis illius animatum continuo de monasterio uelut funda rotante fugiturum.

40. Cassian, *Institutes*, 4.5. Quamobrom ita nudatur quisque, cum receptus fuerit, omni pristina facultate, ut ne ipsum quidem quo opertus est indumentum habere permittatur ulterius.

41. Cassian, *Institutes*, 4.5. Sed de sanctis ac piis monasterii largitionibus militiae suae stipendia percepturum atque inde se deinceps uestiendum alendumque cognoscens et uihil habere et nihilominus de erastino non esse sollicitus secundum euangelii discat sententiam, nec erubescat pauperibus id est corpori fraternitatis aequari, quibus connumerari Christus quorum se fratrem non erubuit nuncupare, quin potius glorietur domestieis eius faetum se esse consortem.

42. *Codex Theodosianus*, IMPERATORIS THEODOSII CODEX liber decimus sextus, Accessed November 25, 2019. http://ancientrome.ru/ius/library/codex/theod/liber16.htm, 16.2.4. Habeat unusquisque licentiam sanctissimo catholicae venerabilique concilio decedens bonorum quod optavit relinquere.

certainly have been a boon to those churches which had formerly had no legal rights, it left ambiguous the line between church and bishop. To whom did the money from such a legacy belong? Was the bishop merely the steward of the money on behalf of the church, or was he able to use it for his own personal purposes as well? Peter Brown notes that although "Roman law had recognized the existence of corporate bodies... Roman lawyers did little to define how these bodies should act in relation to their wealth."[43] In other words, the difference between the money belonging to the church as a corporate body and belonging to the bishop alone was not legally delineated. Therefore, "faced by the problems raised by ambiguously worded legacies, Roman lawyers instinctively... favored the bishop" as the official devisee of any monetary bequest.[44] As one might imagine, this tended to foster a certain amount of corruption by some bishops. In addition to the aforementioned bishop Theophilus's corrupt financial practices in Sozomen's *EH*, there is another case in 475 CE in which Pope Simplicius ordered that the money from a particular bequest be divided equally among the bishop, the clergy, church building maintenance, and the poor. However, from the Pope's letter, we know that the clergy claimed that one bishop kept three years of this money all to himself.[45] Thus, at the very same time that monks were voluntarily and ceremonially stripped of all clothing and possessions in front of all the other monks, bishops had money flowing into their coffers.[46] Of course, not all bishops were so avariciously inclined. However, the very fact that we have historical documentation of bishops being accused of stealing funds intended to support the church and its aims, shows that such theft was always possible. For the proper cenobitic monk, no money at all ever belonged to him as long as he remained a monk. It is difficult to imagine that in highlighting the importance of monks renouncing all possessions, a thinker as astute as John Cassian would have been unaware of the vast gulf separating these two prominent modes of Christian living. I would thus argue that Cassian is purposely, if subtly, drawing attention to the lack of virtue—specifically the total lack of ascetic virtue—required, let alone practiced, in the day-to-day life of many bishops.

The monastic traditions outlined in Cassian's writings above, are both evidence of his desire for separate spheres of influence for monasticism and

---

43. Peter Brown, *Through the Eye of a Needle: Wealth, the Fall of Rome, and the Making of Christianity in the West, 350–550 AD* (Princeton, NJ: Princeton University Press, 2014), 486.
44. Brown, *Through the Eye of a Needle*, 487.
45. Simplicius, *Letter*, 1.1, ed. A. Thiel, *Epistolae Romanarum Pontificum Genuinae* (Braunsberg: E. Peter, 1867; Hildesheim: G. Olms, 1974), 1:176.
46. Cassian, *Institutes*, 4.5.

the institutional church and an indication of his rhetorical power in shaping the subjectivity of the monks who are ultimately his intended audience. In Foucauldian terms, one can see in this category of evidence that Cassian is exercising pastoral power over the Gallican monks. This is evident when we revisit Foucault's criteria of pastoral power.

First, Cassian clearly establishes himself as the rhetorical leader of the monasteries in Gaul, not because they are Gallican or even Western, but because they are monasteries. In other words, Cassian sets himself up as a leader of monks, regardless of their regional origin or any other factors related to their previous identities. He is a leader of all who wish to properly call themselves monks. Second, he gathers, or even rallies the monks around the theme of Egyptian monasticism as the ideal, or indeed the only form of true monastic practice. As such, he is leading them as his flock to the perfect practices of genuine monks and away from the danger of those practices he sees as jeopardizing their salvation. Third, this leads to the responsibility Cassian takes for the salvation of Gallican monks. He outlines both practice and ascetic theology to assure the monks of the salvation he himself has earned thanks to his tenure as a monk in Egypt. Fourth, while he is wielding power over these monks, there is no privilege involved for him in this role. That is, Cassian, as one who received the blessing of living and learning with the monks of Egypt, makes it clear that he is passing along this information and training as a duty. He says as much in the preface to the *Conferences*: "The obligation, which was promised to the blessed Pope Castor in the preface to those volumes which with God's help I composed in 12 books on the *Institutes of the Coenobia*, and the remedies for the eight principal faults, has now been, as far as my feeble ability permitted, satisfied."[47] As a monk clearly dedicated to asceticism, Cassian is unlikely to take on any sort of honor or benefit from this position. Remember that Cassian wrote that humility was the one real requisite for a monastic leader.

Subtle Denigration of Church Hierarchs or their Theological Heroes

While Cassian's jabs at church hierarchs are certainly indirect, this does not subtract from their power. Indeed, as an educated man, Cassian had likely studied the art of rhetoric, and his subtle digs at bishops, clergy, and their literary supporters are arguably more effective and yet less likely to produce

---

47. John Cassian, *Conferences*, preface 1. Debitum, quod beatissimo papae Castori in eorum uoluminum praefatione promissum est, quae de institutis coenobiorum et de octo principalium uitiorum remediis duodecim libellis domino adiuuante digesta sunt, in quo tenuitas nostri suffecit ingenii, utcumque sarcitum est.

punishment for himself than would a more direct approach. He gives an indication that he came from wealth and was thus well-educated when, in the *Conferences,* he complains to an elder monk, Abba Nesteros, about the difficulties he sometimes has during prayer due to memories from his literary education. He writes that

> a special hindrance to salvation is added by that knowledge of literature which I seem already to have in some slight measure attained, in which the efforts of my tutor, or my attention to continual reading have so weakened me that now my mind is filled with those songs of the poets so that even at the hour of prayer it is thinking about those trifling fables, and the stories of battles with which from its earliest infancy it was stored by its childish lessons.[48]

Most significant here is the fact that Cassian sees the educational background he no doubt shares with most bishops as useless for the purpose of living the proper life of a monk.

In his preface to the *Institutes,* Cassian writes that Castor wants the temple built "out of holy souls that shine in the fullness of innocence, righteousness, and chastity and that bear within themselves the indwelling Christ the king."[49] In addition, he writes that Castor wants "to establish in your own province, which lacks such things, the institutes of the Eastern and especially... Egyptian cenobia."[50] Cassian here implicitly admits his superior knowledge of correct monastic practice. However, he makes an important distinction in this section of the preface between the bishop and the monk. Cassian writes that while Castor himself is "accomplished in every virtue and knowledge," Cassian himself is "rude and wanting in word and knowledge."[51] While this may seem insignificant, it builds on a common theme in both the *AP* and Cassian's own writings: knowledge, based on a rich, academic education, is entirely different and far less spiritually valuable than wisdom, which is only gained through the long and arduous practice

---

48. In Cassian, *Conferences,* 14.12. Quibus non dubito infirmos quosque pulsari extrinsecus, speciale inpedimentum salutis accedit per illam quam tenuiter uideor adtigisse notitiam litterarum, in qua me ita uel instantia paedagogi uel continuae lectionis macerauit intentio, ut nunc mens mea poeticis illis uelut infecta carminibus illas fabularum nugas historiasque bellorum, quibus a paruulo primis studiorum inbuta est rudimentis, orationis etiam tempore meditetur.

49. Cassian, *Conferences,* preface, 2. Sed animabus sanctis, quae innocentiae, iustitiae ot castitatis integritate fulgentos regem Christum in semet ipsis circumferant commorantem.

50. Cassian, *Conferences,* preface, 3. Egenum me omnique ex parte pauperrimum ad communionem tanti operis dignaris accersire. In prouincia siquidem coenobiorum experti Orientalium maximeque Aegyptiorum uolens instituta fundari.

51. Cassian, *Institutes, preface,* III. Cum sis ipse cunctis uirtutibus scientiaque perfectus... me quoque elinguem et pauperem sermone atquo scientia.

of asceticism. This is illustrated in one apothegm in which Abba Arsenius, a former Roman scholar and tutor now living as a monk in the Egyptian desert, tells another educated monk that "we indeed get nothing from our secular education, but these Egyptian peasants acquire the virtues by hard work."[52] Cassian similarly establishes that while clergy and bishops may be more classically educated than some monks—although this is apparently not true in the case of Cassian and at least some of his more educated Egyptian cohort—monks are still superior in wisdom, not through the status of an exalted title as may be the case with clergy, but rather through commitment to ascetic practice. As if to reiterate this point, Cassian goes on to write that Castor is "not looking for a pleasing style, with which you yourself are particularly gifted; rather, you are concerned that the simple life of holy men be explained in simple language to the brothers in your new monastery."[53] Again, contrasting the monk's knowledge with that of an institutional church hierarchy, Cassian notes here that while bishops may be both erudite and eloquent, monks attain their wisdom regardless of their previous level of education. In fact, Cassian writes that all of a monk's knowledge "consists in experience and practice alone", by which he likely indicates the practices of proper asceticism.[54] Cassian also writes that "to such an extent is [the] true and spiritual knowledge removed from that worldly learning, which is stained by the filth of fleshly vice, that we know that it occasionally flourishes in wondrous fashion in some rustic and nearly illiterate persons."[55] Lest the reader forget, Cassian also reminds us that the original apostles were said to be uneducated men.[56] Although Cassian was likely well-educated himself, his point is well-made. In contradistinction to most bishops and clergy, monks need not be similarly educated to achieve holiness; indeed, such an education may interfere with the monk's ability to achieve the necessary humility to truly attain intimacy with God.

Cassian is not unaware of other prominent writers who have addressed the topic of the proper monastic and/or ascetic life. The difference between what those writers espouse and his own writings, according to Cassian

52. *AP*, Arsenius, 5. Ἡμεῖς ἀπὸ τῆς τοῦ κόσμου παιδεύσεως οὐδὲν ἔχομεν· οὗτοι δὲ οἱ ἀγροῖκοι καὶ Αἰγύπτιοι ἀπὸ τῶν ἰδίων πόνων ἐκτήσαντο τὰς ἀρετάς.

53. Cassian, *Institutes*, preface, 3. Ita ut ibi nobis a patribus tradita sunt quamuis inperito digeram stilo non leporem sermonis inquirens, in quo ipse adprime es eruditus, sed sanctorum simplicem uitam simplici sermone fratribus in nouello monasterio tuo cupiens explanari.

54. Cassian, *Institutes*, preface, 4. Totum namque in sola experientia usque consistit.

55. Cassian, *Institutes*, 14.16.6. In tantum vero ab illa eruditione saeculari, quae carnalium vitiorum sorde polluitur, vera haec et spiritalis scientia submouetur, ut eam in nonnulis elinguibus ac paene inlitteratis sciamus nonnumquam admirabiliter viguisse.

56. Cassian, *Institutes*, 14.16.7.

5. Cassian's Attempts to Separate Monasticism from the Church 145

himself, is that those "men of outstanding character, endowed with speech and knowledge" have no actual practical experience of the practices of which they write.[57] In other words those authors "tried to describe what they heard rather than what they experienced."[58] Rather than leave the identities of such men hidden, Cassian writes "I refer to the holy Basil, to Jerome, and to several others."[59] Note that the similarity highlighted by Cassian between Basil, Jerome, and Bishop Castor is that all are learned in the classical sense and eloquent in both speech and writing.

Cassian has already differentiated this type of knowledge, and even this type of person, from himself and the wisdom of the monks of Egypt. At this point, it is almost difficult to tell if Cassian is being sarcastic in these references to Basil and Jerome, implicitly questioning their ascetic bona fides. He reiterates the vast gulf of learning, probably specious, between himself and such men of learning: "Coming after these men's overflowing rivers of eloquence, I would not unjustifiably be considered presumptuous for trying to produce a few drops of water were I not spurred on by my confidence in your holiness."[60] Not in question, however, is the bold boundary Cassian draws between "men of learning" and monks, tacitly asserting that the type of knowledge monks possess and attain through ascetic practice is far more significant that that learned through traditional study.

To be sure, both Basil and Jerome were highly educated men. Ignoring, however, the fact that Cassian, given his knowledge of both Greek and Latin, was probably just as classically educated, his insult of the two well-known Christian authors is a bit difficult to comprehend. Basil, or Basil the Great as he is often called, was born to a wealthy Christian family. After a youth spent studying and then teaching law and rhetoric, Basil met a bishop, Eustathius of Sebaste, who inspired him to abandon these secular activities in favor of a life devoted to God.[61] At this point, after studying monasticism and asceticism by visiting monks in Palestine, Egypt, Syria, and Mesopotamia, Basil settled into an ascetic life of solitude near the city of Pontus,

---

57. Cassian, *Institutes,* preface, 5. Huc accedit, quod super hac re uiri et uita nobiles et sermone scientiaque praeclari multa iam opuscula desudarunt.

58. Cassian, *Institutes*, preface 7. utpote qui audita potius quam experta describere temptauerunt.

59. Cassian, *Institutes*, preface, 5. Sanctum Basilium ct Hieronymum dico aliosque nonnullos.

60. Cassian, *Institutes*, preface, VII. Post quorum tam exuberantia eloquentiae flumina, possem non immerito praesumptionis notari, si aliquid stillicidii hujus inferre tentassem; nisi me ad haec fiducia tuae sanctitatis.

61. Stephen Hildebrand, *Basil of Caesarea*: *Foundations of Theological Exegesis and Christian Spirituality* (Grand Rapids, MI: Baker Academic, 2014), 19–20.

a sojourn which proved short-lived.[62] However, based upon those studies and his own ascetic life in Pontus, Basil wrote a set of writings now known merely as *The Ascetic Writings*, meant to encourage and order the ascetic life for those interested.[63]

Afterward, Basil started a monastic community on his family's estate at Annesi and wrote on the communal life. These writings would eventually help to form much of the basis of Eastern monastic thought.[64] We have no knowledge of interactions between Cassian and Basil. Therefore, one can only imagine that Cassian had read both Basil's ascetic and monastic writings and had either found them insufficient compared to his own ideas, or conversely, had found them excellent which had inspired him to jealousy. The case is similar with Jerome.

Jerome converted to Christianity while a student in Rome. Soon after, he left for the Syrian desert to take up the ascetic life.[65] Jerome wrote an enormous corpus of letters, commentaries, translations, and other polemical writings. On the one hand, he was a contentious personality and, as Andrew Cain puts it, "his penchant for polemic did little to win him new supporters in his own day and strained the friendships he already had."[66] On the other hand, it is undeniable that Jerome was committed to the ascetic life; in fact he was a vehement champion of a severe asceticism which even his long-suffering friends found off-putting.[67] This tendency toward extremism in the ascetic life, along with his fervent and frequent polemics, may have rubbed Cassian the wrong way, resulting in his dismissal of Jerome as an authority on asceticism.

None of this information about Basil and Jerome means that Cassian's attack on their authority regarding asceticism and experience is warranted. Both practiced asceticism rigorously and wrote of it to others. Given this, it is fair to assume that this may simply be a rhetorical strategy with Cassian intended to bolster his own authority as a monastic and an ascetic. Regardless, this emphasis on knowledge through experience comes into play when Cassian addresses these and other writers who have also attempted to offer

62. Anthony Meredith, *The Cappadocians* (Eugene, OR: Wipf & Stock, 2009), 21.
63. Philip Rousseau & American Council of Learned Societies, *Basil of Caesarea* (Berkeley, CA: University of California Press, 1998), 190–232.
64. Donald Attwater and Catherine Rachel John, *The Penguin Dictionary of Saints*, 3rd edn (New York, NY: Penguin Books, 1993), 203.
65. Robert Payne, *The Fathers of the Western Church* (New York, NY: Viking, 1951), 91.
66. Andrew Cain, *The Letters of Jerome: Asceticism, Biblical Exegesis, and the Construction of Christian Authority in Late Antiquity* (Oxford: Oxford University Press, 2009), 1.
67. Cain, *The Letters of Jerome*, 2.

5. Cassian's Attempts to Separate Monasticism from the Church 147

advice to monastics but, apparently, without Cassian's vast experience (or at least without the correct experience). Having drawn this line as clearly, if politely, as he can, Cassian pledges to write of "things that have been left utterly untouched by our predecessors."[68]

In addition, Cassian notes that while many of these predecessors have written of amazing miracles performed by eminent monks, he will not do so, "although we have not only heard of many of these and other incredible doings from our elders but have even seem them produced before our very eyes."[69] Not only has Cassian met and practiced assiduously with these honored monastic heroes, but he claims he has also seen their reputed signs and wonders for himself. He establishes himself here as not only a follower of such monks but a very member of their fraternity, one who has the authority to teach proper practice because he has lived it himself, unlike Jerome, Basil, and other authors he names who he claims have written from mere hearsay. Having acknowledged his own firsthand experience with the Desert Fathers of Egypt, Cassian writes that he will not include any of these miraculous tales because his particular purpose in the *Institutes* is "the improvement of our behavior and the attainment of the perfect life, in keeping with what we have learned from our elders."[70] In other words, miraculous deeds and their accompanying fame and power are insignificant and immaterial to the goal of achieving spiritual perfection.

As a final analysis of this category of evidence, I find Foucault's notion of disciplinary power to be a useful tool. As a reminder, Foucault defines disciplinary power as being exercised through surveillance and the creation of new forms of knowledge. How do these criteria manifest in Cassian's subtle insults to clergy and their theological heroes? Furthermore, what does reading Cassian through a Foucauldian lens reveal about Cassian's underlying rhetorical purpose?

First, in addition to the more obvious surveillance enacted upon monks by requiring them to reveal their innermost thoughts and impulses to their superior, I argue that the establishment of ideals and, as in this category of evidence, anti-ideals, functions as a kind of surveillance. In the case of monastic ideals established in the first category, the ideal itself serves to

---

68. Cassian, *Institutes*, preface, 7. ...et ea quae omnimodis intacta relicta sunt ab anterioribus nostris...

69. Cassian, *Institutes*, preface, 7. ...signorumque narrationem studebo contexere: quae quamuis multa per seniores nostros et incredibilia non solum audierimus, uerum etiam sub obtutibus nostris perspexerimus impleta.

70. Cassian, *Institutes*, preface, 8. Propositum siquidem mihi est, non de mirabilibus Dei, sed de correctione morum nostrorum et consummatione vitae perfectae, secundum ea quae a senioribus nostris accepimus, pauca disserere.

give the monks constant feedback on their own monastic practice: Are they living up to the ideals of their forbears? In a similar way, the examples given of how bishops, clergy, and non-monastic theologians fail to practice correctly, the monks are implicitly made to compare themselves with such anti-heroes: are they behaving like a bishop, comporting themselves with pomp and circumstance? Are they flaunting their learning to increase their status among their fellow monks? If so, they know from Cassian's writings the correct way to behave as a true monk. Second, having established the behavior of ideal monks (and their putative progenitors, the prophets and apostles), Cassian establishes a second category of knowledge: the less-than-ideal behavior of bishops, clergy, and their theological heroes. These two forms of knowledge function as correctives to monastic behavior. Monks must steer clear of the behavior of the latter category while doing their best to emulate the former.

Although Cassian never refers explicitly to his own involvement in the Origenist Controversy beyond mentioning one monk's sad lament about Theophilus's original decree that anthropomorphizing God is inappropriate, his doctrinal statements give him away. Remember that the theological heart of the conflict centers around this point: after changing his mind—thanks to an angry mob of monks, apparently—Theophilus goes on to declare that anthropomorphizing God is the official position, at least of the Alexandrian church. This suddenly takes the position of the Tall Brothers, an Origenist position in which God cannot be embodied since it would limit God, and makes it anathema. As mentioned earlier in this book, Cassian was known to be among this group including the Tall Brothers and Evagrius Ponticus, another eminent Origenist monk. However, since Cassian is not openly mentioned as a member of the group in the fifth-century histories of the conflict, we cannot definitively pin him down to that location and time. Nevertheless, some references in the *Institutes* make clear that he must have been on the Origenist side.

In his discussion on anger, Cassian, beginning with an assertion that any scriptural reference to God's wrath must be figural rather than literal, goes on to say the same thing of any references to God as having body parts:

> I pass over ignorance and forgetfulness, which we read are frequently attributed to him in Holy Scripture, and also bodily parts, which are described in terms of human shape and arrangement—namely, hair, head and nose, eyes and face, hands and arm, fingers, belly, and feet. If we wished to take all of this in a crude literal way, it would be necessary to think of God as formed of bodily parts and a bodily shape. But far be it from us to say such a wicked thing.[71]

---

71. Cassian, *Institutes*, 8.3. ut praeteream ignorationem et obliuionem, quae de ipso

5. Cassian's Attempts to Separate Monasticism from the Church   149

This doctrinal statement surely addresses Theophilus's revised decree concerning anthropomorphism which would ultimately result in Origenist monks like Cassian being expelled from the Egyptian desert. Note that this is from a chapter called "How our Fourth Conflict is Against the Spirit of Anger, and How Many Evils this Passion Produces," (*Quod quartum certamen aduersus irae sit uitium, et quanta mala generet haec perturbation*), a topic having nothing explicitly to do with scriptural interpretation as such. Yet, while asserting that God is not limited to a body of any kind and that any such scriptural references are merely allegorical, Cassian goes on to write of the dangers of anger. It seems plausible that his principal referent concerning anger is Theophilus, who is said in the works of church historians Sozomen and Socrates to have frequently acted cruelly toward monks in utter fury. He writes, for example that "we shall be able neither to be untouched by harmful disturbances nor to be free of sin, even though no one ever causes us annoyance, because 'the passionate man begets quarrels, and the wrathful man digs up sins (Prov. 14.17 LXX).'"[72] In a chapter in which Cassian reflects upon the bodiless nature of God, it seems unlikely that this reference to creating conflict and "digging up sins" would be a mere coincidence. Theophilus clearly did both through his decree and its violent enforcement. A further and even more obvious reference is made later in the same chapter: "But what is to be said of those persons (and this I am unable to mention without shame) on whose implacability even sundown itself places no limits and who draw it out for days on end? They maintain a rancorous spirit against those with whom they are upset and, although they deny orally that they are angry, they manifest the deepest anger by their actions."[73] While ostensibly this anger refers to that of monks trying

---

legimus in scripturis sanctis frequenter inserta, deinde liniamenta membrorum, quae tamquam de homine figurali et conposito describuntur, capillis scilicet, capite et naribus, oculis ac facie, manibus et brachio, digitis, utero pedibusque. Quae omnia secundum uilem litterae sonum si uoluerimus admittere, Deum liniamentis membrorum et corporea figura conpositum, quod dictu quoque nefas est quodque absit a nobis, necesse est aestimari.

72. Cassian, *Institutes*, 8.1. [N]ec poterimus carere peccatis, tametsi nequaquam nobis inquietudines ab aliis inferantur, quia uir animosus parit rixas, uir autem iracundus effodit peccata.

73. Cassian, *Institutes*, 8.11. Quid uero dicendum de his - quod quidem dicere sine mea confusione non possum -, quorum inplacabilitati ne hic quidem sol occidens terminum ponit, sed per dies eam plurimos protelantes atque aduersus eos, in quos commoti fuerint, rancorem animi reseruantes negant quidem se uerbis irasci, sed re ipsa et opere indignari grauissime conprobantur? Nam neque eos congruo sermone conpellant nec affabilitate eis solita conloquuntur, et in eo se minime delinquere putant, quod uindictam suae commotionis non expectant.

to perfect themselves, it is instructive that the limitless acrimony Cassian writes of could easily describe Theophilus throughout the Origenist controversy. As mentioned earlier, Theophilus's conduct toward Isidore and the Tall Brothers—and possibly Cassian himself—is said to be motivated by both his political ambitions and anger, presumably at being opposed theologically by popular monks. While Theophilus's changing of his theological decree to one of anthropomorphism shows a cunning, calculating temperament, his violent expulsion of the monks, to the point that their very lives are threatened, shows him acting out of anger. Indeed, Cassian writes that when one hangs onto rage, one is "blinded by its darkness and are unable to let in the light of salutary counsel and knowledge or to be temples of the Holy Spirit, since an evil spirit dwells within us."[74] Cassian here goes so far as to call the kind of raging, violent action that Theophilus performed akin to demonic possession. It would be difficult to imagine a harsher criticism in late antique Christian discourse. Cassian makes one further reference that may be calculated to refer to Theophilus's spiteful deeds when he says, "There are those who fully satisfy their rage and annoyance only if they go as far as they can at the instigation of anger."[75] This is an apt description of Theophilus's actions, to say the least. While this may be a condemnation of Theophilus himself, it is surely also an indictment of the dangers of allowing a bishop to have power over the theology and practice of monks.

The Eucharist: A Case Study for a Closed Monastic System

One possible sticking point in my argument that Cassian is advocating for a separation between monasticism and the institutional church is the celebration of the Eucharist. Since, it might be argued, only the ordained can confect eucharist, how could a monastic system get along without the ordained? First, as mentioned above, I am not arguing that Cassian is claiming that the clergy are obsolete. Rather, I contend that he viewed the monastic calling as a separate sphere which therefore should not be subjected to the authority, theological or otherwise, of bishops or clergy. Second, there is ample evidence that, in the fourth and fifth centuries, clergy were not yet seen as entirely necessary for the celebration of the eucharist. In other

---

74. Cassian, *Institutes*, 8.12. ne tenebris illius obscurati nec consilii salubris nec scientiae lumen admittere, sed nec templum Spiritus sancti, habitante in nobis spiritu nequam, ualeamus exsistere.

75. Cassian, *Institutes*, 8.12. Quasi uero non hic finis unicuique uindictae sit et abunde quis furori proprio uel tristitiae satisfecerit, si id, quod praeualet, ira instigante conpleuerit.

5. Cassian's Attempts to Separate Monasticism from the Church

words, monks (and even laypeople) could serve both themselves and others communion if necessary.

One piece of evidence here is written by the abovementioned Basil of Caesarea (303–379 CE), bishop of Caesarea Mazaca in Cappadocia, Asia Minor. In an epistle to a nobleman, Basil writes

> it is needless to point out that for anyone in times of persecution to be compelled to take the communion in his own hand without the presence of a priest or minister is not a serious offense, as long custom sanctions this practice from the facts themselves. All the solitaries in the desert, where there is no priest, take the communion themselves, keeping communion at home.[76]

This practice of giving oneself communion, then, was sanctioned by no less than a bishop and prominent theologian. It is thus safe to assume that receiving the Eucharist from the hands of a fellow monk, ordained or not, would be equally permitted.

Next, Cassian seems to contradict himself in that he speaks both of daily communion[77] and weekly communion[78] as customs among the monks of Egypt. However, despite this seeming discrepancy, Adalbert de Vogüé points out that these two explanations need not conflict: the daily communion refers to private communion, whether self-administered or given by another monk, while weekly communion is that given by an ordained minister on Saturday or Sunday.[79] Given that both alternatives were allowed as valid at the time of Cassian's writing, it is clear that the monks could serve themselves communion. That is, the distribution of the eucharist was a function that monks could take on themselves rather than relying on an ordained minister.

Conclusion

This chapter examined three types of evidence that John Cassian indeed idealized separation between monasticism and church hierarchy. As with

---

76. Basil of Caesarea, *Epistolae*, in *Patrologia Graeca*, vol. 32, edited by J.-P. Migne (Paris: 1857). Translated by Blomfield Jackson, from *Nicene and Post-Nicene Fathers, Second Series, Vol. 8*. Edited by Philip Schaff and Henry Wace (Buffalo, NY: Christian Literature Publishing Co., 1895), *Ep.* 93. Τὸ δὲ ἐν τοῖς τοῦ διωγμοῦ καιροῖς ἀναγκά ζεσθαί τινα, μὴ παρόντος ἱερέως ἢ λειτουργοῦ, τὴν κοινωνίαν λαμβάνειν τῇ ἰδίᾳ χειρὶ μηδαμῶς εἶναι βαρὺ περιττόν ἐστιν ἀποδεικνύναι, διὰ τὸ καὶ τὴν μακρὰν συνήθειαν τοῦτο δι' αὐτῶν τῶν πραγμάτων πιστώσασθαι. Πάντες γὰρ οἱ κατὰ τὰς ἐρήμους μονάζοντες, ἔνθα μή ἐστιν ἱερεύς, κοινωνίαν οἴκοι κατέχοντες ἀφ' ἑαυτῶν μετα λαμβάνουσιν.

77. Cassian, *Institutes*, 6.8; *Conferences*, 9.21 and 14.8.

78. Cassian, *Institutes*, 3.2 (Saturday and Sunday) and 11 (Sunday), both in cenobitic surroundings; *Conferences*, 18.15 (Saturday and Sunday) and 23.21 (Sunday).

79. Adalbert De Vogüé, "Eucharist and Monastic Life." *Worship* 59.6 (1985): 498–509.

earlier examples in this book, much of Cassian's rhetoric refers to the notion of monasticism as a continuation of apostolic praxis. This is differentiated from the notion of apostolic succession upon which the hierarchy of the institutional church was based. While apostolic succession passed on dogma, title, and authority to each succeeding bishop, apostolic praxis, as established in Cassian's rhetoric, passed on the way to live Christianity, to practice the daily rituals and procedures that gradually transformed a human being into one who could truly unite with God.

First, Cassian presents a number of what he deems monastic exemplars, to draw clear lines between these earlier revered characters and the contemporary monks he so admires. These include biblical figures from the Hebrew Bible, specifically iconic prophets such as Elijah and Elisha, and New Testament figures such as the original apostles and John the Baptist. However, he makes no claim for an abstract authority passed down from these figures to unnamed or elected monks. Rather, he notes the similarities in the way of life between the biblical figures and his exemplary monks of Egypt: their dress, reflecting poverty and humility, their unceasing prayer, including both canonical collective prayers and individual meditation on scripture, and their vigils, connecting back to biblical narratives. Perhaps more significantly, Cassian begins the *Institutes* by identifying himself, and thus, in a sense, all monks, with Hiram, the foreign agent through whom Solomon can build his temple. This example alone demonstrates Cassian's emphasis of the passing down of practical knowledge over that of abstract belief or dogma.

Next, Cassian makes appeals to distinct monastic traditions, differentiating them sharply from the traditions of bishops and clergy. He first denotes the canonical number and character of prayers and Psalms chanted by Egyptian monks together, then notes that the Gallican monks do not follow this standard. This is significant for Cassian because the rule of prayers, according to him, was established long ago by earlier, venerable monks in Egypt. For this reason, there is only one correct canon of prayer for all true monks, leaving the Gallican monks the choice of either following Cassian's dictates or being incorrect, and thus excluded from the true monastic fraternity. In addition, Cassian tells monks to meditate constantly on scripture, to allow their minds and souls to be formed into the "ark of the covenant," worthy of unity with God. This reinforces not only the monk's closeness to scripture, but also his intimacy with the deity. Finally, Cassian notes that the only way for a monk to become the hegemon or leader of a group of monks is to show total humility. This is in stark contrast to the way bishops were chosen in his time, dependent as it was on political maneuvering and intimacy with the previous bishop who would then appoint his own successor.

5. Cassian's Attempts to Separate Monasticism from the Church 153

While becoming a bishop would only add status and wealth to a person, becoming a hegemon was the result of emptying oneself, making oneself lower than everyone, the servant of all.

Finally, Cassian disparages the office of church hierarch and those writers whose theology often informs and supports it. He does this by distinguishing between the knowledge of a classical education which most hierarchs and their theological heroes had, and the wisdom gained, despite such an education or its lack, through the proper practice of asceticism. In Cassian's writings, this ascetic wisdom is far superior to any sort of academic learning, which may even be a hindrance to those trying to attain wisdom. He also subtly disdains theological writers like Basil and Jerome for their eloquence, a characteristic that in his view shows their lack of wisdom and correct practice. This extends to the basis for their writing: mere mental reflection and observation, rather than true, direct experience. Cassian writes that Jerome and Basil write of asceticism and monastic living though both lack the proper experience to speak of these with any authority, unlike Cassian himself.

What all three of these types of evidence have in common is that they are based not upon dogma or orthodoxy, but rather orthopraxy, correct practice. Cassian seems willing to recognize the orthodoxy of the institutional church, or at least never denigrates it, while correct practice is far more significant for him. For this reason, the notion of a bishop ruling over or even getting involved in the affairs of monastics is anathema to him. Monks are ideally their own closed system, based upon correct practices that Cassian traces back to the Hebrew Bible and the original church just as surely as the authority of bishops can be traced to the authority of Peter conferred by Christ. Cassian is ready to allow that episcopal authority to stand, if the bishops do the same for the practices of monastics. It makes little difference that even in his beloved Egypt, different communities of monks in different regions practiced differently. Cassian has built the image of a monolithic monasticism in Egypt which must be evangelized throughout the known world. For this to happen, monks must be properly trained by experienced monks like himself and, more importantly, must be left to their practices by the institutional church.

Finally, what is also significant in Cassian's rhetoric is his establishment of monasticism as a closed discursive system. Cassian refers, of course, to pre-monastic figures from the Hebrew Bible and the New Testament but only while portraying such figures as a kind of proto-monks, the spiritual ancestors of the type of monastic practice that he encourages in his monastic readers in Gaul. All the rest of the stories and sayings in both the *Institutes* and the *Conferences* are drawn from other ascetic monks, rather than any sort of established theologians tied to the institutional church. The few such theological figures he does mention, such as Basil and Jerome, are denigrated as writing about topics—chiefly asceticism—about which they know very little through lack of experience. While this seems disingenuous, given both Basil's and Jerome's extensive histories of asceticism and monasticism, the tacit point Cassian makes is that those monks who practice correctly—the way that he and his teachers did—have no further need of outside input from other church figures, whether practical or theological. Only those who practice correctly, according to Cassian's rule, should participate in the authoritative monastic discourse around which he builds implicit walls to exclude non-ascetic bishops and other clergy. Taken to its logical conclusion, this would ultimately mean that monasticism would develop not as a contributing part of the contemporary institutional church, but rather as a parallel track traveling autonomously.

As I mentioned before, there is no evidence in Cassian's writings that he is attempting to tear down the institutional church. He is instead attempting to separate his own beloved sphere from the institutional one such that monastics have authority over monasticism rather than non-ascetic bishops who may not understand or appreciate apostolic praxis and its implications. For this reason, all references to monks' practices and wisdom in Cassian's oeuvre are bricks in the bulwark he is implicitly building against further encroachment upon monastic territory by uncomprehending bishops and clergy.

Chapter Six

Conclusion

> If it be a season when there are two meals, then as soon as they have risen from supper they shall all sit together, and one of them shall read the *Conferences* or the *Lives of the Fathers* or something else that may edify the hearers... If it be a day of fast, then having allowed a short interval after Vespers they shall proceed at once to the reading of the *Conferences*, as prescribed above
> – Benedict of Nursia, *Rule for Monasteries*

It is a virtually unassailable truth that the monastic *Rule* written by Benedict of Nursia in the sixth century CE is the most influential document in the history of Western monasticism. Because of this rule, Benedict is considered the father of Western monasticism.[1] It is equally true, however, that this document could not have existed in its final form without the writings of John Cassian. As we see in the quotation above, Cassian's *Conferences* was recommended reading after dinner in the monastery, along with the *Vitae* of the Desert Fathers. More significant, however, is how much of Benedict's ideas for monastic living were based on the writings of Cassian. Chapter eight of the *Regula Benedicti*, for example, which was an enormous influence on both Bernard of Clairvaux and Thomas Aquinas, speaks about the 12 levels of humility and the image of Jacob's ladder to salvation. This material was taken directly from Cassian's *Institutes*, 4.39. Much more of Cassian's material, especially his writings on prayer, is included in Benedict's rule. Seeing the influence Cassian had upon Benedict and that Benedict then had upon the world of Western monasticism, the notion that Cassian's influence might have had the power to change the relation between monasticism and the institutional church is not farfetched. In fact, it is not only through Benedict that Cassian's writings influenced later generations of Christian thinkers.

For example, Dominic of Osma (1170–1221 CE), founder of the famed Dominican order, read Cassian's *Conferences* frequently and used them as

---

1. Kevin R. Seasoltz, "Benedict of Nursia." *Encyclopedia of Religion*, edited by Lindsay Jones, 2nd ed., vol. 2, Macmillan Reference USA, 2005, pp. 822–24. *Gale eBooks*, link.gale.com/apps/doc/CX3424500330/GVRL?u=udenver&sid=GVRL&xid=d8637322. Last accessed 22 March 2021.

both the moral and practical basis of his own order's rule. [2] Philip Neri (1515–95 CE), an immensely popular Italian priest and saint, who founded an organization of secular clergy called the Congregation of the Oratory, often read Cassian's writings to the laity and based many of his popular sermons on those writings.[3] In the modern era, Cardinal Newman (1801–1890 CE) quoted liberally from Cassian in his influential book *Apologia Pro Vita Sua*.[4] I point out just a few of the prominent Christian thinkers influenced by Cassian's writings to suggest that Cassian's desire to separate the monastic sphere from that of the institutional church was not merely the pipe dream of one relatively powerless individual. Had this idea been adopted as wholeheartedly as Cassian's moral and liturgical ideas were by so many, there is no telling how vast and impactful the historical result might have been.

However, my analysis of Cassian's writings acknowledges the subtlety of his advocacy for monastic separation which may leave many wondering what greater impact or import this study might have. Cassian was no violent revolutionary, no ecclesial Che Guevara trying to effect a coup within the church. I argue simply that he was shrewdly trying to fashion the subjectivity of the monks of Gaul who made up his intended audience. He wanted to give those monks a shape, familiar to him from his cherished time as a monk in the deserts of Egypt, into which they could pour themselves and thus embody the true, ascetic ideal he himself had learned and come to champion. To do this completely, he wanted to ensure as much as possible, without incurring the wrath of bishops, that monks were allowed to operate their own systems of p1ractice without meddling from the institutional church. I would argue that this subtlety was more practical than self-preserving. Had Cassian stridently and explicitly argued against allowing the authority of the institutional church to reign over monastics, his writings would surely have been suppressed or at least anathematized, causing his argument to fall short of its goal.

Is this study merely a mildly interesting examination of an arcane writer about whose life we know very little? Are there, within my argument, any implications for further avenues of study? I believe there are, and, after a brief recap and synthesis of my principal argument, I discuss these below.

---

2. Rev. Alban Butler, *The Lives of the Fathers, Martyrs, and Other Principal Saints* (Dublin: James Duffy, 1866; Bartleby.com, 2010).

3. Br. Constantius Sanders, "The (Almost) Forgotten Saint," *Dominicana*, February 5, 2021. https://www.dominicanajournal.org/.

4. John Henry Newman and Maisie Ward, *Apologia pro Vita Sua* (London: Sheed & Ward, 1978), 98.

Synthesis

This book discussed the context in which John Cassian wrote both of his best-known works, *The Institutes* and *The Conferences*. The milieu in which these were written was vastly different from the Egyptian context in which his ideas on monasticism were first formed. This would prove to be an obstacle for the elder Cassian in trying to institute the type of reforms that would, in his mind, make the Gallican monasteries to which he was writing true examples of correct practice.

In his Egyptian monastic life, Cassian learned what was to be the bedrock of correct monastic practice for him: asceticism. A true monk was one who renounced all social and family ties, all personal possessions, and even the very identity these ties had ultimately helped to form. That is, a monk was one who lived only for God and thus abandoned every connection or identification with earthly life. It was this concept of renunciation which would undergird every idea, theological and otherwise, that Cassian wrote. Even laypeople and clergy who practiced such asceticism, people like John Chrysostom and several of the bishops and priests written about in the *AP*, were worthy examples. Those who did not practice such committed asceticism—the monks of Gaul, for example—were not worthy of being called monks.

Fifth-century Gaul, where Cassian ended his journey and wrote his seminal writings, had long been something of a political minefield within the Roman Empire. Local Germanic kings had rebelled against the Romans and even achieved a measure of autonomy for a brief period. Even in the centuries leading up to this successful revolt, Roman writers had often written of the Gallican tendency to support usurpers. It was a province that valued its independence highly. However, the culmination of this uprising left the Gallican elite in a bind: to whom should they give their loyalty in oreder to maintain their privileged status? Oddly, for modern sensibilities, it turned out that one way to maintain wealth and status was to enter an ecclesiastical career.

Several well-known Gallican hagiographies aimed at showing the compatibility of monastic/ecclesiastical careers and prodigious wealth and status. In his hagiography of Martin of Tours, Sulpicius Severus wrote that the heavenly world was simply a continuation of the earthly distribution of wealth and status. In both worlds, the wealthy Christian convert continued to live and interact with his social equals. For those monks and clerics who could boast of elite origins, their status was maintained here and in the world to come. Renunciation of wealth, property, and status was therefore completely unnecessary since one's social standing could only improve when one became a monk. Although the *Life of Antony* and other such Egyptian hagiographies were highly popular all over the Roman Empire, the idea of such total renunciation had clearly not been entirely accepted in ecclesiastical circles in Gaul. In fact, the notion of maintaining status and wealth through a religious vocation brought the monks of Gaul into sharp contrast with the Egyptian notions of asceticism and total renunciation as the mark of authority which Cassian espoused.

In Cassian's writing, as well as other early monastic literature from Egypt and Palestine, renunciation was the very foundation of holiness and influence. Cassian made this argument primarily by tying asceticism to the primitive church as depicted in the book of Acts. If indeed Egyptian monks' ascetic practice was merely following the example of the apostles in the Bible (cf., Acts 4.32), then ascetic monastics, as defined by Cassian's Egyptian ideal, had a special claim to a level of authority normally due only to the institutional church and its representatives in the bishopric. Given this, Cassian could only have taken a dim view of the way wealth and status were maintained by the so-called monks he encountered in Gaul.

Essential to my analysis of Cassian's thought and purpose is a discussion of the formation of subjects driven by the thought of Michel Foucault. One consistent and overarching notion Foucault employed is governmentality, the conduct of conduct. For Foucault, governmentality consists of the myriad ways in which individuals are controlled, specifically by manipulating those individuals into controlling themselves. In fact, Foucault wrote that his entire oeuvre consisted of investigations into the way human subjects are thus formed.

Subjects, for Foucault, are not self-directed agents, but rather socially constructed individuals, matrixes of different forms of power. Foucault's interest then was in the techniques by which such subjects were formed. He wrote that this formation was not simply an authoritarian exercise on the part of those in whom power is explicitly concentrated, but rather an intersection between such techniques of power and techniques of self-formation. Accordingly, he identified three methods by which subjects were formed.

First, certain types of analyses create subjects as objects of knowledge. In this monograph, I have argued that Cassian's establishment of the Egyptian monks as the norm by which every other monk is measured in turn creates the Gallican monks who are his intended audience as objects of knowledge. That is, Cassian can use the standards he codifies from the monks of Egypt to measure the spiritual and practical progress (or lack of progress) of the monks to whom he writes. As we see often in Cassian's monastic writings, specific descriptions of Egyptian monastic behavior are then compared with the same (usually deficient) behavior by Gallican monks. This creates the monks of Gaul as subjects in two simple categories. True monks are those who conform completely with those standards, while all others are portrayed as mere pretenders who fail to meet the standards required. Cassian, of course, establishes himself as the arbiter of these subjective categories, the authority who, based on his experience in Egypt, decides both the behaviors necessary for true monks and whether Gallican monks are adequately meeting those standards.

Second, practices and procedures divide subjects both from within, and from other subjects according to standards of norm and deviance. Cassian places all these behavioral standards in the mouths of well-known Egyptian monks, a rhetorical strategy which lends his views more weight. The ideas are portrayed as not merely originating with Cassian's, but rather part of the longstanding traditions of holiness established by the most accomplished and well-known desert ascetics. The Gallican monks are thus given the choice to form themselves as subjects according to these venerable standards or to be excluded from this superior realm. In this sense they are also divided internally: monks must work on themselves, as if one wise, partial self were working on the other, unwise self, in order to achieve an acceptable level of correct practice. At the same time, they are divided from society in that the more correct their practice, the less they resemble laypeople and most bishops/clergy (note the difference here between Gallican monks who remain closely attached to society despite choosing ecclesial careers). True monks undertake very specific types of behavior and Cassian establishes that based upon this standard, one either is or is not a monk—there is no middle ground.

Third, practices and procedures of self-management are introduced, by which subjects transform themselves to meet an externally imposed ideal. Again, the superlative model imposed by Cassian includes meticulous regulation of behaviors and even thoughts by which subjects must regulate themselves. In other words, Cassian provides the template for becoming a correct monk, while setting up the monks as self-regulators, such that his direct supervision ultimately becomes superfluous.

In Foucault's writings, there are also four principal modalities of power. Two of these, disciplinary power and pastoral power, are most appropriate for analyzing the interplay of Cassian's rhetoric.

Disciplinary power is enacted chiefly through surveillance and the creation of certain types of knowledge. By surveillance, however, Foucault does not necessarily mean that subjects must be meticulously watched at all times; rather, subjects must believe they are watched. Foucault's analysis of Bentham's panopticon illustrates this. The panopticon is a type of prison architecture with a surveillance tower in the center surrounded by cells. The guard can certainly see all prisoners from the tower; however, if the windows of the tower are opaque or otherwise obscured, the prisoners, believing they might be watched at all times, will police themselves.

In terms of the gathering and creation of forms of knowledge, subjects are themselves studied as objects of knowledge. This knowledge is then used to form benchmarks of behavior by which subjects can measure themselves as either normal or deviant. The risk of deviance, then, is the risk of exclusion from the majority, and thus the majority are effectively controlled.

In this book, I have argued that Cassian's rhetoric is appropriately, if partially, explained and analyzed by the notion of disciplinary power. Cassian repeatedly emphasizes the behavioral standards of a true monk, including and especially those of total obedience and total mental transparency to one's superiors. By outlining these standards against which a monk may measure himself, he ensures both that the monk will regulate himself—the standards themselves acting as a kind of supervisory agent—and that any secret thoughts will be revealed to the monastic leader, such that everything about the monk will be known and thus ordered. That is, Cassian creates the monastic subject as self-regulating and self-revealing, such that only a certain type of self-created subject will be allowed the honor of being called a monk.

The other type of power evident in Cassian's rhetoric is pastoral power. Pastoral power is noted by Foucault as coming principally out of the Judeo-Christian tradition. He notes that it differs from the ancient Greek political thought contemporary with the rise of Christianity in four ways. First, the shepherd's power relates to a group of people, rather than a land. Wherever those people dwell, the shepherd's power follows them without borders. Second, because of this relationship to a people, the shepherd gathers his people together and helps them to adhere as a people. This includes guiding their behavior and helping them find necessary resources. Third, the shepherd's duty is to effect the salvation of his people. In the most basic sense, this means saving them from danger and/or lack of resources. This also involves paying attention to and monitoring the needs of both individuals and the collective. Fourth, unlike for a king or other autocrat, power for a shepherd is a duty rather than a privilege. He is responsible for the well-being of the whole group as well as that of each individual.

All four of these characteristics apply equally well to Cassian's rhetoric. First, the superior monk, played expertly by Cassian in the sense that his monastic writings are meant to instruct from a place of experiential authority, is responsible for monks, wherever they are. Cassian is responsible for the instruction of monks but also for being an example for them. Second, Cassian, through his writings, gathers and attempts to lead the Gallican monks. He describes and emphasizes the correct modes of practice while reinforcing their monastic identities. Third, Cassian works for the salvation of those monks who are his charges. He does this first by emphasizing the necessity for total obedience to their elders (himself included, presumably). However, for monastic leaders this also meant always being ready to listen to individual monks' confessions. This transparency effected the kenosis or self-emptying which would assure the monks' salvation. Finally, Cassian emphasized that exercising power as a superior monk was an obligation rather than a privilege. For this reason, Cassian noted that if one is to lead a community of monks, one must first prove one's total humility through obedience to others. Having proven this, as Cassian himself did by obeying his Egyptian fathers, the superior monk becomes at last worthy of leading others.

Having established Foucault's thought as a good lens through which to read Cassian's rhetoric, this book appeals to the ample evidence that there were very real conflicts between early monastics and the institutional church. This was not an innovation or a mere assumption on Cassian's part but, like all his ideas on monasticism, a reflection of the lives of monks from whom he had learned and the experiences he had undergone as a monk in Egypt.

Laypeople, in much of the monastic literature, often believed monks to be fonts of both wisdom and virtue while clergy were often disdained on this front, at least in comparison to monks. For this reason, examples abound in which clergy are subordinated to monks, even though clergy clearly held the upper hand in church authority. This belief, this transfer of authority to monks and away from hierarchs and clergy, was generally due to a belief in asceticism as a mark of religious authority. Monks were ideally quite ascetic, while bishops, for example, did not suffer this requirement for their office (which is not to say that there were no ascetic bishops). This ascetic practice was perceived as having created a particular intimacy between the monk and God, conferring a divine wisdom upon monks to which hierarchs were not (necessarily) privy. In many monastic apothegms, in fact, bishops and/or clergy members subordinate themselves to monks, recognizing the superior spiritual acumen of ascetic monks. Monks, in turn, often display a kind of disdain for bishops. This superior monastic authority subjugates even secular authorities such as magistrates.

Another type of evidence occurs in the monastic literature in which monks are often abducted and forcibly ordained by bishops. While for the layperson, ordination into the priesthood would certainly have provided a dramatic increase in status and sometimes wealth, the monks often seem to run for their lives rather than be ordained. One clear problem with monks being ordained was that they viewed this inevitable boost in status to be dangerous to their humility. They were wary of the vice of vainglory and knew that such a change in status would become a mighty temptation. In addition, a key component of monastic identity was the renunciation of family and social ties. While ordination would certainly change the tenor of those ties, it would also entangle the clergy member or hierarch all the more in lay society. The bottom line seems to have been that ordination was perceived as a hindrance to ascetic practice and was thus to be avoided.

Yet another confirmation of such conflicts emerges from monastic hagiographies, especially that of Antony, the nominal father of Christian monasticism. Athanasius, the powerful and contentious bishop of Alexandria, wrote his biography of Antony, not as a historical document, but rather as a rhetorical weapon in his never-ending war against those he perceived as heretics. His portrayal of Antony, therefore, was likely less than accurate. However, it was also highly influential, a bestseller of its day, and thus provided many who had never met the monks of Egypt with a heroic portrait of monks which happened to accord as well with the Nicene theological position.

The letters of Antony, however, problematize this portrait substantially. First, if the letters are indeed genuine, they severely problematize the notion in Athanasius' biography that Antony was illiterate. Several other ancient authors seem to have known of the letters of Antony and thus the general assumption was that Antony was indeed literate and had a rather sophisticated theology, informed mostly by the writings of Origen (although as in Cassian's writings, Origen's name was never explicitly referenced). The general assumption that most Egyptian monks were uneducated peasants has been substantially debunked by William Harmless and others. The notion of monks as exclusively humble peasants could only have supported Athanasius' view of them as his subordinates and as purely ascetic, rather than theologically erudite agents.

According to his letters, Antony held a very Neoplatonic view of the significance of knowing the self in order to know God. This does not easily agree with Athanasius' Nicene position. Even Antony's reference to Arius, Athanasius' theological archenemy, is compassionate in that he notes that while Arius may be wrong about his view of Christ, it is only because he did not know himself sufficiently that he had such incorrect views, not because of willful disobedience.

In addition, while the Antony of Athanasius' *Life* fights embodied demons physically, being almost beaten to death in the process, Antony in his letters describes the demons as disembodied and needing humans in order to embody their sinful thoughts and emotions. In short, the conflict lies here between the way Antony was used as a rhetorical soldier in Athanasius' fight

6. Conclusion   163

against Arianism and the way that monks themselves, Antony among them, tended often to avoid theological conflicts of the day, preferring instead to focus on ascetic practice and to achieve intimacy with God.

The ultimate example of conflict between the institutional church and monks pertains more directly to John Cassian. The Origenist Controversy would cause the exile of Cassian and his mentors, while likely cementing his views on the relation between church hierarchy and monastics. When Theophilus, the bishop of Alexandria, declared that the God was embodied, effectively making this the *de facto* church position, he automatically anathematized the contrary position held by Cassian and the monks of his Egyptian community, a position largely influenced by Origen and certainly identified with him. While in our own time, such an argument might remain in the merely rhetorical realm, in Cassian's time, such divergences had real-world consequences. Cassian and his fellow monks were virtually chased from the Egyptian desert while their cells were burned to the ground. Had Cassian not had a definite opinion on the relation between monks and the institutional church at this time, this incident, as well as others such as the exile of his Constantinopolitan protector and ascetic bishop John Chrysostom by the same bishop Theophilus, would surely have given him pause when considering how monks should relate in terms of authority to the leaders of the church. I argue that this episode was not an anomaly, but rather the culmination and result of conflicts that had long been building between monasticism and the institutional church.

In addition to these explicit examples of conflict portrayed in early monastic literature, Paul Dilley notes that there was, among these early Egyptian monks, a particular monastic theory of mind which differed substantially from that of clergy and laypeople. Monks believed that their minds could be read by God and certain clairvoyant saints, that their thoughts could come from sources outside of themselves, that they could produce morally significant thoughts and reject immoral thoughts by their own free will and that they were exceptionally sensitive to sensory input, especially anything heard. All these propositions, if believed, entailed forms of practice which, again, were generally exclusive to monastics. Surely, if monks were thinking and thus practicing their religion so differently from clergy, this would have contributed to clashes between the two groups.

Finally, this book examines evidence from Cassian's own rhetoric that he indeed believed that a separation of authority between monasticism and the church was necessary. Cassian's monastic writings were the finale of a long voyage from privileged, educated son to novice monk and ultimately, to monastic master. His authority on all matters monastic had been hard-won, and he used it to attempt to bring the new monasteries of Gaul into line with those of Egypt. Rather than let the ascetic way of life he had learned and loved die with his exile from Egypt, he brought it to the Western Empire, and ultimately, to the world. However, this book argues that Cassian fully believed that for this to happen, for the correct way of life to remain alive, monasticism would have to be separated from—indeed, safe from—the meddling of bishops and other clergy. Monks would have to be given free rein over their own affairs, both practical and theological. Only in this way could they truly live the correct life and achieve the necessary intimacy with God that would ensure salvation. Of course, having suffered exile at the hands of an unscrupulous bishop, Cassian knew better than to overtly challenge the church hierarchy in his writings. Rather, he included many subtle references which could be read by future monks as advocating for such a separation.

One way in which Cassian shrewdly argued his case was by including frequent references to the almost ancestral ties he saw between monks and the prophets of the Hebrew Bible and the apostles of the New Testament. He began *The Institutes* by drawing an analogy between Solomon during the building of the Temple and Castor, the bishop to whom this preface was addressed. While the bishop was admirably attempting, like Solomon, to build a new "temple" by constructing Gallican monasticism the way it should be, he had to rely on the work and expertise of a foreigner to actualize this construction. In the case of Solomon, the foreigner was Hiram, to whom Cassian compared himself directly. Again, a bishop may wield the power and resources to begin such a project, but only one truly steeped in the building of such things, only a true monk, could get the job done.

Cassian showed how the clothing and the ascetic lifestyle of monks could easily be traced back to such towering prophetic figures as Elijah, Elisha, and John the Baptist. Like these biblical luminaries, monks dressed poorly but were intermediaries between God and human beings. Their intimacy with God allowed them to intercede for others and to impart divine wisdom to others, which is why monks were so often visited by laypeople and clergy alike looking for "a word." In the same passages where Cassian compared prophets and monks, he also compared the apostles and monks, explicitly claiming that all or most of the traditions of genuine monastic practice were passed down to monks by such foundational biblical figures. Implicit in this was a challenge to the institutional church. While there is no indication that Cassian wanted to deny orthodoxy or the authority of apostolic succession to the bishops, he declared that to monks there was a form of authority far more significant: orthopraxy or, what I have called in this book *apostolic praxis*. The methods of asceticism and prayer, he claimed, were passed down from the early church just as surely as the authority of the apostolic sees. However, since practice was far more important to monks than mere orthodox belief, Cassian was tacitly making a rather grandiose claim: monks are the true possessors of correct Christian living.

This authority was, he stated, passed down through the ages to the Desert Fathers of Egypt from whom Cassian himself had learned. Thus, this knowledge not only tied him and all correctly practicing monks of the future to the venerable monks of Egypt, but indeed to the earliest church. The claim is astounding in its audacity. It is as if Cassian is claiming that those who practice as the Egyptian monks do are the truest form of the church. He stops well short of saying that laypeople and hierarchs are not part of the church. Rather, there are apparent levels to one's involvement in Christ's church, with monks occupying the highest levels.

Cassian takes this claim further by reviewing and outlining the specifics of monastic practice and traditions. He never explicitly says that these practices are only for monks. That is, he differentiates between monks, those who practice correctly, and hierarchs and clergy, who do not, although clearly laypeople and bishops could and sometimes did practice asceticism as well. Again, Cassian draws the line from the primitive church to the monastic practices of Egypt, focusing again not on apostolic succession, the purview of the institutional church, but apostolic praxis, which grants authority principally to monks, assuming those monks practice correctly.

In outlining the correct number and order of prayers for monks, Cassian defines the canon of practices for monks. In doing so, he makes several clear references to the Gallican monks and how their practice is incorrect, whether by the wrong number or type of prayers or by their irreverent conduct during prayer. This is significant for two reasons. First, remember that Cassian is writing his treatises at the behest of Castor, bishop of Apta Julia in Gaul. The monasteries of Gaul that Cassian criticizes were, so Cassian tells us, founded by this bishop. Therefore, a bishop's authority and leadership are clearly insufficient to create an acceptable community of monks. Second, only an experienced monk who learned and practiced in the idealized deserts of Egypt can establish an adequate monastic community of practice. Cassian, though professing humility, notes that his bona fides are impeccable and that he, not the bishop, should oversee the training of monks in best practices.. Gallican monks under the mere authority of the bishop are "uninstructed infants." Only a true father, an *abba*, can form such monks into mature Christian practitioners.

Throughout this discussion of monastic practices, what is constantly evident is the authority that asceticism confers upon monks. Asceticism is an emptying of the self, such that the monk is purified, attaining at last, in Cassian's familiar parlance, purity of heart. As this book established, this seemingly vague phrase is Cassian's translation and/or paraphrase of his teacher Evagrius Ponticus's *apatheia* or passionlessness. When a monk has practiced renunciation, he is left with the absence of passions which allows him to access both the wisdom of the divine and intimacy with that divine. Since such strict asceticism is not required for bishops or clergy, the implication is that monks are far closer to God and thus possess God's wisdom to a greater extent. In other words, correct practice ultimately allows the practitioner to participate in the divine, whereas the title and authority conferred upon bishops and clergy are no guarantee of such holiness. Monks, through practice, have greater spiritual authority than representatives of the institutional church.

Finally, Cassian, throughout his writings, subtly denigrates church hierarchs and their theological heroes. In the preface of *The Institutes*, for example, Cassian writes that his benefactor, Castor, Bishop of Apta Julia, is accomplished in both virtue and knowledge while Cassian himself is lacking such knowledge. Forgetting that Cassian was most likely well-educated as a young man, the distinction here is more significant than is initially apparent. Cassian here makes the first reference to the difference between knowledge, the result of secular education and wisdom, the far more important result of ascetic and monastic practice. In his writings, church representatives are often said possess the former while monks possess the latter. He goes on in the same preface to note that while Castor is blessed with the gift of eloquence, Cassian himself will explicate the wisdom of monastic life in simple words. He further notes that even those who are illiterate are often capable of great wisdom. This is true because, as Cassian says, a monk's wisdom comes only from experience and practice, not from books. Indeed, too much education can be an obstacle to true wisdom.

Cassian goes on to write of some of the most prominent Christian writers of his day, Jerome and Basil. While he notes that their eloquence is so impressive that he is afraid to write anything that might be compared with it, he makes it clear that what monks gain in experience and practice is far superior to anything learned in a classical education. Such articulate writers nevertheless write of things of which they have no direct experience, while Cassian is writing only of that which he has himself experienced. Experience, for the monk, trumps mere speculation every time.

Implications for Further Study

Despite the primitive state of technology in the fifth century CE, I would argue that Cassian had a very sophisticated sense of how to create certain types of subjects. Foucault, meanwhile, decades before the invention of the internet, developed a complex, nuanced analysis of the type of subject creation of which Cassian's writings are an example. Fast forwarding to today, I believe that despite our technological advances we have not appreciably improved upon Cassian's method of shaping subjects or Foucault's analysis of this process.

In our own time, ubiquitous television networks and social media accounts have, depending on their orientations, done an impressive job of shaping the subjectivity of their viewers. Both TV networks and social media, for example, define what it means to be an American. They provide this definition not only through simple platitudes but by defining what Americans should believe, how they should appear, and what they can and cannot do with their bodies.

My first question, therefore, is how one can resist such explicit and implicit shaping of one's identity? The too-obvious answer, of course, is to disconnect from these technologies. In our current milieu, however, disconnecting has consequences. If one does not watch Fox or CNN news or the latest comedy and drama programs, one may be excluded from much of the social interaction around the watercooler. Furthermore, not having any social media accounts may prevent an applicant from being hired for certain jobs these days.[5]

Having established the power of shaping subjectivity, I believe there should be further scholarly attention paid to forms of resistance. In Cassian's milieu, for example, did anyone resist his definition of the ideal monk? Did anyone contradict his prescriptions for monastic behavior and/or ascetic purity? As I have shown in this book, Cassian defined his authority and used it successfully to shape not only fifth-century monks from Gaul but also, and probably inadvertently, subsequent monks throughout history. Resistance to his authoritative fashioning could very well have changed the history of monasticism and thus the church in general. Moreover, examples of such resistance might give scholars a window into our own time, in which the shaping of subjects is even more omnipresent.

Another of my queries at the inception of this study was whether Cassian had conceptualized a larger, overarching basis for this separation he sought, a line that could easily be drawn between monks and most bishops or clergy. The obvious answer, not just within Cassian's oeuvre but within the *AP* and the whole corpus of monastic writings of the fourth and fifth centuries, was

---

5. Jennifer Parris, "Why No Social Media Presence Is Bad for Job Seekers," *Flexjobs* (blog), January 20, 2015, accessed April 4, 2019, https://www.flexjobs.com/blog/post/no-social-media-presence-is-bad-for-job-seekers/. This blog claims that having no social media accounts signals to a potential employer that an applicant may be hiding something or may be technologically inept, apathetic, or simply have nothing to offer.

asceticism. Indeed, in some of the monastic literature there are examples revealed to monks of laypeople and bishops who, merely by virtue of their exceptional ascetic practices, are as worthy of intimacy with God as any good monk. Two examples clarify this emphasis on ascetic practice:

> It was revealed to Abba Anthony in his desert that there was one who was his equal in the city. He was a doctor by profession and whatever he had beyond his needs he gave to the poor, and every day he sang the Sanctus with the angels.[6]

In another example, two monks are sent to a married couple, a shepherd named Eucharistus and his wife, who God says have exceeded the two monks in righteousness. The married couple, out of humility, are loath to reveal their way of life to the monks, but when the monks insist, Eucharistus says

> Here are these sheep; we received them from our parents, and if, by God's help we make a little profit, we divide it into three parts: one for the poor, the second for hospitality, and the third for our personal needs. Since I married my wife, we have not had intercourse with one another, for she is a virgin; we each live alone. At night we wear hair-shirts and our ordinary clothes by day. No one knows of this till now.[7]

This may also explain how there are bishops included in the *AP* as well as the reason Cassian felt comfortable advocating for John Chrysostom, himself an ascetic bishop. What truly divided the sheep from the goats was not status or title but commitment to ascetic practice.

In the Late Antique period in which monasticism began and flourished, we see the beginnings of heresiology as well as fights over Christology and the Creeds. What ties these well-known conflicts together is the notion of orthodoxy or correct belief. Orthodoxy was emphasized in this period of Christian thought, often at the expense of correct practice. While monks such as Cassian would no doubt have agreed that orthodoxy mattered—and Cassian certainly never contradicts that notion and even writes a treatise against the Nestorian heresy[8]—what was clearly more significant for them was correct practice. A monk had to pray, both in the liturgical group setting and frequently on his own. A monk had to fast, preferably every day until

---

6. *AP*, Antony, 24.
7. *AP*, Eucharistus the Secular, 1.
8. John Cassian, *De incarnatione Christi*, in *Patrologia Latina*, vol. 50, edited by J.-P. Migne (Paris: 1865). Translated by C.S. Gibson. From *Nicene and Post-Nicene Fathers, Second Series*, Vol. 11. Edited by Philip Schaff and Henry Wace. (Buffalo, NY: Christian Literature Publishing Co., 1894).

the ninth hour (3 PM). A monk had to meditate on scripture until scripture became part of his very constitution.

What is more, these practices in Cassian's writing were all explicitly linked to the larger history of the church. The monks dressed like Elijah and John the Baptist. They renounced all personal possessions like the apostles in the book of Acts. They prayed without ceasing as Paul had encouraged. They were a community of practice emphasized over belief. Because these practices had, according to Cassian, been passed down from the apostles, I coined a phrase in this book: *apostolic praxis*. While the bishops could and did lay claim to their authority by virtue of its being passed down from the apostles to each successive bishop, Cassian on the other hand laid claim to authority because he and other monks continued to employ the holy practices of the early church which he claimed had likewise been passed down from prophets to apostles to monks.

While there has been ample discussion of the notion of apostolic succession and its conferral of authority upon bishops, I see a further avenue of exploration, principally but not only in the field of monastic studies, in exploring the notion of apostolic praxis. Since Cassian's writings were the basis of much of monastic history in Europe, how does the picture of early and even later monasticism change when we view it through the lens of apostolic practice? While Christian theology throughout history is normally constructed from orthodoxy, what happens when it is viewed through orthopraxy as a mark of authority? On a larger scale, can Christianity throughout the ages be interpreted as a series not only of developing beliefs, but also developing practices? If so, how does this affect our interpretation of the schism between East and West, between Catholicism and Protestantism, between monk and bishop, between any and all Christian groups with respect to the authority of practice? I think this could be a fruitful avenue for further exploration. In this context, I reiterate my earlier suggestion that Cassian put forward an idealized, solitary monk as a synecdoche for monasticism separated from the institutional church. While there is no explicit proof for this argument in Cassian's writings, it appears reasonable to me that Cassian, who had clearly studied the methods of classical rhetoric in his youth and employed them in his writings, could have been subtly attempting to show that if a monk could sit alone in his cell and thus learn everything necessary to become spiritually perfect, a monastic system such as he sought to establish and propagate could separate from the clergy and thus become spiritually perfect in its own right. I offer this, as well, as a suggestion for further study.

Finally, a third question I think could inform future scholarship is historical. Given the enormous wealth developed by the Western church and its subsequent influence on the sociopolitical milieux in which it thrived, what effect would a true separation between monasticism and the institutional church have had? To wit, if monasticism had indeed formed its own institutional body on par with the church of the Late Antique period, would its emphasis on asceticism and renunciation have made it, and perhaps Christianity in general, less powerful, less influential than it became? Put another way, might the emphasis on material renunciation so vital to Cassian's monasticism have changed the development of a European economy? Would something like the apostolic ideal in Acts 4.32 have been attempted on a larger scale in villages, towns, cities, and perhaps even nation states? Or conversely, would such a development have merely downgraded the significance of Christianity in economic affairs, such that it eventually died out as did Buddhism in India in the 12th century?

While merely speculation, I think such questions might lead us as scholars to pay more attention to the interplay throughout the course of history between religious forms and economic forms. Do the two influence each other equally or do economies, practiced often on such large scales, merely dominate whatever types of religion are present? Again, I hope such questions will guide my further work on monasticism and perhaps inspire further scholarly work for others.

Bibliography

Primary Sources

Ammianus Marcellinus. *Res gestae*. LCL Cambridge, MA: Harvard University Press, 1940. trans. John C. Rolfe.

Ammon. *The Letter of Ammon*. In *The Letter of Ammon and Pachomian Monasticism*, ed., tr. James E. Goehring. *Patristische Texte und Studien* 27. Berlin/New York, NY: Walter de Gruyter, 1986.

Antony. *The letters of St. Anthony the Great*. Translated by Derwas James Chitty. Fairacres: SLG Press, 1983.

—*The Letters of St. Antony: Monasticism and the Making of a Saint*. Translated by Samuel Rubenson. Minneapolis, MN: Fortress Press, 1995.

Apophthegmata Patrum (Greek Alphabetic). Edited by Jean-Baptiste Cotelier. In *Ecclisiae Graecae Monumenta*. Paris: 1677. 1.338–712. Reprinted by Jacques-Paul Migne. In *Patrologia Graeca* 65: 71–440. Paris: J.-P. Migne, 1864. Edited by Jean-Claude Guy. *Recherches sur la tradition grecque des* Apophthegmata Patrum, 13–58. Subsidia Hagiographica, 36. Brussels: Société des Bollandiste, 1962. Translated by Benedicta Ward, *The Sayings of the Desert Fathers: the Alphabetical Collection*. Kalamazoo, MI: Cistercian, 2004.

Aristotle. *On the Soul. Parva Naturalia. On Breath*. Translated by W. S. Hett. Loeb Classical Library 288. Cambridge, MA: Harvard University Press, 1957.

—*Problems, Volume II: Books 20–38. Rhetoric to Alexander*. Edited and translated by Robert Mayhew, David C. Mirhady. Loeb Classical Library 317. Cambridge, MA: Harvard University Press, 2011.

Athanasius. *Vita Antonii*. Edited and translated by G.J.M. Bartelink. Sources Chrétiennes, 400. Éditions du Cerf, 1994. Translated by Robert C. Gregg. *Athanasius: The Life of Antony and the Letter to Marcellinus*. Mahwah, NJ: Paulist Press, 1980.

Augustine. *De civitate Dei contra paganos*. (*City of God*), *Volume I: Books 1–3*. Translated by George E. McCracken. Loeb Classical Library 411. Cambridge, MA: Harvard University Press, 1957.

—*Confessions, Volume I: Books 1–8*. Translated by Carolyn J.-B. Hammond. Loeb Classical Library 26. Cambridge, MA: Harvard University Press, 2014.

—*Enarrationes in Psalmos*. In *Patrologia Latina*. vol. 36. Edited by J.-P. Migne. Paris: 1865. Translated by J.E. Tweed. From *Nicene and Post-Nicene Fathers, First Series*. Vol. 8. Edited by Philip Schaff. Buffalo, NY: Christian Literature Publishing Co., 1888.

—*De gratia et libero arbitrio*. In *Patrologia Latina*. vol. 44. Edited by J.-P. Migne. Paris: 1865. Translated by Peter Holmes and Robert Ernest Wallis, and revised by Benjamin B. Warfield. From *Nicene and Post-Nicene Fathers, First Series*. Vol. 5. Edited by Philip Schaff. Buffalo, NY: Christian Literature Publishing Co., 1887.

—*De Opera Monachorum*. in *Patrologia Latina*. vol. 6. Edited by J.-P. Migne. (Paris, 1865). Translated by H. Browne. From *Nicene and Post-Nicene Fathers, First Series*,

Vol. 3. Edited by Philip Schaff. Buffalo, NY: Christian Literature Publishing Co., 1887.
—*De praedestinatione sanctorum*. In *Patrologia Latina*. vol. 44. Edited by J.-P. Migne, Paris: 1865. Translated by Peter Holmes and Robert Ernest Wallis, and revised by Benjamin B. Warfield. From *Nicene and Post-Nicene Fathers, First Series*, Vol. 5. Edited by Philip Schaff. Buffalo, NY: Christian Literature Publishing Co., 1887.
—*Sermones de Tempore*, in *Patrologia Latina*, vol. 38, edited by J.-P. Migne (Paris: 1865), CCXXIV.3. Translated by R.G. MacMullen. From *Nicene and Post-Nicene Fathers, First Series*, Vol. 6. Edited by Philip Schaff (Buffalo, NY: Christian Literature Publishing Co., 1888).
Basil. *Ascetica.* In *Patrologia Graeca*. Edited by J.-P. Migne, vol. 3. Paris: 1885. Translated by W.K.L Clarke. Basil of Caeserea, *The Ascetic Works of St. Basil*. London: Macmillan, 1925.
—*Epistolae*. In *Patrologia Graeca*, vol. 32. Edited by J.-P. Migne (Paris: 1857). Translated by Blomfield Jackson. From *Nicene and Post-Nicene Fathers, Second Series*, *Vol. 8*. Edited by Philip Schaff and Henry Wace. Buffalo, NY: Christian Literature Publishing Co., 1895.
Benedict of Nursia, Timothy Fry, O.S.B. translator. *The Rule of Saint Benedict*. New York, NY: Vintage, 1998.
Bonaventure. *Apologia paupertum*. in *Opera omnia*, vol. 14. book 2. Rome: Citta Nuova, 2005. English translation: *Defense of the Mendicants*, trans. Jse de Vinck and Robert J. Karris. St. Bonaventure, NY: Harper 2005.
Cassian, John. *Conferences*. Edited and translated by E. Picherry. *Conférences*. 3 vols. Sources Chrétiennes, 42, 54, 64. Paris: Éditions du Cerf, 1955–59. Translated by Boniface Ramsey. *John Cassian: The Institutes*. Ancient Christian Writers, 57. New York, NY: Paulist Press, 1997.
—*Institutes.* Edited and translated by Jean-Claude Guy. *Institutions cénobitiques* Sources Chrétiennes. 109. Paris: Éditions du Cerf, 1965. Translated by Boniface Ramsey. *John Cassian: The Institutes*. Ancient Christian Writers, 58. New York, NY: The Newman Press, 2000.
—*The Institutes,* translated by Colm Luibheid, *Conferences*. New York, NY: Paulist Press, 1985.
—*De incarnatione Christi*, in *Patrologia Latina*, vol. 50, edited by J.-P. Migne (Paris: 1865)*.* Translated by C.S. Gibson. From *Nicene and Post-Nicene Fathers, Second Series*, Vol. 11. Edited by Philip Schaff and Henry Wace. Buffalo, NY: Christian Literature Publishing Co., 1894.
Codex Theodosianus, IMPERATORIS THEO1DOSII CODEX liber decimus sextus. Accessed November 25, 2019. http://ancientrome.ru/ius/library/codex/theod/liber16.htm.
Dorotheus of Gaza. *Discourses and sayings*. Translated by Eric P. Wheeler, OSB. Collegeville, MN: Cistercian Publications, 1977.
Epictetus. *Epictetus: Discourses: book 1*. Translated by Robert F. Dobbin. Oxford: Clarendon Press, 1998.
Epistula Ammonis. Ed. J. Goehring, *The Letter of Ammon and Pachomian Monasticism*. Berlin, 1986.
Epistolae Romanarum Pontificum Genuinae. Thiel, A., ed. Peter E. Braunsberg, 1867; Hildesheim: G. Olms, 1974.
Eusebius. *Historia ecclesiastica*. In *Patrologia Graeca*, vol. 20. Edited by J.-P. Migne (Paris: 1857). Translated by Arthur Cushman McGiffert. From *Nicene and Post-*

Nicene Fathers, Second Series, Vol. 1. Edited by Philip Schaff and Henry Wace. Buffalo, NY: Christian Literature Publishing Co., 1890.

Evagrius Ponticus. Ο ΓΝΟΣΤΙΚΟΣ Η ΠΡΟΣ ΤΟΝ ΚΑΤΑΞΙΩΘΕΝΤΑ ΓΝΩΣΕΩΣ. *The Gnostikos*. Ed. A. & C. Guillaumont, Évagre le Pontique, Le Gnostique ou A celui qui est devenu digne de la science. Sources Chrétiennes, n° 356. Paris: 1989.

—*The Praktikos; Chapters on Prayer*. Translated by John Eudes Bamberger. Piscataway, NJ: Gorgias Press LLC, 2009.

Evagrius Ponticus, R. Sinkewicz, translator, *Evagrius of Pontus the Greek Ascetic Corpus*, Oxford: Oxford University Press, 2006.

Hilary of Arles. *Sermo de Uita S. Honorati*. in *Patrologia Latina*, vol. 50. Edited by J.-P. Migne. Paris: 1845.

Historia Monachorum. Translated into Latin by Rufinus of Aquilea. Printed in *Patrologia Graeca*, vol. 21. Edited by J.-P. Migne. (Paris, 1849). Translated by Norman Russell as *The Lives of the Desert Fathers*. Trappist, KY: Cistercian Publications, 1980.

Hugh of Digne. *De finibus paupertatis auctore Hugone de Digna*. Edited by C. Florovski, in *Archivium Franciscanum Historicum* 5 (1912): 277–90. Spontanea propter Dominum abdicacio proprietatis.

Historia Monachorum. translated into Latin by Rufinus of Aquilea. in *Patrologia Graeca*, vol. 21. Edited by Migne (Paris, 1849). Translated by Norman Russell as *The Lives of the Desert Fathers*. Trappist, KY: Cistercian Publications, 1980.

Irenaeus. *Adversus Haereses*. In *Patrologia Graeca* vol. 7. Edited by J.-P. Migne (Paris: 1857). Translated by Alexander Roberts and William Rambaut. From *Ante-Nicene Fathers*, Vol. 1. Edited by Alexander Roberts, James Donaldson, and A. Cleveland Coxe. Buffalo, NY: Christian Literature Publishing Co., 1885.

Jerome. Translated by C. Mierow. *Epistles*. Paris: Belles Lettres, 1949.

—*Liber de Viris illustribus*. In *Patrologia Latina*, vol. 23. Edited by J.-P. Migne (Paris: 1845). Tanslated by Thomas P. Halton as *On Illustrious Men,* translated by Thomas P. Halton (Fathers of the Church; v. 100) (Washington, DC: Catholic University of America Press, 1999).

—*The History of the Monks who Lived in the Desert of Egypt*. Whitefish, MT: Kessinger Publishing, 2005.

John Climacus. *John Climacus: the Ladder of Divine Ascent*. Colm Luibheid, Norman Russell, and Kallistos Ware, ed. London: SPCK, 1982.

Macarius the Egyptian. *Homiliae PG* 34, 449–822. English translation: *Fifty Spiritual Homilies of St. Macarius the Egyptian*. Trans. A.J. Mason. Translations of Christian Literature: Series 1, Greek Texts. London: SPCK; New York, NY: Macmillan, 1921.

Origen. *Homilae en Leviticum*. 2.4. In *Patrologia Graeca,* series 12. Edited by J.-P. Migne. Paris, 1862. Translated by Gary Wayne Barkley. *Homilies on Leviticus*, 1–16. Washington, DC, Catholic University of America Press, 2010.

—G. W. Butterworth and Henri De Lubac, translators. *On First Principles*. New York, NY: Harper & Row, 1966.

Pachomius. *Regula et Praecepta*. In *Patrologia Graeca*. vol. 40. Edited by J.-P. Migne. (Paris: 1863).

Palladius. *Historia Lausiaca*, in *Patrologia Graeca*. Vol. 65. Edited by J.-P. Migne, Paris: 1864. Translated by Robert T. Meyer. *Palladius, the Lausiac History*. Westminster, MD: Newman Press, 1965.

Plotinus. *Ennead, Volume I: Porphyry on the Life of Plotinus. Ennead I*. Translated by A.

H. Armstrong. Loeb Classical Library 440. Cambridge, MA: Harvard University Press, 1969.
Prosper of Aquitaine. *Liber contra collatorem*. In *Patrologia Latina*. vol. 51. Edited by J.-P. Migne (Paris: 1861).
Simplicius, *Letters*, 1.1, ed. A. Thiel, *Epistolae Romanarum Pontificum Genuinae*, Braunsberg: E. Peter, 1867; Hildesheim: G. Olms, 1974.
Socrates Scholasticus. *Historia Ecclesisastica.* In *Patrologia Graeca*. Edited by J.-P. Migne, vol. 3. Paris: 1864. Translated by A.C. Zenos. From *Nicene and Post-Nicene Fathers, Second Series*, Vol. 2. Edited by Philip Schaff and Henry Wace. Buffalo, NY: Christian Literature Publishing Co., 1890.
Sozomenus, Salaminius Hermias. *Historia ecclesiastica*. Turnhout: Brepols, 2004.
Shenoute. *Selected discourses of Shenoute the Great: Community, Theology, and Social Conflict in Late Antique Egypt.* Translated by David Brakke and Andrew Crislip. Cambridge: Cambridge University Press, 2015.
Sulpicius Severus. *Dialogi*. In *Patrologia Latina*, vol. 20, edited by J.-P. Migne (Paris: 1845). Translated by Alexander Roberts. From *Nicene and Post-Nicene Fathers, Second Series*, Vol. 11. Edited by Philip Schaff and Henry Wace. (Buffalo, NY: Christian Literature Publishing Co., 1894).
—*Epistle 3*. In *Patrologia Latina*, vol. 20. Edited by J.-P. Migne (Paris: 1845). Translated by Alexander Roberts, from *Nicene and Post-Nicene Fathers, Second Series*, Vol. 11. Edited by Philip Schaff and Henry Wace. Buffalo, NY: Christian Literature Publishing Co., 1894.
Theophilus of Alexandria. "Epistulae Festales". In *The Corpus Scriptorum Ecclesiasticorum Latinorum* 55 (1912): 159–81, 185–211, 213–32.
Tertullian. *De poenitentia*, IX.3–4. In *Patrologia Latina*. Edited by J.-P. Migne. *Series 1*, Paris, 1844. Translated by S. Thelwall. From *Ante-Nicene Fathers*, Vol. 3. Edited by Alexander Roberts, James Donaldson, and A. Cleveland Coxe. (Buffalo, NY: Christian Literature Publishing Co., 1885).
Vincent of Leríns. *Commonitorium*. Translated by R. Demeulenaere. Turnholti: Brepols, 1985.
Vita Pachomii (1953) Bohairic: *Pachomii vitae bohairice scripta*, ed. L.T. Lefort, CSCO 89, Louvain; (1932). Greek: *Sancti Pachomii vitae graecae*, ed. F. Halkin, Brussels and *Le corpus astenien de Saint Pachome* (1982).
Ward, Benedicta, ed. *The Wisdom of the Desert Fathers: Systematic Sayings from the Anonymous Series of the Apophthegmata Patrum*. Seoul: Kyujang Publishing, 2006.
—*The Sayings of the Desert Fathers*. Kalamazoo, MI: Cistercian Publications, 1975.
White, Carolinne, Athanasius, Jerome, Sulpicius Severus, and Gregory. *Early Christian Lives*. London: Penguin Books, 1998.
Xenophon. *Memorabilia. Oeconomicus. Symposium. Apology.* Translated by E.C. Marchant, O.J. Todd. Revised by Jeffrey Henderson. Loeb Classical Library, 168. Cambridge, MA: Harvard University Press, 2013.

Secondary Sources

Attwater, Donald and Catherine Rachel John. *The Penguin Dictionary of Saints*, 3rd edition. New York, NY: Penguin Books, 1993.

Barnes, T.D. "Angel of Light or Mystic Initiate? The Problem of the Life of Antony." *Journal of Theological Studies*, xxxvii (1986): 353–68.
Brakke, David. *Athanasius and Asceticism*. Baltimore:, MD, Johns Hopkins University Press, 2009.
—*Demons and the Making of the Monk: Spiritual Combat in Early Christianity*. Cambridge, MA: Harvard University Press, 2006.
—"Macarius's Quest and Ours: Literary Sources for Early Egyptian Monasticism." In *Cistercian Studies Quarterly* 48.2 (2013): 239–51.
—"The Problematization of Nocturnal Emissions in Early Christian Syria, Egypt, and Gaul." *Journal of Early Christian Studies* 3.4 (1995): 419–60.
Brennan, B. "Athanasius' Vita Antonii: A Sociological Interpretation." *Vigiliae Christianae* 39.3 (1985): 209–27.
Brown, Peter. *Authority and the Sacred: Aspects of the Christianisation of the Roman World*. Cambridge: Cambridge University Press. 1997.
—*The Body and Society: Men, Women, and Sexual Renunciation in Early Christianity*. New York, NY: Columbia University Press, 1988.
—"The Rise and Function of the Holy Man in Late Antiquity." *Journal of Roman Studies* 61.11 (1971): 80–101.
—*The Making of Late Antiquity*. New York, NY: ACLS History E-Book Project, 2005.
—*Through the Eye of a Needle: Wealth, the Fall of Rome, and the Making of Christianity in the West, 350–550 AD*. Princeton, NJ: Princeton University Press, 2014.
Budge, E.A.W. *The Wit and Wisdom of the Christian Fathers of Egypt: The Syriac Version of the Apophthegmata Patrum*. London: Oxford University Press, 1934.
Butler, Rev. Alban. *The Lives of the Fathers, Martyrs, and Other Principal Saints*. Dublin: James Duffy, 1866; www.Bartleby.com, 2010.
Bultmann, Rudolf. *The History of the Synoptic Tradition*. Trans. John Marshfrom, 1931 German ed.; Oxford: Basil Blackwell, 1972 revised ed.
Burton-Christie, Douglas. *The Word in the Desert: Scripture and the Quest for Holiness in Early Christian Monasticism*. New York, NY: Oxford University Press, 1993.
Cain, Andrew. *The Letters of Jerome: Asceticism, Biblical Exegesis, and the Construction of Christian Authority in Late Antiquity*. Oxford: Oxford University Press, 2009.
Casiday, Augustine. *Reconstructing the Theology of Evagrius Ponticus. beyond Heresy*. Cambridge: Cambridge University Press, 2013.
—*Tradition and Theology in St John Cassian*. Oxford: Oxford University Press, 2010.
Chadwick, Owen. *John Cassian*. 2nd ed. Cambridge: Cambridge University Press, 1968.
—"Origen, Celsus, and the Resurrection of the Body." *Harvard Theological Review* 41 (1948): 83–102.
Chesnut, G.F. *The First Christian Histories: Eusebius, Socrates, Sozomen, Theodoret and Evagrius*. Macon, GA.: Mercer University Press, 1986.
Chitty, Derwas James. *The Desert a City: An Introduction to the Study of Egyptian and Palestinian Monasticism under the Christian Empire*. Crestwood, NY: St. Vladimir's Seminary Press, 1999.
Clark, Elizabeth A. *Origenist Controversy*. Princeton, NJ: Princeton University Press, 2016.
—"The Place of Jerome's Commentary on Ephesians in the Origenist Controversy: The Apokatastasis and Ascetic Ideals." *Vigiliae Christianae* 41 (1987): 154–71.
—*Reading Renunciation Asceticism and Scripture in Early Christianity*. Princeton, NJ: Princeton University Press, 2001.

Clements, Niki Kasumi. *Sites of the Ascetic Self: John Cassian and Christian Ethical Formation.* Notre Dame, IN: University of Notre Dame Press, 2020.
Cribiore, Rafaella. *Gymnastics of the Mind:* Greek *Education in Hellenistic and Roman Egypt.* Princeton, NJ: Princeton University Press: 2001.
Crum & Bell. *Wadi Sarga: Coptic and Greek Texts.* Gyldendal, Nordisk Forlag: Copenhagen, 1922.
De Vogüé, Adalbert. "Eucharist and Monastic Life." *Worship* 59.6 (1985): 498–509.
Dilley, Paul C. *Monasteries and the Care of Souls in Late Antique Christianity: Cognition and Discipline.* Cambridge: Cambridge University Press, 2017.
Driscoll, Jeremy. "Gentleness in the *Ad Monachos* of Evagrius Ponticus." *Studia Monastica* 32 (1990): 295–321.
Elm, Susanna. "Evagrius Ponticus' *Sententiae ad Virginem*." *Dumbarton Oaks Paper* 45 (1991): 265–95.
Ferguson, Everett. "Origen and the Election of Bishops." *Church History* 43.1 (1974): 26–33.
Folliet, G. 'Les Trois Catégories des Chrétiens, Survie d'un Theme Augustinien', *L'Année théologique augustinienne*. V14, 1954.
Forlin Patrucco, Marcella. "Bishops and Monks in Late Antique Society." *Zeitschrift Für Antikes Christentum* 8.2. (2004): 332–45.
Foucault, Michel. *About the Beginning of the Hermeneutics of the Self.* Chicago, IL, University of Chicago Press, 2016.
—Sheridan, Alan, translator, *Discipline and Punish: The Birth of the Prison.* New York, NY: Vintage Books, 1995.
—*The Government of Self and Others: Lectures at the Collège de France, 1982–1983.* Houndmills, Basingstoke, Hampshire: Palgrave Macmillan, 2010.
—*The History of Sexuality: An Introduction.* Translated from the French by Robert Hurley. (New York, NY: Vintage Books, 1990).
—*The History of Sexuality.* vol. 2. Translated from the French by Robert Hurley. 1st Vintage Books ed. New York, NY: Vintage Books.
— "Nietzsche, Genealogy, History." In *Homage a Jean Hyppolite* (Paris: Presses Universitaires de France, 1971), 145–72.
—"The Subject and Power." *Critical Inquiry* 8.4 (1982): 777–95.
Foucault, Michel with Frédéric Gros, and Graham Burchell, ed. *The Courage of Truth: The Government of Self and Others II: Lectures at the Collège de France 1983–1984.* Basingstoke: Palgrave Macmillan. 2012.
Foucault, Michel. with Michel Senellart, François Ewald, Alessandro Fontana, and Graham Burchell. On the Government of the Living: Lectures at the Collège de France, 1979–1980. Basingstoke: Palgrave Macmillan, 2014.
Foucault, Michel. with Michel Senellart, François Ewald, Alessandro Fontana, and Graham Burchell. *The Order of Things: An Archeology of the Human Sciences,* New York, NY: Vintage Books, 1995.
Foucault, Michel with Jeremy Carrette, translator. *Religion and Culture*, Florence: Taylor and Francis, 2013.
Foucault, Michel with François Ewald. *Society Must be Defended: Lectures at the Collége de France, 1975–76.* London: Penguin, 2008.
Frank, Georgia. *The Memory of the Eyes: Pilgrims to Living Saints in Christian Late Antiquity.* Berkeley: University of California Press, 2008.
Frede, Michael and A.A. Long. *A Free Will: Origins of the Notion in Ancient Thought.* Berkeley, CA: University of California Press, 2012.

Gamble, Harry. *Books and Readers in the Early Church: A History of Early Christian Texts.* New Haven, CT: Yale University Press, 1995.
Goodrich, Richard J. *Contextualizing Cassian: Aristocrats, Asceticism, and Reformation in Fifth-century Gaul.* New York, NY: Oxford University Press, 2007.
Gregg, R and D. Groh. *Early Arianism—a View of Salvation.* Philadelphia, PA: Fortress Press, 1981.
Guy, Jean-Claude. *Jean Cassien. Vie et Doctrine Spirituelle.* Collection Theologie, Pastorale et Spiritualite, Recherches et Syntheses IX. Paris: P. Lethielleux, 1961.
Harmless, William. *Desert Christians: An Introduction to the Literature of Early Monasticism.* New York, NY: Oxford University Press, 2004.
Hildebrand, Stephen. *Basil of Caesarea: Foundations of Theological Exegesis and Christian Spirituality.* Grand Rapids, MI: Baker Academic, 2014.
Hunt, Hannah. *Clothed in the Body: Asceticism, the Body, and the Spiritual in the Late Antique Era.* Farnham: Ashgate, 2012.
Inwood, Brad, and Lloyd P. Gerson, eds. *The Stoics Reader: Selected Writings and Testimonia.* Indianapolis, IN: Hackett, 2008.
Jaeger, Werner. *Early Christianity and Greek Paideia.* Cambridge, MA: Harvard University Press, 1961.
Kennedy, George A. *Classical Rhetoric & Its Christian and Secular Tradition.* Chapel Hill: The University of North Carolina Press, 1999.
Keith, Alison and Leif E. Vaage. "Imperial Asceticism: Discipline of Domination." in Leif E. Vaage and Vincent L. Wimbush, eds. *Asceticism and the New Testament.* Abingdon: Routledge, 1999.
Kirschner, Robert. "The Vocation of Holiness in Late Antiquity." *Vigiliae Christianae* 38.2 (1984): 105.
Krawiec, Rebecca. "Monastic Literacy in John Cassian: Toward a New Sublimity." *Church History* 81.4 (2012).
Krueger, Col. G.P. "Psychological Issues in Military Uniform Design." In *Advances in Military Textiles and Personal Equipment*, 64–78. Philadelphia, PA: Woodhead Publishing, 2012.
Lausberg, Heinrich. *Handbook of Literary Rhetoric: A Foundation for Literary Study.* eds. David E. Orton and Dean Andersen. trans. Matthew T. Bliss, Annemiek Jansen, and David E. Orton. Leiden: Brill, 1998.
Leyser, Conrad. *Authority and Asceticism from Augustine to Gregory the Great.* Oxford: Clarendon, 2007.
Macalister, Robert Alexander Stewart. *Ecclesiastical Vestments: Their Development and History.* Charleston, SC: Nabu Press,1896.
Mathisen, Ralph. *Roman Aristocrats in Barbarian Gaul: Strategies for Survival in an Age of Transition.* Austin, TX: University of Texas Press, 1993.
McGuckin, John Anthony. *The Westminster Handbook to Origen.* Louisville, KY: Westminster John Knox Press, 2004.
Meredith, Anthony. *The Cappadocians.* Eugene, OR: Wipf & Stock, 2009.
Newman, John Henry, and Maisie Ward. *Apologia pro Vita Sua.* London: Sheed & Ward, 1978.
O'Laughlin, Michael. "The Anthropology of Evagrius Ponticus and Its Sources." In *Origen of Alexandria*, ed. C. Kannengiesser and W. Petersen, q.v., 357–73.
— *Origenism in the Desert: Anthropology and Integration in Evagrius Ponticus.* Th.D. dissertation, Harvard University, Cambridge, USA, 1987.
Parris, Jennifer. "Why No Social Media Presence Is Bad for Job Seekers." *Flexjobs*

(blog), January 20, 2015. Accessed April 4, 2019. https://www.flexjobs.com/blog/post/no-social-media-presence-is-bad-for-job-seekers/.

Parry, Ken, ed. *The Wiley Blackwell Companion to Patristics*. (Oxford, UK: John Wiley & Sons, Incorporated, 2015).

Payne, Robert. *The Fathers of the Western Church*. New York, NY: Viking, 1951.

Rapp, Claudia. *Holy Bishops in Late Antiquity: the Nature of Christian Leadership in an Age of Transition*. Berkeley: University of California Press, 2005.

Rea, Robert F. "Grace and Free Will in John Cassian." PhD dissertation, St. Louis University: 1990.

Rousseau, Philip. *Ascetics, Authority, and the Church in the Age of Jerome and Cassian*. Notre Dame, IN: University of Notre Dame Press, 2010.

—*Basil of Caesarea*. Berkeley, CA: University of California Press, 1998.

— "Cassian, Contemplation and the Cenobitic Life." *Journal of Ecclesiastical History* 26 (1975): 113–26.

—"Cassian: Monastery and World." In *The Certainty of Doubt: Tributes to Peter Munz*, 68–89. Wellington, NZ: Victoria University Press, 1996.

Rubenson, Samuel. "Christian Asceticism and the Emergence of the Monastic Tradition." in *Asceticism*. Edited by Vincent L. Wimbush and Richard Valantasis. Oxford University Press, New York, NY: Oxford University Press, 1995.

—*The Letters of St. Antony: Monasticism and the Making of a Saint*. (Minneapolis: Fortress Press, 1997).

Sanders, Br. Constantius. "The (Almost) Forgotten Saint." Dominicana, February 5, 2021. https://www.dominicanajournal.org/.

Schroeder, Caroline T. *Monastic Bodies: Discipline and Salvation in Shenoute of Atripe*. Philadelphia: University of Pennsylvania Press, 2007.

Seasoltz, Kevin R. "Benedict of Nursia." *Encyclopedia of Religion*. edited by Lindsay Jones. 2nd ed., vol. 2, Macmillan Reference USA, 2005, 822–24. *Gale eBooks*, link.gale.com/apps/doc/CX3424500330/GVRL?u=udenver&sid=GVRL&xid=d8637322.

Sellars, John. *Stoicism*. Hoboken: Taylor and Francis, 2014.

Shaw, Teresa M. *The Burden of the Flesh: Fasting and Sexuality in Early Christianity*. Minneapolis: Fortress Press, 1998.

Simon, Richard. *Histoire Critique du Vieux Testament* 1.3.1 (1685 edn, p. 403).

Smith, Zachary B. *Philosopher-Monks, Episcopal Authority, and the Care of the Self: The 'Apophthegmata Patrum' in Fifth-Century Palestine*. Turnhout, Belgium: Brepols, 2018.

Sterk, Andrea. *Renouncing the World Yet Leading the Church: the Monk-Bishop in Late Antiquity*. Cambridge, MA: Harvard University Press, 2004.

Stewart, Columba. *Cassian the Monk*. New York, NY: Oxford University Press, 1999.

Stroumsa, Guy. "The Scriptural Movement of Late Antiquity and Christian Monasticism." *Journal of Early Christian Studies* 16.1 (2008): 61–77.

Trigg, Joseph W. *Origen*. London: Taylor and Francis, 2012.

Turner, William. "Neo-Platonism." In *The Catholic Encyclopedia*. New York, NY: Robert Appleton Company, 1911. Retrieved May 17, 2019 from New Advent: http://www.newadvent.org/cathen/10742b.htm

Vahlen, Johannes, ed. *Corpus Scriptorum Ecclesiasticorum Latinorum*. Imperial Academy of Sciences: Vienna, 1866.

Van Dam, Raymond. 'The Pirenne Thesis and Fifth--Century Gaul.' in *Fifth--Century*

Gaul: A Crisis of Identity? Edited by John Drinkwater and Hugh Elton. Cambridge: Cambridge University Press, 1992.

Vladislav, Suvák, Flachbartová Lívia, and Pavol Sucharek. "The Care of the Self and Diogenes' Ascetic Practices," in *Care of the Self. Ancient Problematizations of Life and Contemporary Thought.* (Leiden: Koninklijke Brill NV, 2017).

Williams, M. "*The Life of Antony* and the Domestication of Charismatic Wisdom." in *Charisma and Sacred Biography*. Journal of the American Academy of Religion. Thematic Studies Series, 48.3. Chico, CA: Scholars Press, 1982, 23–45.

Williams, Rowan. *Arius: Heresy and Tradition.* (London: SCM Press, 2005).

Wimbush, Vincent, and Richard Valantasis, ed., *Asceticism*. New York, NY: Oxford University Press, 2002.

Index of Ancient Sources

Hebrew Bible

Genesis
1.26   1, 22, 110

Deuteronomy
4.24   21

1 Kings
5.1-18   129

2 Kings
1.1-8   131

Psalms
7.10   117

23.1   83
25.18   67
109.1   115

Proverbs
14.17 (LXX)   149

New Testament

Gospel of Matthew
4.1-2   28
5.39   29
7.1   119
19.21   28
22.36-40   42

Gospel of Mark
1.4-6   28

Gospel of Luke
14.11   18

Gospel of John
17.21   22

Acts of the Apostles
2.44   42
4.32   52, 133, 158, 170
4.32-5   39

1 Corinthians
9   28
7.29-35   28
10.13   118
10.15   106

2 Corinthians
6.5-6   139

Ephesians
4.28   77

6.11-20   53

Philippians
2.5-8   64

1 Thessalonians
5.8   53
5.17   132

2 Thessalonians
3.11   77

1 John
4.8   139

Revelation
2.23   117

Other Ancient Sources

Ammianus Marcellinus
  Res gestae 35, 45
Amoun of Nitria 5
Antony
  Letters of St. Antony 11, 50, 105–9, 162
Apophthegmata Patrum
  Agathon 119
  Ammonius 101
  Antony 18, 28–30, 37, 81, 114, 168
  Appy 38, 96
  Arsenius 30, 93, 96, 144
  Bessarion 17, 32–33
  Daniel 108
  Epiphanius, Bishop of Cyprus 100, 114
  Eucharistus the Secular 168
  Gelasius 30, 94
  Isaac, Priest of the Cells 28, 99
  John the Short 18, 66, 77, 81
  Macarius the Great 33–4, 81, 90–1, 99
  Mark, Disciple of Abba Silvanus 16
  Matoes 91, 99
  Moses 67, 79, 93, 96, 119–20
  Longinus 32
  Poemen 16, 95–6, 114
  Sisoes 95
  Spyridon 100
  Theodore of Pherme 99
  Theophilus the Archbishop 95
  Xanthias 120
Aristotle
  On the Soul 120
  Problems 20
Athanasius
  Vita Antonii 15, 26, 28, 37, 39, 42, 50, 52, 104–6, 109, 121, 157, 162
Augustine
  De civitate Dei contra paganos 40, 43–4
  Confessions 39, 105
  Enerrationes in Psalmos 42
  De gratia et libero arbitario 40
  De Opera Monachorum 40
  De praedestinatione sanctorum 41
  Sermones de Tempore 138

Basil   21
  Ascetical 36–7
  Epistolae 35–6, 151
  Longer Responses 113
Benedict of Nursia
  Regula Benedict 3, 59, 81, 155
Bonaventure
  Apologia paupertu 57

Cassian, John
  Conferences ix, 3, 5
  Preface   142–3
  Reg 73.5   4
  1.9   51
  2   73
  2.10   72, 77–8, 116
  2.10.2   126
  2.11   78
  2.17   73
  2.23   67
  3   73
  3.1   18
  3.17   118
  4   73
  5.4.3   26
  9.21   151
  10.2.2   111
  10.3   111
  10.5   111
  14.1.2   24
  14.4.1   130
  14.8   151
  14.8.2–5   23
  14.10.2   136
  14.12   143
  14.14.2   137
  14.16.8   139
  18.3   84
  18.5   52
  18.5.1   133
  18.6   69
  18.6.2   131
  18.15   151
  19.6   85
  19.8.4   4

Index of Ancient Sources 183

20.1 15
21.1.2 86
23.21 151
24.26 53
De incarnacione Christi 168
Institutes
ix, 3, 5–6, 9
Preface 9, 19, 31, 73, 80, 127, 129, 143–5, 147
1.1 53–4, 130
1.1.1 130
1.1.2 130
1.2 54
2 74
2.1 59, 134
2.2 59, 135
2.2.2 135
2.3 136
2.3.2 62
2.3.3 86
2.4 59–60, 81
2.4.5 61
2.5.2 62
2.5.3 61
2.6 61
2.10 82
2.10.1 63, 137
2.11.2 63
2.12 62
2.12.1 137
2.12.2 62
2.14 63
2.15.1 138
3.1 81
3.2 81, 132, 151
3.4.1 81
3.4.2 15, 81
3.9.1 132
4.3.1 58, 64, 139
4.3.2 64, 139
4.4 58
4.5 55, 64, 140–1
4.6 54, 58
4.7 65
4.24 66
4.39 155

Institutes (cont.)
5.3 13
5.24 15–16
5.39 50
6.8 151
8.1 149
8.3 148
8.11 149
8.12 150
10.2.1 79
10.25 79
11.14 124
11.16 123
11.18 ix, 11–12, 99, 125
14.16.6 144
14.16.7 144
18.11.3 138
Cassiodorus
De inst div. litt. (PL 70.1144) 4
Epistula Ammonis 91
Epistolae Romanarum Pontificum Genuinae 141

Epitomes operum Cassiani 4
Eusebius
Historia ecclesiastica 60
2.16 60
Evagrius Ponticus
Evagrius of Pontus 54
Ο ΓΝΟΣΤΙΚΟΣ Η ΠΡΟΣ ΤΟΝ ΚΑΤΑΞΙΩΘΕΝΤΑ ΓΝΩΣΕΩΣ 24
The Praktikos and Chapters on Prayer 24–5

Hilary of Arles
Sermo de Uita S. Honorati 47
Historia Monachorum in Aegypto (HM) 103–4
Hugh of Digne
De finibus paupertatis 56–7

Irenaeus ix, 4, 60,
Adversus Haereses 60

Jerome 39, 106, 145–7, 153–4, 166
Liber de Viris illustribus 106

Lausiac History
Ammonios 102

Evagrius Ponticus 103
Isidore 101
Macarius of Alexandria 102
Nathanael 102
Palladius 16, 91

Origen
Homilae en Leviticum 31
On First Principles 21–3

Pachomius
Regula et Praecepta 106, 114
Plotinus
Enneads 27, 107–8
Porphyry
Vita Plotini 34
Prosper of Aquitaine
Liber contra collatorem 40, 44

Simplicius
Letters 141
Socrates Scholasticus
Historia Ecclesiastica (EH) 1, 98, 111
Sozomenus, Salaminius Hermias
Historia Ecclesiastica 3, 112, 125, 141
Sulpicius Severus 157
Dialogi 46
Epistle 3 47

Tertullian
De poenitentia IX.3-4 30

Thomas Aquinas
Summa Theologiae 4
Vita Pachomii 116, 118

Xenophon
Memorabilia 27

Index of Subjects

1 Corinthians 181–2, 195–6, 267
Aegyptia Instituta 82, 121
Alexandria 1–2, 6, 9, 12–15, 20, 26, 60, 91, 101–2, 104, 109, 111, 124, 127, 136, 148, 162–3
  Great Library of 14
allegory, -ical interpretation of scripture 4, 23–24, 149
anaogy, -ical interpretation of scripture 23
Anthony 8, 18, 29, 168
Antony 11, 15, 26, 28–30, 37, 39, 42, 50, 52, 89, 97, 104–9, 114, 121–2, 130, 157, 162–3,
Apostles 5, 52–53, 59–61, 126, 128, 130, 132–4, 144, 148, 152, 158, 164, 169
apostolic praxis ix, 5, 28, 128, 131, 134, 152, 154, 164–5, 169
apostolic succession ix, 5, 12, 60, 131, 134, 152, 165, 169
Apphy 39, 96
Arians, Arianism 37, 109, 163
  anti-Arianism 104
Arsenius 30, 93, 96, 144
Asceticism ix, 2, 6–19, 21, 23–40–45, 47, 49, 51–54, 57, 59, 61, 63, 65, 73–74, 80, 90, 92, 94–104, 110, 112–3, 117, 121, 124, 126, 129, 131, 134, 138–9, 141–2, 144–6, 153–4, 156, 158, 161–4, 166–8
Athanasius 15, 26, 37, 39, 50, 101, 104–6, 109, 119, 122, 137, 162
Augustine of Hippo 6, 19–20, 39–44, 105, 110, 138,
Authority ix, 4, 5–6, 9, 11–12, 14, 28, 37–8, 43, 46, 53, 59–60, 66, 68, 74, 84, 89, 93, 98, 103, 126, 128, 136–7, 142, 144, 151–4, 161–7

Basil of Caesarea 21, 34–38, 39, 44, 113, 145–7, 151, 153–4, 166
Benedict of Nursia 3, 59, 80, 155
Bessarion 17, 31–33
Bethlehem ix, 3, 15–16
Bishops ix
body, -ies 1, 8–9, 12, 14, 21–3, 26–9, 32–3, 36–3, 42–4, 47, 54, 61–3, 67, 75, 77–9, 81, 84, 86–7, 100, 103, 108–9, 110–1, 119–21, 141, 148–9, 156, 162–3, 167
  appearance of 14, 16, 36
  resurrection of 110
Bonaventure 57

Cappadocia 35, 151
Castor, Bishop of Apt 9, 20, 80, 127–9, 142–5, 164–6
cell 2, 15, 50, 62, 66–67, 74, 78–81, 97–99, 102, 123, 135, 159, 163, 169
Church fathers, ix, 3
Chrysostom, John 3, 8, 13, 97, 112, 124–5, 127–8, 134, 157, 163, 168
class 7, 42–43, 46, 48, 51, 68, 111
community 6, 11, 14–17, 30, 35, 39, 42–3, 46, 48–9, 54, 56, 62–3, 77, 80–1, 84–93, 95, 97, 102, 113–4, 118, 122, 124, 126, 129, 133, 136, 146, 151, 153, 161, 163, 165, 169
cognitive, 92, 112–20
confess, -ion 29, 31, 39, 72, 74, 77–9, 85, 87–9, 116, 161

Constantinople 3, 9, 13, 25, 34, 92, 103, 112, 124–5, 127
contemplation, contemplative 9, 11, 24, 36, 69, 99, 108, 116

demons, demonic 26, 32, 50, 69, 77–9, 82, 90, 97, 102, 105–6, 109–10, 150, 162
deprivation 26, 34, 56, 105, 140. *See also* renunciation.
Desert Fathers ix, 5, 17, 20, 28, 31, 37, 51, 62, 65, 82, 103, 122, 124, 132, 135, 147, 155, 165
devil, *see* demons.
Dioscorus, 2–3
discernment 103, 122, 126
discipline 15, 29, 54, 75, 112–4, 124, 133, 138–9
  disciplinary power *see* power.
  self- 27, 38
discourse ix
  as closed ix
  monastic ix, 5, 91, 93, 95, 154

Eastern Orthodox Church 3
education 1–3, 6, 20, 34–5, 39, 48–52, 90, 105–6, 111, 114–5, 127, 142–5, 153, 162–3, 166
Egypt, -ian ix, 1–5, 7–11, 13–16, 19–21, 23–6, 28, 30, 35–7, 40–3, 47, 50–53, 58–63, 66, 68, 72–3, 76–7, 80–3, 88–90, 92–4, 97–9, 103–6, 110–2, 115, 117–9, 121–2, 124–9, 131–7, 142–5, 147, 149, 151–3, 156–9, 161–5
  Egyptian Institutions *see Aegyptia Instituta*.
  monasticism 1
embodiment *see* body, -ies.
ethics 8–9, 78
  ethical agency 8
  ethical formation 8, 107
Eustathius 35–7, 145
Evagrius of Pontus 13, 16, 20–5, 34, 54, 56, 79, 82, 102–3, 111, 124, 148, 166
exemplification, exemplars 8, 27, 35, 37, 39, 59, 66, 82, 96, 126, 128, 133, 152
exile 16–17, 24, 91–2, 110, 112, 125, 127–8, 163–4
exomologesis 29–30

fasting 14–16, 18, 25, 28–30, 46, 67, 74, 82, 94, 102, 137–9, 155, 168
Francis of Assisi 57

Gaul ix, 3–4, 7–10, 12–15, 16, 18–20, 44–53, 59, 61–63, 68–69, 73–4, 80–5, 88–9, 115, 125–9, 131, 133–7, 139, 142, 152–3, 156–60, 163–5, 167
Gelasius 17, 30, 94, 121
Germanus 3, 15–16, 19, 25, 125
Gnosticism 110
grace 6–7, 38, 40–4, 96, 107
Gregory the Great 4, 39

hagiography 15, 26, 34, 104–5, 116, 157
heaven 9–10, 39–40, 42, 46–7, 60, 105, 157
hedonism 27, 35
heresy 11, 21, 35, 40, 53, 105, 109, 111, 168
  heresiology 5, 168
hierarch, -y ix, 5–6, 9, 11, 14, 38, 43, 46, 53, 60, 66, 68, 89, 93, 98, 126, 128, 136, 142, 144, 151–3, 161–6
hospitality 16, 51, 65, 94, 120, 168
humility 15, 18, 32–33, 35, 38, 56, 59, 63–5, 67, 76–7, 79, 84, 88–90, 99–100, 106, 119–20, 127, 130–1, 136, 142, 144, 152, 155, 161–2, 165, 168

ideal, ideals, idealization ix, 3, 5–6, 12, 34, 37, 39, 42, 51, 63, 70–71,

74, 76, 79, 83, 105, 112, 131–4, 136, 142, 147–8, 151, 153, 158–9, 165
  apostolic 170
  ascetic 35, 156
  monastic, monk, monastery 3, 5, 50–1, 67–8, 80, 86, 128, 136, 142, 161, 167, 169
  moral 119
identity 10, 16–17, 42, 45, 49–51, 53–69, 63–5, 67, 70, 79, 85, 120, 130, 140, 157, 167
instruction 9, 16, 23, 28, 31, 46, 48–50, 59, 74, 82, 84, 114–5, 119, 128–9, 135, 139, 160, 165
Irenaeus ix, 4, 60

Jerome 39, 106, 145–7, 1534, 166
John the Baptist 27–8, 54, 131, 152, 164, 169
John the Short 18, 66
judgment 41, 63, 75, 77–8, 99, 115–7, 119–21, 126, 136

knowledge 2, 9–11, 51, 71, 73–5, 80–3, 86–7, 103, 116, 125, 133, 139, 143–8, 150, 153, 158–60, 165–6
  and power 73, 87
  creation of 10, 73–4
  practical 152
  self-knowledge 70, 107–8
  spiritual 144

laypeople 11, 31, 37, 43, 73, 91, 96–7, 112, 114, 121, 125, 131, 137, 151, 157, 159, 161, 163–5, 168
leader, -s, -ship 27, 30, 34–37, 45, 52, 62, 84–86, 92, 96, 101, 116, 128, 130, 136–7, 142, 152, 160–1, 163, 165
  of abbots 85–86

literacy 49–52, 105–6, 114–5, 144, 162, 166
literal, -ism, interpretation of the bible 23–4, 148
liturgy 60–1, 125

Macarius the Great 33–4, 90–1, 98–9, 102
manual labor 15, 37, 50–1, 76–81, 92, 113, 126, 138
Marseilles 9, 13, 63, 125
Martin of Tours 46–7, 68, 157
martyr, -dom 3, 26, 30, 60, 94, 156
mercy 16, 29–30, 41, 51, 57, 118, 123
Middle Ages 4
miracles 31–4, 99–101, 103–4, 147
  healing 31–2, 103, 109
monastic manual 3, 9, 126
Moses, Abba 19, 66–7, 77, 79, 89, 93, 96, 119–20

nakedness 54, 56
Nicea 5, 37, 100, 105, 110, 122, 162
  anti-Nicene 35
novitiate, novices 3–4, 54–5, 59, 64–6, 78, 84–5, 124, 139–40, 163

obedience 8, 18, 43–5, 54, 63, 66, 72, 76–7, 79, 85–6, 93, 104, 160–2
ordination, ordain 11, 16, 38, 91, 95–103, 109, 121, 124–5, 139, 150–1, 161–2
  forced 2, 11, 38, 95–6, 98, 101, 109, 121, 124
Origen, Origenism 1, 13, 20–5, 50, 107–8, 110, 124, 136, 162–3
  Origenist Controversy 2, 11, 16, 20–1, 25, 50, 110, 125, 148–50, 163
orthodoxy 3, 12, 25, 37, 106, 110, 153, 164–5, 168–9
ownership 52, 55–8, 95
  communal 54–6

Index of Subjects 189

Pachomius 15, 49, 114–8
Palestine 4, 15, 28, 36–7, 42, 66, 93, 103, 128, 145, 158
Paphnutius 18, 118
passions 1, 35, 56, 79, 111, 116, 149, 166
penance, penitence 25, 29–31, 94
perfection 4, 6, 13–14, 20, 22–3, 28, 31, 42–3, 48, 53, 56, 60–1, 69, 73, 77, 80, 82, 85–7, 105, 119, 142, 147, 150, 169
philosophy, -ers 2, 14, 27, 34–5, 39, 50, 72, 75, 106, 117
piety, -ous 2–3, 13, 51, 61, 105, 113
Plato, -nism 20, 27, 106
  Neoplatonism 34, 50, 106–8, 162
Plotinus 14, 27, 34, 107–8,
police, -ing 11, 75, 77–8, 127, 134, 160
prayer ix, 14, 18, 28–30, 33, 37, 46, 48, 59–63, 67, 73, 80–2, 97, 100–1, 108, 113, 116–7, 131–5, 137–8, 143, 152, 155, 164–5
pride 43–4, 55, 102
property 48, 52, 56–7, 140, 157
Pelagianism 6, 19, 40
Poemen 95–6, 99, 119
poverty 45, 47, 54–5, 57, 112, 129–30, 140–1, 152, 168
power ix, 6–12, 18, 21, 26, 31–2, 37, 41, 45, 58, 63, 69–72, 74–8, 80–1, 83–8, 90–6, 100–1, 104, 112, 116, 120–2, 124–6, 128–9, 133, 136, 142, 147, 150, 155–6, 158–62, 164, 167, 170
  biopower 11, 69, 74, 86–8
  divine 33–4
  disciplinary ix, 11, 69, 75–7, 80–1, 83–4, 86, 88, 121, 126, 147, 159–60
  intercessory 31
  pastoral ix, 11, 69, 74, 83–4, 86, 88, 126, 142, 159–60
  rhetorical 7, 80, 96, 142
  sovereign 74, 121–2

  spiritual 32, 104
prophets, prophecy 5, 54, 126, 128–30, 133, 148, 152, 164, 169
Prosper of Aquitaine 6, 19
purity, -ification 25, 30–1, 34, 36–37, 41, 56–7, 67, 78–9, 99, 103, 130, 137, 162, 165, 167
  impurity 113, 137

reform 7–9, 12, 157
renunciation 7–8, 16–18, 46–48, 50, 52–3, 55–9, 62, 65–8, 124, 139, 141, 157–8, 162, 166, 169–70
rhetoric ix, 7–8, 11, 18, 20, 34, 45, 48–9, 51–2, 54, 59–60, 62, 65–6, 68, 71, 73–4, 77–8, 80, 83–4, 86, 88, 91, 96, 104–5, 109, 115, 117–9, 121, 123, 127, 133–5, 142, 145–7, 152–3, 159–63, 169. *See also* rhetorical power.
Roman Catholicism 3, 169
Rome 10, 14, 26–7, 29, 44–5, 47–8, 51–3, 60, 63, 97, 101, 112–4, 120, 125–6, 129, 140–1, 144, 157–8
Roman Egypt 14
Rufinus 21, 25, 103

sacraments 14, 30, 37, 79, 90, 95, 100, 116, 125, 150–1
salvation 5–6, 10, 23, 37, 40–1, 44, 77–8, 83–5, 87, 97, 142–3, 155, 160–1, 164
Scythia 3
seclusion 27, 42, 61, 65, 97
self-control 27–8, 40, 62, 116, 120, 158
separatism ix, 5–6, 8, 10–13, 57, 61, 65, 68, 71, 74, 89, 96–7, 107, 121–3, 125–9, 141–2, 150–1, 154, 156, 163–4, 167, 169–70
Serapion 25, 111
sex, -uality 35, 39–40, 44, 65, 74
silence 4, 64, 82, 93, 95, 114, 137–8
sin, -fulness 13, 19, 23, 30–31, 35, 43–4, 54, 56, 69, 79, 82, 87, 95,

99, 103, 107, 117, 119–20, 137, 144, 149, 162
shepherd, -ing 11, 83–5, 100, 160, 168
sleep 14–15, 18, 32, 35, 62, 76, 81–2, 84, 100. *See also* vigils.00
Socrates Scholasticus 1, 98, 111–2
solitude 4–5, 11, 14, 17, 26, 33, 37–38, 42, 44, 62, 67, 69, 75, 96–8, 104–5, 123, 126, 130, 145, 151, 169
soul 23, 26–7, 29, 34, 42–4, 53–4, 63, 67, 78, 87, 97, 103, 107–9, 112–3, 116, 120, 133, 143, 152
Sozomen 3, 112, 125, 141, 149
status 7, 17, 31, 37–8, 43, 45–6, 50, 52–3, 62–3, 68, 90, 93, 96, 100, 103, 106, 113, 115, 120, 139–40, 144, 148, 153, 157–8, 161–2, 168
subjectification 10, 86
subjectivity ix, 2, 4, 6–8, 10–12, 68–74, 84, 88, 121–2, 126, 131, 133, 142, 156, 167
  as socially constructed 70–71, 158
  collective 71
  ethical 8
surveillance 11, 74–5, 77, 79, 81, 87, 89, 116, 147, 159
Symeon Stylites 36
synaxis 63, 104
Syria, -c 35–6, 106–8, 117, 145–6

Tall Brothers, the 2–3, 16, 24, 98, 111, 125, 148, 150
temptation 11, 23, 26, 40, 50, 65, 72, 99, 103, 113, 118–9, 162
Tertullian ix, 4, 29–30, 60, 119, 129
theology 1, 6, 8, 12–13, 21, 24–5, 37, 44, 66, 84, 92, 94, 97, 100, 105, 109–10, 118, 121–2, 124–6, 128, 142, 147–8, 150–1, 153–4, 157, 162–4, 166, 169
  anthropology 63
  tradition 4
  of divine corporeality 1–2, 12, 21–4, 109–11, 124, 148–9, 163
Theophilus, bishop of Alexandria 1–3, 12, 16, 24, 95, 98, 111, 112, 124–5, 127–8, 148–50, 163

vice *see* sin.
vigils 25, 67, 132–3, 152. *See also* sleep.
virtue, -osity 14, 18, 26, 34, 51, 54, 56, 58, 62–63, 66, 72, 85–86, 103, 107–8, 113, 118, 127, 134, 139, 141, 143–4, 161, 163, 166, 168–9
vocation 10, 79, 97, 119, 158

wealth 2, 7, 10, 12, 17, 45–6, 50, 52–3, 55, 62, 68, 98, 139–141, 143, 145, 153, 157–8, 161, 169
West ix
will 7, 18, 27, 29, 38, 40, 43–4, 53, 55, 66, 79, 98, 100, 102, 120, 124, 153, 162
  divine 44
  free will 6, 40, 113, 116, 138, 163
  surrender of 18, 72
wisdom 11, 19, 28, 67, 93, 95, 103, 109, 121, 126, 128–9, 131, 143–5, 153–4
women ix, 6–7, 11–12, 32–3, 65, 90–1, 99, 103, 125

Index of Modern Authors

Attwater, Donald 146

Barnes, T. D. 104
Brakke, David 96
Brennan, B., 105
Brown, Peter 16–17, 65, 91–2, 94, 141
Budge, E. A. W. 117
Butler, Rev. Alban 156
Bultmann, Rudolf 31
Burchell, Graham 70, 72
Burton-Christie, Douglas 49

Cain, Andrew 146
Carrette, Jeremy 83
Casiday, Augustine 7, 21
Chadwick, Owen 3
Chesnut, G. F. 34
Clark, Elizabeth A. 16, 110
Clements, Niki Kasumi 8
Cribiore, Rafaella 115
Crum & Bell 115

De Vogüé, Adalbert 151
Dilley, Paul C. 91–2, 112–8, 122, 163

Ferguson, Everett 136–7
Folliet, G. 43
Forlin Patrucco, Marcella 92
Foucault, Michel ix, 8, 10–11, 68–72, 74–7, 79–81, 83–9, 121–2, 126, 133, 142, 147, 158–61, 166–7

Gamble, Harry 49
Goodrich, Richard 7–8, 45–8, 59, 85

Gregg, Robert C. 26, 105
Groh, D. 105
Guy, Jean-Claude 6, 17, 49

Harmless, William 14–15, 106, 162
Hildebrand, Stephen 145
Heaton, Robert 5

Jaeger, Werner 27
John, Catherine Rachel 146

Kennedy, George A. 20
Keith, Alison 27
Kirschner, Robert 34
Krawiec, Rebecca 48–52
Krueger, Col. G. P. 54

Lausberg, Heinrich 49
Leyser, Conrad 39–44
Lívia, Flachbartová 27

Macalister, Robert Alexander Stewart 130
Mathisen, Ralph 45
McGuckin, John Anthony 21
Meredith, Anthony 146

Newman, John Henry 156

Parry, Ken 25
Parris, Jennifer 167
Payne, Robert 146

Rapp, Claudia 31
Rea, Robert 6–7
Rousseau, Philip 4, 28, 52, 146
Rubenson, Samuel 50, 105–7, 109

Sanders, Br. Constantius 156
Seasoltz, Kevin R. 155
Simon, Richard 25
Smith, Zachary B. 65–6, 93, 99, 128
Sterk, Andrea 27, 34, 36
Stewart, Columba Andrew 6–7, 15–16
Stroumsa, Guy 49
Sucharek, Pavol 27

Trigg, Joseph W. 21
Turner, William 108

Vaage, Leif E. 27
Vahlen, Johannes 115
Van Dam, Raymond 45–6
Vladislav, Suvák 27

Ward, Maisie 156
Williams, M. 105
Williams, Rowan 109
Wimbush, Vincent 27

Studies in Ancient Religion and Culture

Series Editors:
Philip L. Tite, University of Virginia
Michael Ng, Seattle University
https://www.equinoxpub.com/home/studies-in-ancient-religion-and-culture/

Published:
Critical Theory and Early Christianity
Edited by Matthew G. Whitlock

Death's Dominion: Power, Identity, and Memory at the Fourth-Century Martyr Shrine
Nathaniel J. Morehouse

John Cassian and the Creation of Monastic Subjectivity
Joshua Schachterle

Social and Cognitive Perspectives on the Sermon on the Mount
Edited by Rikard Roitto, Colleen Shantz, and Petri Luomanen

The Complexity of Conversion: Intersectional Perspectives on Religious Change in Antiquity and Beyond
Edited by Valérie Nicolet and Marianne Bjelland Kartzow

Theorizing "Religion" in Antiquity
Edited by Nickolas P. Roubekas

Worth More than Many Sparrows: Essays in Honour of Willi Braun
Edited by Sarah E. Rollens and Patrick Hart

Forthcoming:
An Embodied Reading of the Shepherd of Hermas: The Book of Visions and its Role in Moral Formation
Angela Kim Harkins